Queequeg's Coffin

QUEEQUEG'S COFFIN

Indigenous Literacies & Early American Literature

BIRGIT BRANDER RASMUSSEN

DUKE UNIVERSITY PRESS
Durham & London 2012

Printed in the United States of America
on acid-free paper ∞
Designed by Jennifer Hill.
Typeset in Quadraat by
Keystone Typesetting, Inc.

Library of Congress
Cataloging-in-Publication Data appear on
the last printed page of this book.

Published with the assistance of the
Frederick W. Hilles Publication Fund
of Yale University.

For my children
Eva and Tobias Arne

and

in loving memory of
my mother
Karin Beathe Rasmussen

We Americans have yet to
really learn our own antecedents. . . .
They will be found ampler as
has been supposed, and in widely
different sources. Thus far, impress'd
by New England writers and
schoolmasters, we tacitly abandon
ourselves to the notion that our
United States have been fashioned
from the British Islands only—which
is a very great mistake.

WALT WHITMAN

CONTENTS

ACKNOWLEDGMENTS

Writing a book is a long journey, and often a solitary one. Yet, as I look back at the road I have traveled to get here, I see many individuals and institutions that have provided me support and sustenance along the way. It is good to finally have a chance to give thanks.

This book would not be what it is without Ken Wissoker, who believed in the project long before I could articulate its intervention. A brilliant editor, Ken was supportive and challenging at just the right times. I am also grateful for the comments and suggestions made by the anonymous Duke Press readers, who helped make this a significantly better book. Also thanks to Mandy Early, Jade Brooks, Amanda Sharp, Jennifer Hill, Mark Mastromarino, Susan Deeks, and Lori Delazan.

Crucial funding and resources came from many quarters. I received Summer Research grants and a funded semester leave from University of Wisconsin, Madison. I am thankful to my colleagues in the University of Wisconsin, Madison English department for that early vote of confidence. I used it to spend a valuable year at Stanford's Center for Comparative Studies in Race and Ethnicity. I thank the center for permitting me to be an affiliated fellow and for providing me office space and other resources. A Frederick W. Hilles Publication grant from Yale University helped pay for images and other publication costs. Finally, I will always be thankful for the support I received from The Danish Research Academy. Without that early fellowship, this book would not exist today.

I owe a big debt of gratitude to my colleagues at University of Wisconsin, Madison. Leslie Bow and Russ Castronovo went above and beyond in many ways. They read drafts and made brilliant suggestions, gave great practical advice, and embodied excellent mentorship. I am so grateful for their guidance and their collegiality. Camille Guerin-Gonzales was an outstanding colleague, ally, and mentor; I am thankful to her and the entire Chican@ and Latin@ Studies Program community for taking me in. Tom Schaub and Heather DuBrow read the first chapter, Roberta Hill and Deborah Brandt read the second chapter, Teresa Kelley read an early draft. All made valuable suggestions. I am grateful to Deb Brandt for sharing her expertise on literacy studies. Frank Salomon was a patient and challenging interlocutor for chapter 3, frightening and fabulous at just the right times. Also great thanks to Jeff Steele, Susan Friedman, and Michael Bernard-Donals.

Dean Gary Sandefur authorized accommodations for disabilities. Without such accommodations, this book would not exist, and I would not be a scholar today. Thus, I owe a great debt to many people I will never meet, who struggled for the passage of the Americans with Disabilities Act (ADA). Because of you, my severe repetitive strain injury did not end my career. Connie Chiba at University of California, Berkeley and Barbara Lanser at University of Wisconsin, Madison helped me navigate the administrative waters of ADA accommodations. Hannah Nyala West, Lisa Photos, and Samaa Abdurraqib typed much of the manuscript when my own limbs failed me.

Anne McClintock and Rob Nixon became more than colleagues. Thanks for tea, talks, continued friendship, and inspiration in the scholarly, culinary, horticultural, and political sphere. Grace Hong is fierce and brilliant. Certain passages in the manuscript can be traced directly to our conversations.

I am also grateful for my wonderful colleagues and students in American Studies and Ethnicity, Race, & Migration at Yale. Jonathan Holloway, Matt Jacobson, Alicia Smith Camacho, and Steven Pitti were instrumental in bringing us here. Special thanks to Alicia and Steve for reading the afterword and fortifying my resolve. Rani Neutill helped me remember and reconnect.

Aisling Colón is a special kind of angel. I am honored to count her among that sisterhood that carries me along through good times and bad. Lotte Kaa Andersen, min livslange veninde. Heidi Cohensen. Helle Rytkø-nen. Sara McClintock. Pernille Ipsen. Og nu også Benedicte Aarestrup.

Although graduate school is many years behind me, my time in the Bay Area and at University of California, Berkeley was formative. The department of Ethnic Studies provided an exciting and challenging space in which to become a scholar, and clarified the stakes of education and research. I am deeply grateful to the professors, the staff, the undergraduate students, the Bay Area activist community, and my fellow graduate students for all they taught me. In particular, José David Saldívar, Saidiya Hartman, Michael Omi, Sam Otter, Michael Rogin, Gerald Vizenor, Troy Duster, Abdul JanMohammed, Eric Hsu, Ron Lopez, Tomás Summers Sandoval, Jason Ferreira, Cat Ramirez, Jasbir Puar, Matt Wray, Rachel Stryker, Toeutu Faaleava, Marisa Belaustegegoitia, Chris Bracken, and Charlotte Coté guided, inspired, challenged, supported, and shared with me; blew my mind; and left their imprints on my heart and mind. Here, I was born into consciousness.

Ida Klitgaard, Janni Larsen, and Lærer Greve nurtured my love of learning from an early age. They, too, were formative influences. Roseanne Clark and Rose Brown helped put me back together when I broke. Shelley Fisher Fishkin has been supportive in many ways for many years—I hope this book lives up to her expectations.

I came to early American studies relatively late. Ralph Bauer was instrumental and has remained a role model and a source of inspiration. Thank you for your wise words and your support. Annette Kolodny read an early and incomplete incarnation of this work; her grace and generosity was deeply appreciated. Also big thanks to Dennis Moore and the entire SEA community of scholars, a welcoming and supportive group. Thanks to Matt Cohen and Jeffrey Glover for inviting me to the Early American Mediascapes Symposium, and for reading work on Guaman Poma. A special thanks to Ivan Boserup for permitting me to view Guaman Poma's original manuscript. I am thankful to all the librarians and archivists who helped me during this process.

Without the peace of mind and the quiet work hours that good childcare provides, this book would not have been possible. Thanks to Peggy and Cindy, the folks at Big Oak, Lapham, Stanford Arboretum, Appletree, and Cold Spring School for bringing as much love and dedication to nurturing my children as I bring to my students.

First, last, and always, the love of my family makes everything possible and meaningful. Lene, Vibeke, Jane. You are the most wonderful sisters in the world; you sustain me through hard times and share all my joy. My father, Knud Erik Brander Rasmussen, taught me early on to question authority and to believe in justice. This may all have started with that conversation about Columbus! My mother, Karin, was bright and studious, but a high-school education was beyond her family's means. But she gave me her *flidspræmie*, the autobiography of Madame Curie, to read when I was a young girl. I lost her much too soon, but her dreams and continuing education efforts inspired my own educational trajectory. In many ways, my degrees and accomplishments are for her.

Also thanks to my extended family, my wonderful brothers-in-law, my nieces and nephews, my Godmother Kœthe, Tom, Flemming, Lissie, my cousins, and my entire family-in-law. A special thanks as well to Bodil og Børge, who have always been there for me. Although my grandparents, Lilly and Arne Nielsen and Peder and Ottomine Brander Rasmussen, have all passed on by now, I am forever grateful for their love.

Ned Blackhawk was there at the beginning of this journey and is there still. I faltered many times along the way. His faith in this project, and in my ability to carry it through, never did. Words are inadequate.

My children, Eva and Tobias Arne, have expanded my capacity for love immeasurably. They are the reason for everything and make everything worthwhile. This is for them and for all our children.

Parts of an earlier version of chapter 2 appeared in *American Literature* 79, no. 3 (2007): 445–73.

"A New World Still in the Making"

In 1524, twelve Spanish friars met with Mexica dignitaries just out-side recently conquered Tenochtitlan, now known as Mexico City.[1] The friars were there as emissaries of the pope and Charles V to convert the indigenous people and to disseminate the written word of the Bible. The Mexica listened as the Spanish told them about their divine book. Then their *tlamatinime*, or scholar-priests, went on to explain how the Mexica concep-tualized the relationship between divinity and their own archive of books. Over the next two weeks, these peoples from radically dissimilar worlds engaged in a dialogue across linguistic and epistemological chasms about knowledge, memory, and writing.[2]

This dialogue happened in the year of Three House, according to the sacred calendar or "day-count" kept by the tlamatinime. The shockwaves from such early exchanges would set in motion the European conquest of the Americas and ripple across the centuries to follow. In the process, the entire world was radically altered. For all of the peoples involved, a new and shared world emerged, a world so violently transformed that epistemologi-cal, geographical, and cosmological maps would be changed forever.

Like other early colonial encounters, this meeting between friars and tlamatinime inaugurated "a new world still in the making," as well as a new world literature rooted in the exchanges between different peoples and their literary traditions.[3] The Spanish-Aztec dialogue about written words was not unique. In North America, Europeans also came into contact with peoples who had their own, distinct forms of writing. In 1652, for example, Jesuit missionaries in what is now eastern Canada noticed that the Mi'kmaq took notes on birch bark with charcoal in order to learn prayers. The Jesuits would call these marks "hieroglyphics," linking them to other non-alphabetic scripts with which they were familiar.

A few decades later, another French missionary named Christian Le Clerq also noticed the use of "Micmac hieroglyphics," which the Mi'kmaq call komqwe-jwi'kasikl.[4] Hoping to use this indigenous writing system to spread his faith, Le Clerq set out to learn it from children, presumably by pointing to various marks on their birch bark and asking what sounds or words the marks represented. No records survive of these early notes, either on birch bark or in Le Clerq's account. Eventually, Le Clerq added his own signs and characters to the original Mi'kmaq writing system in order to better record and transmit the catechism, Catholic prayers, and other Christian materials. The resulting Oukateguennes Kignamatinoer, or Hieroglyphic Prayer, represented a novel experiment in writing that brought together and into dialogue the writing systems of two distinct cultures through the collaboration between Le Clerq and anonymous Mi'kmaq writers. Several hundred years later, another missionary would learn the Mi'kmaq language and writing system, adding Greek and Roman alphabetic elements as well as his own designs and publishing the result in Vienna in 1866.[5] This publication would in turn be shipped back to the Mi'kmaq, testifying to several hundred years of semiotic exchange between two different writing systems.

Such textual and literary exchanges constitute an important and neglected aspect of American literary history in large part because scholars have inadequately explored the extent to which Europeans who arrived in the Americas encountered literate cultures.[6] The destruction of much of this archive following conquest—and its non-alphabetic nature—make such dialogic literary studies difficult. In addition, colonial records and subsequent scholarship have elaborated the notion that America's indigenous people had no writing. These material and discursive practices have converged to link terms such as "writing" and "literature" predominantly to alphabetic script. Consequently, most literary scholarship on the colonial period has paid attention to European literature about the Americas, writing about Europe's own experience of discovery and conquest. This literature is significant and important; however, it paints only a partial picture of the colonial era. It records a monologue rather than a dialogue.

But the literature that emerged out of the colonial conflict is far more than just such colonialist monologues. Contrary to common belief, the confrontation between European and indigenous people in the Americas was often a clash between literate cultures. From Tenochtitlan in central Mexico to the northeastern shores inhabited by the Mi'kmaq and across the American continents, indigenous people and European newcomers engaged each other in dialogue about ways to write and record knowledge. Such exchanges could become the foundation for a new kind of early American literary studies.

Perhaps what we now call "American literature" began that day in 1524 outside Tenochtitlan with a dialogue about different kinds of writing. This means not that there was no literature in the hemisphere before the colonial period but, rather, that there was no "America." Until recently, anthologies of North American literature have often located the literary beginnings of the United States with the Puritans, but such New England settlers were relative latecomers to the continent and a small, if prolific, minority of its writers. Latin American anthologies have often begun with the writings and miscommunications of Spaniards like Christopher Columbus, who was not the first European to set foot in the hemisphere, but whose journeys and epistolary monologues set off a European dream of gold and conquest that shaped the subsequent history and literature in significant ways. This book proposes a shift away from such monologues of conquest to the often fraught and conflictual dialogues instantiated by colonialism and the confrontation between different textual traditions.

Indigenous literary traditions have been documented across the Americas.[7] These writings are diverse and range from Mayan pictoglyphs to Haudenosaunee wampum, from Ojibwe birch bark scrolls to Incan quipus. This literature has largely remained outside the purview of American literary studies because writing often has been defined primarily as alphabetism. But that equation is flawed, as a number of scholars have demonstrated.[8] During the colonial process, literacy became a signifier, as well as the "sine qua non," of civilization, and "writing" became a crucial dividing line between colonized and colonizer.[9] The ways in which literary scholars have constructed their object—and abject—of inquiry remain deeply entangled with the history of European imperialism. As long as literary scholars continue to think about writing predominantly as the alphabetic system used by Europeans, we uphold that legacy by defining other forms of recording knowledge and narrative out of existence.

A dialogic study of multiple forms of literacy recasts early American literature by placing the clash between heterogeneous textual practices, rather than the European literary tradition, at the center of inquiry. Such a project entails, first, putting critical pressure on the foundational category of literary studies: "writing." As the field is currently configured, writing is too often conceptualized as synonymous with alphabetic script. The common equation between writing and the alphabet relegates other forms of recording and transmitting knowledge outside the boundaries of literary inquiry, leaving uncontested the monologues of colonial agents and diminishing our understanding of the reciprocity of the colonial encounter. It denies the agency, knowledge, and sometimes even the existence of indigenous perspectives recorded in non-alphabetic texts. Equally significant, the equation between alphabetism and writing maintains the colonial mythology of a meeting between "civilized" and "savage" peoples, marked respectively by literacy and its absence.

Broadening the definition of writing in the Americas beyond a particular semiotic system—the alphabet—disrupts a whole complex of cultural meanings, as well as dynamics of dominance. A more dialogic study of colonial confrontations makes visible the presence, agency, and knowledge of America's indigenous peoples who can move from seemingly mute objects to literate subjects in the colonial sphere. It further unveils the material and epistemological violence through which the myth of indigenous non-literacy has been produced and maintained. Reckoning with non-alphabetic forms of writing as literature destabilizes the binary between "civilized" and "savage" peoples, characterized by literacy or the lack thereof. Such recognition in turn reveals how "literacy" has often been a colonizing discourse, as Western civilization has defined itself in part through exclusive claims to "writing" and "literature." Finally, an engagement with non-occidental forms and theories of writing changes our understanding of textuality and the colonial encounter in important ways.

Such a shift recasts the field of early American literary studies by placing indigenous forms of writing alongside, and in dynamic relation to, more familiar alphabetic texts. This change has a number of important consequences. It brings into focus a vast new archive, foregrounding the presence of indigenous forms of writing and the violence and exclusion which have made them invisible to literary studies. These materials bring to crisis not only American literary studies but also the category of literature itself and require the development of new methods of reading and analysis adequate for this expanded archive.

Changing our conception of early American literature in this way has important implications for the study of later periods as well. Taking account of indigenous forms of writing and their relationship to alphabetic scripts can transform understandings of later American literature, because indigenous people continue to use and assert the relevance of their own records and literary forms. Such texts deserve the sustained attention of literary scholars, in their own right and as part of the hemisphere's larger literary history.[10] A more dialogic critical practice can also begin to map how alphabetic and indigenous literatures inter-animated each other. Finally, many indigenous literary forms survive and continue to remain relevant to Native communities today in various ways.

The Haudenosaunee, for example, continue to use wampum in tribal affairs and maintain an archive of wampum belts as evidence of treaty and sovereignty rights. Some contemporary Native American authors, such as Louise Erdrich, locate their work within ancient, local traditions of indigenous writing on rock and birch bark. Arguing that "books are nothing all that new" in the region, Erdrich notes the relationship between the Ojibwe word for "rock paintings" (Mazinapikiniganan) and "books" (Mazina'iganan).[11] The literary scholar Lisa Brooks's etymologies of Ojibwe and Abenaki words for books and writing show that, indeed, neither are exterior to traditional native culture in the area.[12] Like Erdrich, Leslie Marmon Silko links her contemporary work to earlier indigenous literary traditions in the Americas, like the Mayan codices. In a discussion of how the codices and contemporary Mayan struggles, such as the Zapatista uprising in 1994, informed Almanac of the Dead, Silko notes that "books were and still are weapons in the ongoing struggle for the Americas." She adds: "In 1540, the great libraries of the Americas were burned by the European invaders, most of whom were illiterate but not stupid. They burned the great libraries because they wished to foster the notion that the New World was populated by savages. . . . International law regulated the fate of conquered nations but not of savages."[13]

If even the earliest colonial records document the existence of indigenous literatures, and if native people themselves have continued to use and honor their own indigenous forms of writing, how did so many develop the common misconception that, while native people in the Americas had an "old and richly developed oral literature; they did not write?"[14] The oral literature of America's native people is indeed rich and ancient, but there is also, as Craig Womack notes, "a vast, and vastly understudied, written tradition" that merits the attention of literary scholars, as well.[15]

This book sets out to consider that written tradition and to counter the enduring notion that indigenous Americans did not write before the arrival of Europeans. It begins by contemplating a colonial archive of literary encounters and conflicts which reveals not only that "they" did write, but also that colonial agents were aware of such writings and at times deliberately destroyed them. In addition, scholars through the ages have defined writing in ways that exclude indigenous American records. But writing is neither a neutral category nor "the tranquil locus on the basis of which other questions . . . may be posed." Rather, it is a category that itself poses "a whole cluster of questions."[16] Scholarly definitions of writing have excluded indigenous American records, and such exclusion, in turn, came to underpin colonial—and, for that matter, national—identities. Indeed, the term "writing" has a history and a genealogy that merits interrogation. A critical engagement with philological and linguistic scholarship reveals how and why indigenous forms of writing, though diverse and widespread across the hemisphere, were excluded from definitions of "writing," exposing the "possessive investment" that this term has held for generations of literary scholars.[17]

Recognizing this possessive investment and its roots in the colonial process enables a more capacious understanding of American writing, one that takes account of indigenous literacies before and after the arrival of Europeans. In the past few decades, North American literary scholars have critically interrogated the national boundaries of the field, bearing out Walt Whitman's prediction that "Americans" would eventually expand their sense of literary heritage beyond "New England writers."[18] In terms of geography and text selection, this project ranges from what is now Canada in the north to the Andes in the south. While paying attention to diverse geographic locations, the book moves critical pressure from "American" to "writing" and offers a definition of writing that can account for the radical diversity of literary forms in the American hemisphere. Such an approach paves the way for a comparative engagement with different American literary traditions and for understanding the traffic between distinct kinds of writing, such as pictographic and alphabetic texts, as well as between alphabetic scripts and radically different records, such as Northeastern wampum or Andean quipus.

America's literary antecedents are indeed far "ampler than has been supposed," as Walt Whitman noted, and to be found in "widely different sources." But we cannot read such materials and trace their cross-cultural syncretism using only conventional literary methods. This book begins to sketch a method for reading this new archive through a series of case studies that analyze the inter-animation between alphabetism and indigenous forms of writing. This approach proceeds by drawing on, and putting into dialogue, a range of disciplines, such as history, archeology, anthropology, linguistics, literary studies, and philology—often read against the grain—as well as interdisciplinary fields such as Latin American studies, Native American studies, and postcolonial studies. It is ethically and methodologically rooted in the field of American ethnic studies and aligned with hemispheric and global efforts to instantiate what Linda Tuhiwai Smith calls "de-colonizing" scholarship.[19]

The history of imperialism and colonialism has shaped not only "the indigenous experience," as Smith argues, but also the "Western" experience. Colonial categories and methods of analysis have structured the identities and epistemologies of the colonizing cultures as much as those who were colonized. It is immensely fruitful, then, to work through foundational categories such as writing and literature in order to recognize that the challenges posed by texts that traditionally have been excluded from the field represent, at the same time, an opportunity to develop a new critical practice. After such a "working through" of scholarship on writing, chapter 1 analyzes indigenous American pictography, the most ubiquitous form of writing in the Americas before and long after the arrival of Europeans. What is pictography and what does it mean to attempt a literary history of "Native American picture-writing"? Chapter 1 considers such questions and reveals how pictography expands current understandings of the relationship between language, sign, and signified.

Having offered a definition of writing that includes pictographic texts, the chapter then traces how pictographic writing changed in response to the arrival of Europeans and the introduction (and imposition) of alphabetic writing. It also considers how, conversely, Native American pictography has shaped alphabetic texts in ways that literary scholars have yet to recognize. The brief discussions provided in the chapter reveal the enormous potential indigenous literacies possess to change understandings of early and nineteenth-century American literature. On the one hand, pictographic narratives, such as the sketchbooks produced by Native American prisoners in military forts, complicate traditional histories, genealogies, and understandings of nineteenth-century North American literature. On the other hand, the inter-animation between alphabetic and pictographic texts links, in unrecognized ways, canonical works such as Henry Wadsworth Longfellow's *The Song of Hiawatha* with *The Traditional History and Characteristic Sketches of the Ojibway Nation*, by the Ojibwe writer Kah-ge-ga-gah-bowh (George Copway).

Pictographic and alphabetic writing were two important textual forms that organized the transmission of knowledge in the colonial woodlands and beyond, but not the only ones. In chapter 2, another kind of indigenous record further challenges understandings of writing and refines methods used to read texts produced in the context of colonial struggle. Focusing on a peace council in 1645 recorded by the French in *The Jesuit Relations* and by the Haudenosaunee in wampum, the chapter extends the book's concerns with the inter-animation between alphabetic and indigenous literacies. Erroneously known mainly as "Indian money," wampum belts consist of shells and beads strung together and are maintained by Haudenosaunee nations as important documentary, legal, and cultural records. Throughout the colonial era, Haudenosaunee spokesmen negotiated diplomatic and cultural relations with French (as well as Dutch, British, and later American) colonists and settlers, who recognized that wampum belts "have the same use that writing and contracts have with us."[20] Organized by situationally specific adaptations of Haudenosaunee narrative and political traditions, particularly the Condolence Council and the Epic of the Peacemaker, this and later French-Haudenosaunee peace councils revolved around the exchange of wampum, as well as the construction of mutually intelligible forms of communication. Exploring the ways that people involved in this negotiation made sense of their respective textual systems internally, as well as cross-culturally, chapter 2 discusses how the radical alterity of these literacies shaped the records of this particular peace council.

The proceedings are partially recorded in *The Jesuit Relations*, a small passage in an enormous archive of Jesuit activity in "New France." The *Relations* have been a key resource for historical studies of colonial North America. As carefully composed and edited writing, the archive deserves greater critical attention from American literary scholars, as does the complex textuality of Haudenosaunee wampum. Just as wampum is more than a cultural artifact, alphabetic script is not simply a record of facts. As chapter 2 describes, both are documentary media and forms of literacy—one printed, the other beaded and strung. Records of such textual negotiations must be conceived together as a conjoined archive and as mutually informed texts rooted in distinct cultural and textual contexts.

Anyone familiar with *The Jesuit Relations* or with French-Haudenosaunee history will recognize that this is not a representative moment in Jesuit texts or in Franco-Haudenosaunee relations. In fact, relations between the two communities were more often hostile, and this particular peace accord did not last. However, the council and its records belong to a historical moment in which neither party held enough power to solely dictate the terms of engagement. Myra Jehlen proposes that in such "literature of the undetermined encounter," we can recover the contingency of early colonial negotiations before European settlers had achieved hegemony and the success of conquest came to seem overdetermined.[21] Such early moments make it possible to trace the multiple textual forms that organized cross-cultural meetings, a dialogism that is increasingly difficult to trace once alphabetism becomes more dominant.

The meeting in 1645 offers a window through which we can glimpse that which might have been and that did momentarily come into being: a multicultural and multi-semiotic literary sphere of dialogue and exchange. Such instances are not as singular as they seem, and they enable us to reimagine early American literary studies in profound new ways.[22] Recovering these moments of negotiation and reciprocity does not negate or diminish the enormity of the violence that attended conquest. On the contrary, it recognizes the tremendous loss sustained by indigenous people as a consequence of colonialism, without relegating their agency and records to obscurity. After conquest, the cultural and textual traditions of America's indigenous peoples often became invisible in historical and literary studies. Recovering such textual interactions and reading them in dialogue with indigenous records enable us to imagine a literary tradition rooted in negotiation and dialogues—rather than simply conquest and colonial monologues—at the foundation of American literature.

Chapter 2 closes by considering the implications of such insights for more canonical American literature, such as the foundational captivity narrative by Mary Rowlandson. Her brief, and understudied, representations of wampum as mere finery constitute a refusal to recognize its status as an alternative textual medium that is oddly analogous to the traditional inability of many American literary scholars to recognize indigenous forms of literacy in colonial America.

This is, however, a moment of possibility. In the past few decades, scholarship on literacy has undergone an internal critique which has resulted in new, culturally located ways to understand literacy and literary practices. Likewise, scholars of book history have expanded the material basis of their work to include a diversity of media. Such work has made possible important new ways to understand the literary landscape of colonial America.[23] Two studies have particularly helped shape this project. *The Darker Side of the Renaissance: Literacy, Territoriality, and Colonization* by Walter Mignolo describes how writing has been a key site of colonial struggles, and *Writing without Words: Alternative Literacies in Mesoamerica and the Andes*, edited by Elizabeth Hill Boone and Walter Mignolo, suggests what a radically revised sense of literary archive and method in the Americas might yield.[24] These two volumes offer methodologically enabling concepts that broaden textual studies of colonial encounters organized by both alphabetic and indigenous scripts. In *The Darker Side of the Renaissance*, Mignolo proposes the concept of "colonial semiosis" to "redraw the boundaries of a field of study mainly inhabited by texts alphabetically written by the colonizers."[25] In this way, Mignolo expands the notion of colonial discourse to account for "semiotic interactions between different writing systems."[26] This project brings Mignolo's concept of "colonial semiosis" to bear on North America; it conceives of early American literature as hemispheric and puts indigenous and alphabetic texts into dialogue. Such analysis is enabled by the term "alternative literacies," which Hill Boone and Mignolo use to describe non-alphabetic forms of writing with the potential to radically disrupt a colonial legacy maintained by narrow definitions of writing and literacy.

This project adapts and extends that term to encompass multiple forms of writing at play in colonial conflict. Hence, "alternative literacies" here refers not only to those forms of writing that are different from alphabetic script but to each system of writing that, in the space of colonial conflict, becomes relativized and, at times, mutually inter-animated. Only in its own cultural context is a given writing system normative, and as different systems of writing come into contact, each becomes strange and unfamiliar. Such moments reveal how "alternative literacies" relativize each other in a process here termed "colonial dialogization."[27] This book traces the processes of colonial dialogization at various stages in the establishment and contestation of alphabetic hegemony and suggests the diversity of literary early America while analyzing the internal logic of specific forms of indigenous writing in selected case studies.

Needless to say, no single monograph can adequately engage the full spectrum of indigenous literacy in the Americas before and during colonial conflict. Rather, select moments provide methodological tools for a textual study of the reciprocity of colonial encounters and for understanding the relationship between textuality and coloniality more generally.

Such an approach is possible in part because the difficulties we face today when we attempt such recovery to some extent parallel the challenges faced by writers long ago. Confronting radically different ways to write and record knowledge, they also theorized, by necessity, the dynamics of the cross-cultural and inter-semiotic communications they were negotiating. Such were the challenges confronting an Andean author who called himself Don Felipe Guaman Poma de Ayala, who in 1613 composed the manuscript El primer nueva corónica y buen gobierno addressed to King Philip III of Spain.[28]

Marked by both Andean and Spanish literary conventions, Guaman Poma's Corónica has much to teach us about indigenous Andean forms of literacy, as well as the textual implications of coloniality. In his use of multiple languages, alphabetic script, illustrations, and indigenous records of knowledge, Guaman Poma simultaneously validates and places all these perspectives and modes of communication into dialogue, making his manuscript an important site of colonial semiosis theorized and negotiated by a native Andean writer. As such, it is a uniquely important document in early American literature, one of the earliest produced by a native author from the continent who witnessed, lived through, and, indeed, was a product of conquest.

In his manuscript, Guaman Poma brings multiple and often competing voices, perspectives, and textual traditions into dialogue and an uneasy co-existence. As signaled by its title, the Corónica is self-consciously new in both its local and transnational contexts. This strangely modern text instantiates what Mikhail Bakhtin has called dialogization in its attempt to make the book a narrative space where Andean epistemology and quipu textuality can coexist with European cultural and narrative forms.[29] Thus, Guaman Poma's literary achievement goes beyond the mastery of a foreign system of literacy—alphabetism—as he brings different textual traditions into dialogue to produce a new chronicle of the colonial conflict between Spain and the Andes and a new vision of the American book.

The text is admittedly difficult for anyone trained in North American literary studies—there are no full English translations—and yet it offers a model for scholars whose field of training may be outside Latin America because Guaman Poma was not a native Spanish speaker, either. He has much to teach us about the inter-animation between European and indigenous American forms of literacy precisely because he attempted to navigate the two and instantiate a dialogue between them. Chapter 3 thus analyzes the intersection between indigenous and European forms of writing within the pages of a single, monumental text. The chapter locates Guaman Poma in the context of my larger argument about alternative literacies and colonial dialogization by tracing the relationship between Guaman Poma's *Corónica* (copiously illustrated and written in Spanish, Quechua, and Aymara in Latin scripts) and the indigenous Andean textual tradition embodied in quipus. In writing a history centered in the Andean world, Guaman Poma attempts to recoup the rupture of the Spanish conquest by reconciling Andean and Spanish textual forms within the pages of his manuscript.

As I trace Guaman Poma's efforts to negotiate and theorize the encounter of diverse literary traditions, I discuss in some detail the kind of textual tradition quipus represent. Using contemporary scholarship on quipus, I attempt to recover and explicate evidence of quipu literary modes and conventions in his alphabetically written manuscript. This analysis brings early Americanist scholarship into dialogue with Latin American texts and attempts to recover indigenous literacies in the context of highly asymmetric relationships of power—what we might call the overdetermined encounter.

Although useful and relevant at times, terms such as "encounter" and "contact" can elide the degree of violence that structured cross-cultural exchanges in the context of colonialism. Indeed, recovery efforts like this one are needed because of the tremendous levels of violence and destruction that attended conquest. Likewise, the methodological difficulties of such work result directly from the historical decimation that sometimes rendered entire epistemologies and writing systems illegible. For that reason, this project revises Mary Louise Pratt's influential notion of a "contact zone" and proposes that we understand someone like Guaman Poma as writing in a "conflict zone."[30] We can think of texts that emerge out of such conflict zones, via Galen Brokaw, as "textual conflict zones," where we can trace the messy and conflictual exchanges between forms of writing in the context of the unequal relations of power.[31]

Because of the asymmetry of power relations that organize the production of American literature, indigenous forms of writing are often marked by various kinds of discontinuity and disruption, leaving us with fragments rather than complete literary archives. Sometimes these fragments take the form of rare extant texts isolated in museums and collections; at other times, they are encoded or inscribed within alphabetic texts. In some cases, alphabetic script has become the vehicle for the preservation of ancient indigenous texts, as is the case with the Mayan Books of Chilam Balam.[32] In other cases, indigenous forms of textuality remain important within tribal communities even to the present day. Haudenosaunee representatives, for example, took wampum to Ottawa during the First World War to protest military conscription and then to Geneva in 1923–24 to argue before the League of Nations. As recently as 1988, a Haudenosaunee envoy presented and explicated a wampum belt at the United Nations as evidence of sovereignty rights secured during treaty negotiations.[33]

The Ojibwe Midé continue to use pictographic scrolls, although these sacred documents are not shared with the public. In the Andes, villages still use and maintain quipus, although their function has been dramatically altered since pre-colonial times.[34] Sometimes, as in the case of Midé scrolls, such texts are not meant for outsiders. At other times, as in the case of wampum, efforts to educate Europeans about wampum and assert its legitimacy as a binding document constitute longstanding traditions.

It is clear, then, that as different European and indigenous peoples came into contact across the American continents, they discovered not only worlds beyond those they had previously known but also new forms of literary and textual expression. Although the arrival of Europeans and the subsequent colonization of America brought about enormous changes, we can still trace these textual practices, ironically sometimes because they are inscribed within a colonial archive which is forever marked by its confrontation with indigenous forms of writing. Returning to exchanges such as the French-Haudenosaunee Peace Council and to texts such as Guaman Poma's *Corónica* enable us to recover the often overlooked textual dialogism at work in early colonial literature. The focus on dialogue and the dialogic in this project is thus simultaneously a methodological and an ethical move.

Although the inter-animation between alphabetic and indigenous forms of writing becomes less apparent as the colonial project advances, the recognition of its significance in early colonial texts has important implications for our understanding of other and later American literature. As evident in the writings of Mary Rowlandson and Henry Wadsworth Longfellow, indigenous textual forms have marked alphabetic settler literature in ways that are significant yet often unrecognized. The paradigm of "alternative literacies" and the methods developed here thus enables new understandings of American literature beyond the early colonial period. From an epic manuscript written by a man who called himself Don Felipe Guaman Poma de Ayala, the project concludes with another American epic, told by a narrator who calls himself Ishmael.

Whether or not we consider it the "unavoidable centerpiece of the American tradition," Moby-Dick remains one of the great novels of the English language, one of the great classics of the nineteenth century, and one of the great epics of the colonial world.[35] Because of Herman Melville's attention to the relationship between writing and coloniality, Moby-Dick and his first book, Typee, reveal the relevance of an "alternative literacies" approach to American literature outside the early colonial period. In both books, Melville represents Polynesian tattoos as forms of writing that are contrasted with and linked to alphabetic texts. Chapter 4 analyzes Typee and Moby-Dick and traces continuities and changes in Melville's representation of Polynesian tattoos and their relationship to writing.

Chapter 4 argues that tattoos on bodies and Polynesian hieroglyphs on wood are textual practices and that Melville's youthful encounters with indigenous, non-alphabetic systems of inscription constitute a "vital center" of his authorship. The term "vital center" recalls the climactic conclusion of Moby-Dick in which Queequeg's coffin, inscribed with the hieroglyphic marks of an unnamed Polynesian culture, emerges out of the vortex and saves the narrator, Ishmael. The coffin emblematizes the presence of Polynesian writing in the text. Queequeg's coffin cannot be deciphered because it is divorced from its original context. Nonetheless, it represents a critical key to the novel, which likewise cannot be understood separately from the Polynesian text at its "vital center." Indeed, to fully make sense of either, we must read them together as linked, mutually informed, and inter-animated yet rooted in the distinct context and cultures from which they derive their unique logics.

Like the previous chapters, chapter 4 pays careful attention to the specificity of non-alphabetic textual traditions—in this case, Polynesian tattoos. The final chapter returns to pictography and builds on the lessons and insights from chapter 1. The analysis uncovers direct correspondences between textual images in Moby-Dick and Polynesian tattooing motifs, revealing how Melville explores the possibility that writing and inscription, rather than marking colonial difference, can function as sites of commonality through the shared element of imagery.

Buoyed by a "coffin" that has been carved by his friend Queequeg with Polynesian "hieroglyphics," the narrator resurfaces from the vortex that has swallowed the Pequod and its crew. Melville represents this inscribed coffin as a form of writing, a "treatise," a literary document. What possibilities, what loss, and what potential recovery might Queequeg's coffin and the text inscribed on it represent? This book invokes Queequeg's coffin as a metaphor for indigenous forms of writing that also have the potential to resurge and form a "vital center" of American literature. Because the inter-animation among divergent forms of writing remains visible in early American literature, we can reconstruct some sense of the reciprocity that organized the interactions among different kinds of writing and literary traditions in the colonial period.

Paying particular attention to Native American pictography, Haudenosaunee wampum, Andean quipus, and Polynesian tattooing, this book explores the interaction between alphabetic script and indigenous forms of writing. Such textual traditions have their own cultural specificities and internal logic. At the same time, they marked and shaped the literary cultures of settler colonists. Early American literary studies—and studies of colonial literature—become richer and more nuanced fields when they are conceived as radically plural in linguistic and semiotic terms. Texts such as the interlinked records of the Haudenosaunee-French peace negotiations of 1645, Guaman Poma's *Corónica*, and Melville's *Moby-Dick* represent opportunities to recover aspects of non-alphabetic, indigenous forms of writing and to understand their dynamic relation to alphabetic scripts. Such work need not be limited to the American context. It has the potential to reconfigure our understanding of other colonial locations as well.[36]

As a Polynesian figure, Queequeg stands for more than just American indigeneity, and the title of this book points not just beyond the borders of the United States but also beyond the shores of the continent. Indeed, much of Melville's work is located in international waters and the multiracial and multinational crew of the *Pequod* travel a world made by colonialism. In that world, Queequeg is identified somewhat ambiguously as a Polynesian hailing from an unnamed island that is not on any map and thus, presumably, is not possessed, colonized, or even known by imperial powers.[37] The text on his coffin remains similarly beyond the comprehension of colonial categories, maps, or schemas because it is never deciphered. Queequeg's coffin serves as a leitmotif for this study, which seeks not to recuperate categories such as "writing" and "literature" but, rather, to recognize how such categories have constituted themselves through colonial relations. In this book, Queequeg's coffin represents the non-alphabetic, indigenous text in the colonial world, as well as the possibility for recovery and resurgence of subaltern literacies, texts, and knowledges. The coffin soars to the surface of the ocean after great struggle and destruction. Thus, it is a fitting trope for the transformative potential of understanding and narrating the American past differently to make possible a future that is not shaped by its colonial tropes and logic.

CHAPTER ONE

Writing and
Colonial Conflict

The indigenous peoples of what is now Mexico were not surprised when the Spanish arrived with their paper and ink. They had a similar, centuries-old tradition of writing on agave bark paper, *amatl*, to keep records.[1] As in Europe, such literacy was not widespread. Scribes, *tlacuilo* or *amatlacuilo*, were a distinct professional class, serving the elite as scribes generally did in Europe. Because the manuscripts of Mesoamerican peoples resembled European scrolls, they attracted the attention and interest of the Spanish. Indeed, the earliest reaction on both sides seems to have been philological curiosity. The Franciscan friar Bernardino de Sahagún, for example, worked with Mexica students at Colegio de Santa Cruz de Tlatelolco, compiling indigenous histories, translating them into alphabetic script, and teaching Mexica students how to write in Spanish.[2]

Sahagún used native scribes and employed parallel texts in Spanish and alphabetized Nahuatl. He gathered information through dialogue and conversation. Thus, Sahagún and his fellow workers created a site of linguistic and semiotic exchange where different forms of writing inter-animated each other on the pages of the manuscripts they produced. In the Florentine Codex, alphabetic and pictoglyphic Nahuatl writing were "part of a dialogue" that was linguistic, oral, and textual.[3] Nahuatl speakers in the process acquired alphabetic literacy, which they subsequently used to produce some of the earliest alphabetic texts written in the region.[4]

Indigenous people in North America also lived in a literate universe of documents, contracts, and public signs. Jesuit priests observed and sometimes used these established systems of writing in early missionary efforts.

For example, Sébastien Râle noted that the Abenaki of Maine communicated via pictography "as well as we understand each other by our letters."[5] Likewise, Barthélemy Vimont wrote that the Montagnais at Quebec recorded missionary teachings with "certain figures which represented for them the sense of some clause."[6] Boasting of the eagerness with which his Abenaki students took to Catholic teachings, Father Gabriel Druillettes stated in a report in 1652 that they "wrote out their lessons in their own manner. . . . They carried away this paper with them to study their lesson in the repose of the night."[7] Abbé J. A. Maurault, who edited Druillettes's report, added in a footnote that he had noted similar activity among other native Woodlands people: "We often saw during our instructions or explanations of the catechism that the Indians traced on pieces of bark, or other objects very singular hieroglyphs."[8] According to Maurault, the students would then spend the night studying "what they had so written, and in teaching it to their children or their brothers. The rapidity with which they by this manner learnt their prayers was very astonishing."[9]

Regardless of whether seventeenth-century missionaries were bragging about the eagerness of children to learn the gospel or attempting to translate it into indigenous scripts, such accounts testify to the existence of already established systems of literacy in the Northeastern Woodlands. As in central Mexico, these non-alphabetic, indigenous forms of writing remained viable in the area long after initial contact. Almost a century later, Joseph-François Lafitau documented the continued and ubiquitous use of such "hieroglyphic" marks not only for private purposes but also for public notices and other forms of communication. For example, Lafitau described how warriors on war expeditions would strip the bark from trees and use a specially prepared waterproof ink to leave messages for other, separate groups following behind them.[10] Upon returning home, warriors might similarly debark trees to create a surface on which to post an account of their exploits.[11] The fact that warriors traveled with waterproof ink and produced numerous public postings suggests, along with accounts of children taking private notes on birch bark, that literacy was common and not limited to certain privileged classes, as in Mesoamerica. The Northeastern Woodlands can then be understood as a site of widespread literacy used for public and private purposes.

We can surmise the extent of such literacy based on a brief passage in *The Jesuit Relations* from 1636, which reveals that the Huron had a word that meant "to write." Jean de Brébeuf uses the verb "*ahiaton*" to exemplify one class of conjugations in a discussion of Huron grammar. The existence of a word for writing is significant because societies name practices with which they are familiar. Equally important for understanding indigenous literacy in the region is the fact that the verb can be conjugated for all subject positions, indicating that "to write" was a common and familiar practice in Huron society.[12] Brébeuf discusses at length the difficulty of talking about phenomena with which the Huron are not familiar. He requests permission to translate "the Father" as "our Father" in his missionary work because the Huron insist on indicating relation when using the term "father." If the missionary use of a word like "father" must accommodate Huron linguistic practices, and if a word for "to write" exists with a full range of conjugations, writing must have been a practice familiar to the Huron, not needing special translation or linguistic invention. Conjugations for the subject positions I, you, he, they, and we indicate that this activity was practiced by all, or many, members of society.[13]

The use of hieroglyphic writing was not limited to the Huron. Algonquin people throughout the Northeastern Woodlands employed similar forms of writing, as did indigenous people west of the Great Lakes, along the Atlantic seaboard, and as far south as the Choctaw homelands in what is now Alabama and Mississippi. In the sub-Arctic region, indigenous people also used forms of hieroglyphic writing to communicate and to record information. Evidence of similar forms of writing has been found across the hemisphere, from the Andes to what is now Panama. Indeed, such hieroglyphic writing appears to have been widespread throughout pre-Columbian America, and petroglyphs suggest its antiquity.[14]

European newcomers to the American continents thus found the indigenous people writing on birch bark and in screenfold books, in public and in private, on matters both sacred and profane. The diversity of literary expression and the textual implications of a confrontation between different literate cultures constitute an important and neglected aspect of early American studies. How did we lose sight of this heritage and come to believe, as many do, that Europeans encountered a hemisphere without writing? The answer must be found in the complex history of colonialism. As a consequence of the struggle over territory and resources, Europe and its descendants in the Americas developed a "possessive investment" in writing as a marker of reason and civilization. Its purported absence in areas where Europe established colonies often served as a justification for conquest. Indigenous forms of writing eventually came to be defined as pictures or mnemonic aids, while alphabetic script, by contrast, has become nearly synonymous with "writing." However, such a narrow understanding of writing diminishes the literary diversity of colonial America and perpetuates the legacies of cultural imperialism.

Like the marks on Queequeg's coffin in *Moby-Dick*, indigenous forms of writing reveal something important about the textual, about the colonial process, and about the semiotic exchanges that took place when different cultures came into contact and conflict. Europeans initially marveled at, and catalogued, indigenous forms of writing, and America's native people likewise observed and engaged the literary culture of Europe. We can recover the dialogic potential of these early interactions by recognizing indigenous ways to record and transmit information as writing and by taking seriously the internal logic of such non-alphabetic writing systems. This chapter rejects the common historical equation between alphabetic script and "real writing" and advances a definition of writing that better comprehends the full diversity of America's literary heritage. Recognizing the colonial process as one shaped by the conflict between different cultures of literacy in turn allows us to tease out the ways in which dialogic, and sometimes reciprocal, exchanges shaped colonial literature and subsequent settler literature written in the Americas. The literature of the hemisphere thus appears as a vast and rich tableau in which the inter-animation between different forms of writing plays an important role in shaping literary production.

"The Science of Reading These Inscriptions":
Writing and the Legacy of Colonialism

Lafitau referred to the Algonquin scripts he observed as "hieroglyphics, writing, and records," but writing soon became a vexed and contentious terrain.[15] In the centuries that followed, other terms emerged—such as pictography—that reflected a different understanding of indigenous American scripts and implicitly questioned whether these "hieroglyphs" should be considered writing at all. Yet it seems clear that numerous indigenous communities used conventionalized systems of graphic marks capable of recording and communicating specific and detailed information. These marks could be read by others who were not present at the time of their production, so they were not simply mnemonic in nature. Rather, they functioned as systems of writing.

Historically, however, the term "writing" has been reserved primarily for alphabetic and syllabic scripts. "Pictographs" have been either classified as "forerunners of writing" or dismissed as "limited, dead-end means of communication."[16] American indigenous texts that are non-alphabetic have thus fallen outside the boundaries of literary study because they have not been considered "real" writing. Philologists and linguists have generally defined writing as recorded speech and posited the alphabet as its best and most complete form.[17]

This definition of "real writing" as recorded speech, actualized alphabetically, is deeply ingrained in the Western scholarly tradition. However, it is somewhat misleading. Alphabetic writing does not capture speech; it captures some elements of speech and leaves out others, such as intonation.[18] Familiarity with the conventions of a given writing system and its relationship to speech and culture can blind us to gaps between arbitrary signs (like letters), meaning, and pronunciation. Non-native students of English are often confounded by the divergence between its spoken and written forms. Nor is there ever a single and fixed relationship between alphabetic letters and sounds. For example, the letter "a" represents different sounds in Denmark, the United States, and, for that matter, any other country that uses the Roman alphabet. The relationship between writing, speech, culture, and scholarship is far more complex than immediately apparent, and indigenous American writing systems have not been well understood by scholars of writing.[19] To consider what constitutes writing, and what is at stake in such definitions, we must come to terms with long-standing assumptions about writing, as well as the history of colonialism, out of which such ideas have emerged.

A brief survey of the terms that organize scholarship on writing enables us to critically engage basic definitions and understand their colonial underpinnings. Scholars have generally distinguished between two overarching types of writing—namely, glottographic and semasiographic writing.[20] Glottographic, or sound-based, writing uses graphic signs to represent spoken language. It is subdivided into phonographic and logographic writing. Phonographic writing, such as the alphabet, consists of arbitrary signs that refer to linguistic micro-elements such as syllables, vowels, or consonants. When signs represent whole words, they are called logographs. In English, the symbols "&" and "%" are examples of logographic signs.[21] The signs can be arbitrary (e.g., "&") or they can be phonetic similes, like using the image of an eye for the concept "I." In practice, phonographic and logographic forms of writing are often combined. An example would be a sentence such as, "Save $$$! 25% off the original price."

Semasiographic writing, on the other hand, uses graphic signs to refer to larger chunks of information such as ideas or concepts and combines these signs to create narrative.[22] This term pairs the Greek words *semasia* (meaning) and *graphikos* (to write) to account for writing systems that graphically represent meaning without reference to sound.[23] Such forms of writing are also called picture, idea, or word writing. The relationship between graphic sign and meaning can be iconic or it can be arbitrary and conventional, as is the case with musical and mathematical notations. Iconic writing is often used in "brainteasers" such as rebuses and pictogram puzzles. A picture of an eye may represent an eyeball, the act of seeing, or the pronoun "I." Sometimes, when a picture of an eyeball means "eye," the relationship between sign and signified can be understood across linguistic boundaries, a potential advantage in linguistically diverse environments such as the precolonial Americas. At other times, when a picture of an eye represents the pronoun "I," familiarity with the language in which the two are homonyms is necessary to interpret the graphic sign correctly.

Like glottographic writing, semasiographic scripts may use arbitrary signs to refer to concepts via a conventionalized code. In mathematics, for example, numerals, letters, and specialized signs such as "+" are conventionally understood as numbers, things, and actions such as "add." In public spaces such as airports, semasiographic signs for restrooms, telephones, and baggage often appear alongside alphabetic writing in multiple languages. Airports represent a site where phonographic and semasiographic forms of writing coexist in our contemporary world. Nonetheless, scholars have historically theorized glottographic and semasiographic writing as distinct and temporally separate forms and posited as superior writing that represents speech, with alphabetic writing at the pinnacle.

Because alphabetic writing uses a relatively small number of signs that combine to represent an almost infinite number of sounds, scholars have traditionally considered it more efficient and accurate than all other forms of writing. Semasiographic forms of writing, on the other hand, has generally been theorized as "forerunners of writing," an earlier stage in the development of full-fledged sound-based writing (see figure 1).

These categories and distinctions may, however, say more about our limited understanding of non-alphabetic forms of writing than about the

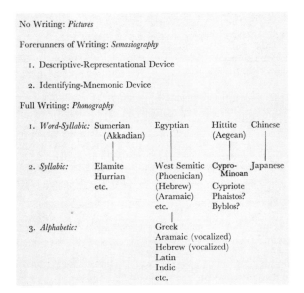

No Writing: *Pictures*

Forerunners of Writing: *Semasiography*

  1. Descriptive-Representational Device

  2. Identifying-Mnemonic Device

Full Writing: *Phonography*

  1. *Word-Syllabic:* Sumerian   Egyptian   Hittite   Chinese
                     (Akkadian)   (Aegean)

  2. *Syllabic:*   Elamite   West Semitic   Cypro-   Japanese
                    Hurrian   (Phoenician)   Minoan
                    etc.   (Hebrew)   Cypriote
                                (Aramaic)   Phaistos?
                                etc.   Byblos?

  3. *Alphabetic:*   Greek
                                Aramaic (vocalized)
                                Hebrew (vocalized)
                                Latin
                                Indic
                                etc.

1. Schematic representation of the history of writing, from *A History of Writing* by Ignace J. Gelb. Courtesy of the University of Chicago Press.

scripts themselves. Only a few decades ago, for instance, Mayan writing was presumed to be entirely semasiographic. As deciphering has progressed, we have learned that it combines purely phonetic and logographic elements.

The pictorial elements of what Garrick Mallery called "Native American picture-writing" may have blinded philologists to the possibility that these scripts can also combine phonetic and logographic elements. This would indeed make them similar to the Egyptian script to which Lafitau and others implicitly compared them: hieroglyphics. Egyptian hieroglyphs employ a number of signs that seem to represent animals or natural objects, such as reeds. Despite their superficial appearance as mere images, such "pictures" represent sounds rather than objects. For example, two successive "reeds" stand for the vowel "e." Likewise, a simple representation of a hand stands for the sound "t," and what appears to be a naturalistic representation of a lion stands for the sound "l." Other signs are logograms that stand for ideas or words.[24] While European thinkers had known about Egyptian hieroglyphic writing for centuries, a crucial breakthrough in deciphering came only in the early nineteenth century with the realization that the script was not only pictographic, but also phonographic. Even when such crucial insights initiate deciphering of a script, it can take decades or more for deciphering to proceed. While Diego de Landa correctly perceived a phonetic basis to what he called the "Maya alphabet" as early as 1566, he misunderstood the nature of the script, which was syllabic rather than alphabetic. Various misperceptions obstructed attempts at deciphering well into the twentieth century, until scholars began to unravel its syllabic nature.[25]

When Ignace J. Gelb first published his magisterial monograph A Study of Writing in 1952, he cited the inability of Western scholars to decipher Mayan script as evidence of its failure to have developed into a full-fledged writing system. "The best proof that the Maya writing is not a phonetic system results from the plain fact that it is still undeciphered," Gelb argued, and declared himself "in complete accord with the opinions of two eminent Americanists" that " 'no native race in America possessed a complete writing'; 'the Maya hieroglyphs are by no means a real writing in our sense.' "[26] Only late in the twentieth century did scholars such as Michael Coe and Linda Schele establish beyond a doubt the phonetic nature of Mayan script. Even so, this complex writing system remains only partially deciphered.[27]

The case of Maya writing should caution us against dismissing as non-writing graphic forms of communication that we do not understand. While Maya script in the last half of the twentieth century moved from the category of "pre-writing" into the realm of "writing" proper, nothing intrinsic to the script itself changed. Despite its inclusion in the category of "full writing" in recent synthetic publications, many scholars continue to maintain a basic division between "full writing" and "proto-writing," such as "Amerindian pictography" (see figure 2).[28]

These categories remain problematic and potentially misleading. Like Mayan writing, other indigenous American scripts that appear to be entirely semasiographic may eventually turn out to be more phonetic than thus far understood. Because indigenous American scripts have received relatively little attention from scholars of writing, appropriate terminology remains a vexing and unresolved issue. While some forms of writing from the North American Plains and from Mesoamerica do appear to be largely semasiographic, others may be combination scripts that combine semasiographic and phonetic elements, or they may be entirely phonetic. Research to answer such questions is stymied in part by the lack of extant documents and the general destruction that attended conquest.

In The Jesuit Relations from 1636, Jean de Brébeuf explicitly notes a relationship between Huron language and script: "They have a letter to which we have nothing to correspond—we express it by Khi; the use of it is common to the Montagnés and to the Algonquins."[29] We do not know what hieroglyphic sign corresponded to the sound "khi," and yet de Brébeuf's

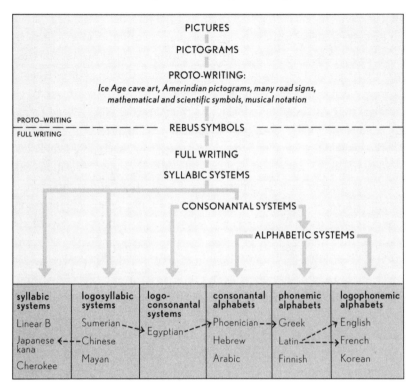

2. Schematic representation of the classification of writing systems. From *Lost Languages: The Enigma of the World's Undeciphered Scripts* by Andrew Robinson. © 2002, 2009 Andrew Robinson. Published by Thames and Hudson Ltd, London.

observations suggest it was more like a letter than like a picture. Unable to study this particular letter or the writing system of which it was part, we can nonetheless theorize that "Huron hieroglyphs" functioned at least partly as a sound-based system of writing. This prospect opens up the possibility that what Mallery called picture writing was either fully or partially phonetic in nature. Mallery's contemporary, Daniel Brinton, argued just that in 1893, when he cautioned that "the term 'picture-writing' as applied to this graphic material conveys an erroneous impression. These delineations were intended and are to be regarded as letters, not as pictures. The object of the artist was not to paint or draw but TO WRITE. . . . This is an all-important distinction, as upon it turns the science of reading these inscriptions."[30] Brinton, a linguist, archeologist, and ethnographer, goes on to note that such Native American scripts, like Egyptian hieroglyphs, employ a combination of elements, including some that are "emblematic," with the relationship between the sign and the signified being as arbitrary as in alphabetic writing. Furthermore, Brinton argues that the forms of North American writing he studied represent, and correspond to, the structure of spoken language. Unfortunately, Brinton's insights were not widely accepted. Few scholars took such scripts seriously as writing and therefore failed to interrogate their internal logic or their relationship to language.

The question of whether indigenous American "hieroglyphs" constitute writing remains entangled with a fraught history of colonial relations that have organized intellectual inquiry. Indeed, definitions are not neutral elements of epistemology but sites of power and traces of struggle. Far from being simply a technology that captures and preserves the spoken word, the term "writing" has a history, a genealogy; just like "pictography," it is embedded in relations of power and reflects a complex history of struggle and resistance. Traces of this struggle can be read in terms such as "real writing" and its inferior other, "pre-writing." Such philological terms provide entry points for understanding the discursive "work involved in the construction of social phenomena," such as the ostensible absence of indigenous writing.[31] What textual practices are negated by categories such as "real" or "complete" writing used in classic scholarship? Read against the grain, such terms represent a semantic trace of the process of erasure, the negation of forms of writing that have been delegitimized by centuries of scholarship informed by a colonial unconscious.[32]

Isaac Taylor's publication The History of the Alphabet (1899) exemplifies such scholarship.[33] Taylor organized different writing systems into various categories conceptualized as sequential, "successive," and hierarchic. This evolutionary model posited simple pictures as the beginning of a progression toward alphabetism, with pictorial symbols, simple verbal signs, and then syllabic signs as intermediary stages.[34] The production of simple pictures marked "the first permanent step that was taken in the progress towards civilization," while alphabetism marked the highest stage in this journey of "human progress."[35] Alphabetic script, then, represented the most advanced stage in writing and, by extension, the highest level of human evolution. All other forms of writing were conceptualized as pre-alphabetic and indicated lower stages of human development and achievement in the journey toward "progress" and "civilization."[36]

For Taylor and many other thinkers of his day, different forms of writing corresponded to evolutionary and racial hierarchies. Such scholarship mapped difference around the world onto an evolutionary timeline in which peoples living in the same historical moment represented different stages of human development. In this way, categories of writing came to mirror racial categories, with the alphabet and Europe at the apex of human civilization. Indigenous American writing systems came to represent a precursor to the "real" writing used by those who colonized the hemisphere, just as the indigenous people themselves were categorized as representatives of earlier stages of human development who possessed only "prehistory." This denial of coevalness, as Johannes Fabian terms it, negates contemporaneous existence and makes a displacement in time complicit with a displacement in space. Recent critiques of disciplinary ethnocentrism such as Fabian's in anthropology and Eric Wolf's in history can also be brought to bear on scholarship of writing, which has largely failed to deal with the context of military conquest and colonialism in which the alphabet "triumphed" over and "conquered" other forms of writing.[37]

"We Found a Great Number of Books in These Letters, and . . . We Burned Them All"

When Europeans arrived in the Americas, they found a range of writing systems radically different from the alphabet in both form and function.[38] As a consequence, new ways to understand literacy and the textual could have emerged. That was one potential outcome of Sahagún's *Colegio*. However, writing soon became a site of conflict and struggle, where cultural colonization attended and supplemented military conquest.[39] Spanish colonial agents destroyed indigenous records and attached such significance to writing as a tool of colonization that they established a printing press in New Spain almost immediately after conquest began.[40]

Unlike Sahagún, many other friars investigating indigenous writing systems did so primarily in order to determine whether the scripts were idolatrous or otherwise in conflict with the teachings and authority of the Bible. On the Yucatan peninsula, for example, Diego de Landa documented Maya writing and history. His short book *Yucatan before and after the Conquest* (1566) describes the Maya writing system, along with local history, culture, and science as related to him by native informers.[41] According to de Landa, the Maya "used certain characters or letters, with which they wrote in their books about their antiquities and their sciences; with these, and with figures, and certain signs in the figures, they understood their matters, made them known, and taught them."[42] De Landa concluded that Mayan writings on historical, scientific, and religious matters constituted a threat to Christian teachings and thus Spanish rule: "We found a great number of books in these letters, and since they contain nothing but superstitions and falsehoods of the Devil we burned them all, which they took most grievously, and which gave them great pain."[43]

With this action, de Landa heeded the call of one of the first Franciscans to arrive in Mexico. A leader in the "spiritual conquest" that accompanied military occupation, Toribio de Benavente Motolinía studied the indigenous literary traditions and identified a range of genres such as ritual calendars, cosmogonies, religious ceremonies, and historical annals. He then appealed to his fellow missionaries to destroy all but the historical books, which were seen as reliable historical sources for European chroniclers.[44] All other documents were categorized as works of the devil, designed to lead America's indigenous people from Christianity. De Landa answered Motolinía's call to destroy most native texts with his famous *auto-da-fé* of July 1562 at Maní, which ordered the wholesale destruction of indigenous documents in the Yucatan, including twenty-seven glyphic rolls.[45]

Despite the plenitude of early accounts about indigenous writings and despite scattered sites of literary exchange such as the Colegio Tlatelolco, other voices and projects thus prevailed. De Landa's careful record of indigenous literacy and knowledge seems in conflict with his own orders to destroy the sources of that knowledge, but the two acts are in fact complementary. De Landa's book about Maya writing, and his destruction of Mayan books, functioned dialectically to displace indigenous writing and replace it with colonial and alphabetic authority.[46] As the sixteenth century wore on, indigenous Americans were becoming in the European imaginary people without letters or books, without writing or civilization. At Valladolid in 1550, Bartolomé de Las Casas claimed that, while America's native people had reason and were therefore able to rule themselves, they did "not have a written language that corresponds to the spoken one, as the Latin language does with ours. . . . For this reason they are considered to be uncultured and ignorant of letters and learning."[47] Such testimony marks the early stages of a process that would conceptualize colonized people in the Americas and elsewhere as non-literate, making writing an index of difference between savagery and civilization. The French philosopher Jean-Jacques Rousseau summarized this teleology with the statement that "the depicting of objects is appropriate to Savage people; signs of words and propositions, to a barbaric people, and the alphabet to civilized peoples."[48]

As Europeans began to develop a sense of themselves as different from those they colonized, that difference became not only racialized but also linked to the possession of writing, defined narrowly as alphabetism. The persistent use of the possessive in the discourse on writing is notable. Eighteenth-century and nineteenth-century writers repeatedly stressed that Europe *had* history, writing, and literature, that others did not *possess* it. This possessive investment in writing eventually came to underpin white racial identity, particularly in North America, where it was elaborated through anti-literacy slave codes.[49] As Europe and its descendants in the Americas claimed exclusive possession of writing and linked the possession of this technology to a hierarchy of humanity, "writing" became a maker and marker of racial difference.[50]

The distinction between peoples with and without writing has underpinned colonial myths of civilization and savagery for centuries and shaped literary production in important ways. Even critiques of European civilization posit writing as one of its defining characteristics. For example, in his despondent, post–First World War poem "Hugh Selwyn Mauberley," Ezra Pound makes "a few thousand battered books" the mark of Europe's "botched civilization."[51] But the lack of writing among America's indigenous peoples was, both materially and discursively, a European production. Indigenous documents, historical records, and other evidence of writing systems were destroyed, stolen, discredited, or simply defined out of existence by centuries of scholarship.

Taylor's work thus emerged out of a longstanding sense among European and Euro-American thinkers that alphabetic writing was a mark of higher civilization. His work also reflected a movement from philology to linguistics that would prioritize speech and equate only alphabetism with "real writing." The American linguist Leonard Bloomfield used this term in his study *Language* (1933) to specify writing meant to represent speech.[52] Taking up Taylor's evolutionary schema, Bloomfield drew a crucial distinction between phonetic-alphabetic writing and all other writing systems. Such work would be supplemented throughout the twentieth century by studies in Germany, France, and the United States. This development simultaneously privileged phonetic scripts in scholarship on writing and marginalized seemingly non-phonetic scripts, now conceptualized as outside the realm of "real" writing.

In one of the most ambitious and influential of these studies, A Study of
Writing, Ignace J. Gelb coined the term "grammatology" to mark the depar-
ture from philology and argued that "writing is, as some linguists assume, a
device for the recording of speech. . . . All the stages in which writing does
not serve this purpose are only feeble attempts in the direction of writing,
but not real writing."[53] The indigenous people of the Americas were among
the peoples Gelb designated as having managed "only feeble attempts" at
writing, although he ironically devotes no fewer than thirty-one pages to
describe the variety of such "not real writing." Such inclusion, however,
only serves to buttress his argument that non-phonetic notation systems
represent "pre-writing," mere "feeble attempts."

Gelb's use of the adjective "feeble" echoed a longstanding tradition linking writing to cognitive difference. In the twentieth century, the work of
literacy theorists such as Eric Havelock, Jack Goody, and Walter Ong, among
others, reinforced such notions by linking alphabetic literacy to cognitive
abilities such as rational thought and formal logic.[54] Although Goody and a
number of other literacy theorists eventually modified these ideas, the cor-
relation between literacy and cognition retained currency even in the late
twentieth century. In The Conquest of America, an erudite and widely read book,
Tzvetan Todorov argues that the numerically inferior Spaniards defeated the
Aztecs because of their superior ability to manipulate signs, and he maintains that writing can serve as an "index of the evolution of mental structures."[55] Such work affirms the importance of refuting the myth that America's indigenous people did not write. This notion not only excludes from
the purview of literary and colonial studies a rich archive of non-alphabetic
texts; it also reproduces notions of essentialist difference between groups of
human beings.[56]

Ironically, such difference is established in part through the consistent
demand for equivalence that organizes comparative studies of writing, re-
quiring "their" writing to be like "ours" in order to count. Almost all classic
studies of writing take up pictographic writing only to dismiss it, casting it
as the relative form that mirrors, and thus establishes, the privileged status
of phonetic writing.[57] In fact, phonetic writing must be contrasted with
pictography (or some other kind of writing) for this hierarchy of value to be
instituted; alphabetic writing becomes "real" and normative, while pictographic writing serves as its conceptual "other."[58] In the context of colonialism, we can observe a similarly specular relationship in which the colonizing culture begins to understand and express itself in relationship to a

colonial "other." This reflects a larger dialectic of colonizer and colonized in which the colonizing culture constructs and establishes itself as normative, the "value form" of humanity.

The historical context of conquest helps explain why philologists mapped different types of writing onto a hierarchical, evolutionary scheme, constructing linear, unified, and monogenetic histories of writing that culminated in the Roman alphabet and made it normative. Such histories paralleled evolutionary models of the development of mankind that placed Europeans at the pinnacle of human progress. Thus, classic scholarship on writing emerged within a closed hermeneutic circle organized by cultural bias and logocentrism. However, the purported limitations of indigenous writing do not actually inhere in the writing systems themselves. Rather, they reflect (while simultaneously masking) the limited understanding and cultural bias of the scholars who constructed histories and theories of writing around a teleological vision rooted in European civilization. Thus, literacy needs to be defined in "variable and culturally determined ways," as Stephen Houston and others have argued.[59]

To be sure, the classic work of literacy scholars such as Havelock and Goody has been soundly critiqued in the past few decades by scholars of literacy working from a range of perspectives and disciplines. The field of new literacy studies, for example, has challenged the early work of literacy theorists and described the diverse ways in which people use and relate to literacy; explored the great variety of literacy practices among different groups; and recognized the relationship between power, identity, and literacy.[60] At the same time, scholars doing comparative studies of writing across cultures have uncovered widely disparate ways to understand and use writing in different societies and described the manifold ways that spoken language and scripts are related in different cultures. Such work reveals the culturally, and temporally, specific and contingent nature of terms such as "writing" and "literacy" and the diverse ways in which different groups understand the relationship between knowledge, language, and permanent records.[61]

Indeed, cross-cultural studies undermine the closed hermeneutic circle of logocentrism. Because they bring into dialogue two or more disparate hermeneutics, cross-cultural encounters require the denial and denigration of "foreign" systems of knowledge to keep a logocentric logic intact. Or they demand the alternative: a recognition that writing and literacy are always culturally embedded and variable practices. Scholars looking to under-

stand the reciprocity of early American literature must come to terms with
how "writing" has functioned as a colonizing discourse if they are to appreciate how different forms of writing interacted with and inter-animated each
other. Such work becomes possible if we abandon narrow, phonocentric
definitions of writing. Therefore, I propose to amend Geoffrey Samson's
and Elizabeth Hill Boone's definition so that "writing" refers to *communication of relatively specific ideas transmitted across space and/or time by use of a conventionalized system of visual or tactile marks understood by a given a community of
readers.*[62] Such a redefinition of writing enables us to take account of a great
variety of indigenous records from the American continents. Indeed, across
the hemisphere, it is possible to move from monologic to dialogic studies of
colonial conflict, because native people across the Americas *did* write and at
times wrote in dialogue with Europeans texts—an archive that invites fascinating studies of textual and cultural inter-animation and reciprocity.

Of course, such redefinition must not be done lightly, as an overly broad
definition of writing might empty the term of any real meaning. At the same
time, it is crucial to become aware of the historical and ideological work
done by this term. Narrow and phonocentric definitions of writing leave in
place ethically troubling assumptions rooted deeply in a colonialist history.
Furthermore, the failure to understand any given writing system limits our
understanding of writing and the textual in general. Because scholars of
writing have often dismissed indigenous American forms of writing, our
understanding of what has been called "pictography" remains limited, yet it
appears to have been among the most ancient and widespread forms of
writing in the hemisphere.

The term "pictography" is problematic for both historical and technical
reasons, as Brinton warned us, yet it is not easily replaced by the term "semasiography," which denotes a lack of phoneticism that will be inaccurate in many,
perhaps even most, cases. Furthermore, while important differences exist
between, say, indigenous writing systems used in the Northeast, on the Plains,
and in Mesoamerica, the term "pictography" does suggest something of the
relatedness and ubiquity of such graphic forms of writing throughout the
hemisphere, in contrast to alphabetic and syllabic scripts that hail from the
post-conquest era and in contrast to other textual traditions that are uniquely
regional, and three-dimensional, such as wampum and quipus. "Pictography," for lack of a better word, is an important part of American's literary
history, and the term will serve as a flawed but capacious placeholder until
more appropriate terminology is developed.[63]

What matters here is that a broader definition of writing makes it possible to revisit "pictography" in North America and move our discussion from whether it constitutes writing to how various semasiographic and hieroglyphic records functioned in relation to the communities that used them and how it changed as a consequence of the arrival of Europeans. The remainder of this chapter will focus specifically on the form and literary history of Native American pictography, which remains a rather neglected field of inquiry. This can be explained not only by past failures to recognize such records as writing, but also by the lack of extant materials, which presents unique methodological challenges. My method will necessarily involve some degree of recovery and reconstruction, although this is neither an archeological nor an anthropological project. Rather, my focus will be on the challenges and possibilities of that part of the archive which emerged as a consequence of the clash between Europeans and indigenous Americans. Parsing through the scattered records of that encounter—from missionary reports to extant Plains winter counts—what can we reasonably infer about pictographic scripts in North America before and after Europeans arrived? How can we understand this surviving archive as a textual site in which the records and the logic of alphabetic and indigenous forms of writing remain forever intertwined? What might we learn about writing and colonial conflict by investigating the forms and histories of indigenous American pictography?

Native American Pictography and Early American Literature

While pictography hails from many parts of the world, it was particularly widespread and varied in the American hemisphere. What about the indigenous American world made it such fertile ground for pictography—or what about pictography was so particularly well suited to this context? The confluence of immense linguistic diversity and intense social interaction across geographic distances brought about by a well-developed network of trade across the hemisphere provide one answer. Elizabeth Hill Boone has theorized that pictographic scripts suited the American context because they can function without recourse to spoken language and can move across linguistic barriers. Anyone literate in the conventions of a given script can sound it out in a variety of languages, as is the case with pictographic signs such as those for "restroom" and "telephone," which we find today in international contexts like airports.[64] Hill Boone focuses on Mesoamerica, an area which has generated much analytic insight. While my focus will be on

North America, it is useful to consider what we can learn from Mesoameri-can pictographic scripts, such as those produced by the Mixtec and Aztec.[65] Such texts best conform to terms like "picture-writing" or "semasiography" in that images are the central elements that communicate meaning and narrative. Despite varying degrees of phoneticism, Hill Boone argues that glyphs are "fundamentally a part of the pictorial presentation. It is the relationship of the disparate pictorial elements that carries the meaning."[66] Hence, phonetic glyphs play a relatively minor role in the construction of narrative, which is able to traverse linguistic barriers precisely because signs represent meaning and idea complexes rather than sounds. While meaning is communicated fairly precisely by these signs and their relative placement, wording remains somewhat flexible.[67] Thus, a narrative produced by Aztec scribes in central Mexico could be read and sounded out in a different language by Mixtec readers in southern Oaxaca as long as they were familiar with the conventions of the text and the culture that informed it.[68] This point is crucial. The images are not simply pictures which communicate meaning transparently, as in the example of an eyeball representing an eye. Rather, they are part of a system of writing which requires its readers to be literate in the meaning of each sign, the way in which the relative placement of signs determines meaning, and the cultural context out of which this meaning emerges.

Europeans such as Sahagún, who arrived in the region and worked with indigenous texts, acquired some working knowledge of these pictographic forms of writing from their native collaborators, who in turn achieved some alphabetic proficiency. These exchanges produced documents uniquely rooted in the colonial dynamic. Texts such as the Florentine Codex and the Books of Chilam Balam emerged out of and testify to such exchanges, which can be seen as characteristic of the earliest "American" literature. While writing became a site of struggle, colonization, and resistance, it was also at times a site of dialogue and rare collaboration. We can recover that potential at the center of early American literature because these texts are themselves shaped and informed by the methodological challenges inherent in such a project. The linguistic, cultural, and semiotic difficulties that confront scholars are, to some extent, the same that confronted Europeans and indigenous Americans trying to communicate and negotiate radically different kinds of writing in the early colonial period.

Writing in America remains more than print and alphabetism, even after such rare collaborations became increasingly uncommon and the colonial project became more entrenched. More than two hundred years after French and other colonial agents first documented literate communities in the Northeastern Woodlands, Garrick Mallery, a U.S. Army colonel and ethnographer, set out to conduct a comprehensive study of such practices. He was able to obtain birch bark records that were "immemorially and still made by the Passamaquoddy and Penobscot tribes of Abnaki [sic] in Maine," as well as among the Montagnais and Nascapees, who lived north of the St. Lawrence River in territories traversed by French colonial agents centuries before. Mallery compared birch bark records produced by the Ojibwe, the Mi'kmaq, and the Abenaki and established "a similarity in the use of picture-writing between the members of the widespread Algonquin stock in the regions west of the Great Lakes and those on the northeastern seaboard."[69]

Mallery documented that, even in the late nineteenth century, Algonquin-speaking peoples in the Northeast continued to use a system of writing on birch bark that predated the arrival of Europeans. In 1893, Mallery's contemporary, the Penobscot writer Joseph Nicolar, listed pictographic writing among traditional practices of the Penobscot and located its origins in genealogy: "Reading and writing were never taught . . . until after they had divided themselves into clans."[70] Algonquin peoples across the region shared not only closely related languages and cultures, but also similar or possibly even identical systems of writing that were partially phonetic. Was this a hieroglyphic system closely related to spoken language in the manner of Mayan script, or was it more pictographic in nature? The answer to that question must remain speculative, given the history of disruption and the tendency of human practices to change over time. It is certainly possible that a shared system of writing traveled across areas of linguistic diversity in a region that shared linguistic roots and cultural traits in the manner of Mixtec pictography. If so, it might have functioned as a kind of lingua franca for people trading and conducting diplomacy across tribal boundaries. As such, it was likely connected to another lingua franca in the region—namely, sign language.

The use of sign language in North America is well known, and colonial observers noted that it was commonly used in multilingual settings where diverse peoples negotiated trade and treaty agreements. Sign language, in turn, appears to have been related to graphic script, with some pictographic signs having a direct correspondence to sign-language gestures. Mallery notes the similarity of pictographic signs and hand gestures for words such as "fear," "chief," and "sun."[71] The "gesture sign for sky, heaven, is generally made by passing the index [finger] from east to west across the zenith.

This curve is apparent in the Ojibwa pictograph" for sky.[72] North American pictographic writing might then have combined hieroglyphic and pictographic elements, with some hieroglyphic elements related to spoken language, and some pictographic elements related to sign language. This possibility confounds standard categories in scholarship on writing, which do not account for the possibility that writing records language without recording sound, as would be the case with pictographic signs representing gestures from sign language. North America thus forces us to reconsider the ways in which we understand writing and its relationship to language.[73] Here, the relationship between graphic units, speech, and the gestures of sign language suggests a triangulated complex in which imagery may be central without being divorced from language.

Travelers in the colonial period remarked repeatedly on the eloquence of native speakers in North America and on the high degree to which speeches were marked and shaped by metaphors.[74] Like many others, Lafitau noted that Haudenosaunee oratory was "full of figures of speech and quite metaphorical."[75] In the nineteenth century, Brinton explained that the sentence "*mooshkin aguwa manitowa*" literally means "I fill my kettle for the spirit" and thus makes sense only when understood as a metaphor meaning, "I prepare to go forth on a medicine hunt."[76] One key sign in the graphic representation of this sentence is a kettle. In order to understand how a graphic image of a kettle represents going on a "medicine hunt," one must know the relationship between the metaphoric language, "fill my kettle for the spirit," and the literal meaning "going on a medicine hunt." This observation permits further insight into the relationship between language and pictographic writing. Languages organized in large part around metaphor would correspond well to writing systems organized largely around images, ideographs, and other staples of pictographic writing. Indeed, the word "image" could equally apply to a spoken metaphor and to a given pictographic sign. Images and metaphors convey meaning in larger conceptual chunks than letters, in part by drawing on cultural references.[77]

The relationship between sign and signified can be relatively direct (i.e., sunrise, noon), or it can be quite abstract (e.g., fear). Sometimes the relationship between graphic sign and signified is established through a complicated interplay of representational, linguistic, and cultural associations. Lafitau's etymological description of a particular glyph reveals a metonymic relationship between language and graphic sign. As he notes,

The Iroquois and Huron call war *n'ondoutagette* and *gaskenrhagette*. The final syllable *gagetton*, found in the compound in these two words and meaning "to carry," marks the fact that people formerly carried to war something so much its symbol that it [war] took its name from it. The word, *ondouta*, means the down taken from marsh reeds and also the whole plant which they use to make mats on which they lie, so that it seems that they apply this term to war, because each warrior carried his mattress with him on expeditions of this sort. Indeed, the mat is still today the symbol that they represent in their hieroglyphic paintings to designate the number of their campaigns.[78]

The glyph for going to war is thus a fairly abstract representation of a mattress, described elsewhere as "cross-hatches," which might be legible across linguistic barriers to readers familiar with that convention. However, it is not pure pictography in Hill Boone's sense, as Lafitau's etymology lesson reveals. The "mattress glyph" has both cultural and linguistic underpinnings. One root word is "*ondouta*," a term which refers to a particular plant, as well as to parts of the plant used to make mattresses. A second root word is "*gagetton*," which means "to carry." Mattresses were conventionally associated with going to war, because each warrior would carry his own mattress. The compound word "*n'ondoutagette*" would literally mean "mattress carrying." The glyph for "going to war" is, then, conceptual *and* linguistic, simultaneously pictographic and phonetic in a compound-logographic manner which combines noun and verb. The relationship between graphic sign and signified is thus metonymic, where a graphic sign resembling a mattress stands for going to war, just as the graphic sign "pen" might metonymically represent the activity of writing. As in all metaphorical relationships, there is a transfer of meaning—in this case, through a chain of linguistic and cultural references so that readers must be familiar with a glyph, a language, cultural practices, and chains of association in order to recognize in an abstract image of crosshatches a reference to a mattress, the compound word "*n'ondoutagette*," and the activity of war.

Compound words, like those Lafitau discusses, are common in many American Indian language families, including Nahuatl, Iroquoian, and Algonquian.[79] Such polysynthesis—the creation of linguistic compounds which combine different roots and modifiers—means that individual words often function like entire sentences, with nouns, verbs, and other linguistic elements. Semasiographic writing, where signs stand for idea complexes and where roots can combine with various modifiers, might correspond well to such polysynthetic languages. Ironically, such analysis, enabled by the non-phonetic definition of writing offered earlier in this chapter, suggests that in this case, there is in fact a fundamental relationship between writing and language.[80] Some pictographic signs in the American Northeast do appear to be related to or to reflect aspects of language, including metaphors, the gestures of sign language, and a linguistic tendency toward compound words. Other signs are conceptual, like that for sunrise, or they combine linguistic and conceptual elements. Even this brief discussion thus reveals the immense potential of engaging indigenous American systems of writing without prejudice and affirms that different kinds of writing represent not different evolutionary stages, but disparate ways to link graphic representation to language and concept. As different forms of writing came into contact during the colonial era, new documents emerged which were fundamentally shaped by exchanges between such different systems. Dispensing with the colonial distinction between peoples with and without writing allows us to recognize at the center of early American literature the clash between different cultures of literacy. While literary scholars generally have only scant knowledge of the rich literary diversity that characterized this period, early and later records of such encounters provide a basis for developing a greater understanding of the textual implications and the literary legacy of colonial conflict and exchange.

A sustained, comparative engagement with different American literary traditions, made possible by a broader definition of writing and a more capacious understanding of the literary sphere, reveals trans-temporal continuities between the colonial and national era in both indigenous and settler literature. Such continuity can be traced, for example, in Plains winter counts, which constitute some of the best-known examples of North American pictography. Called *wan'iyetu wo'wapi* by the Lakota, such pictographic histories, painted on buffalo hides, emerged as a common form of historical documentation among Plains communities in the early decades of the nineteenth century, and a number survive to the present.[81] Hailing originally from the westernmost parts of the Great Lakes area, groups such as the Dakota migrated west during the eighteenth century in response to pressures in their former homelands. The migration westward onto the Plains, which took place throughout the eighteenth century, was characterized by great disruption. It brought changes in these communities as they became nomadic buffalo hunters, and this transformation in turn led to new forms of writing, just as the encounter with the American continents brought about new forms of writing in European narratives. On the Plains, buffalo hides replaced birch bark as the more readily available surface for inscription, and the graphic signs used to compose narrative became more pictographic than hieroglyphic. This form of writing best fits Hill Boone's concept of pictography proper, where phonetic elements play a relatively minor part in the graphic narrative, although they may be supplied by attendant performances. This change may, in some cases, have reflected the ways in which devastated communities reconstituted themselves across tribal and linguistic lines.[82]

Although these migrants likely knew and used birch-bark records before their migration westward, they developed new kinds of writing that reflected their new environment and identity. The emergence of winter counts in the late 1700s and early 1800s suggests that these communities had stabilized in their new homelands and begun to produce historical records that could establish and reflect their identities as Plains people.[83] The production of a winter count was a communal event in which a council of elders would gather and determine which events had been most significant that year. Such events would name the year that would be marked, on the winter count, by the tribal historian with one or more pictographs depicting the event. For example, in American Horse's winter count, 1792–93 is marked by pictographs representing death in childbirth, because many women that year died while giving birth. In Cloud Shield's winter count from 1825–26, one highly abstract pictograph represents a flood which killed many Lakota camped by the Missouri River as it swelled above its banks.[84]

Such histories mark key events in a community's collective experience by linking graphic sign to experience and collective memory.[85] Winter counts record not only specific information but also the cultural logic of a community as it determines the relative significance of events in the collective experience. For example, Mallery notes with some surprise that in Lone Dog's winter count, the defeat of Custer's army, a cataclysmic event in the national imaginary of the United States, was deemed less important than the acquisition, through theft, of a great number of horses. Lone Dog's winter count was widely understood and used in Lakota society at the time.[86]

In contrast to the individualism of, say, coup tales on buffalo robes and tipis, winter counts represent a communal vision of a collective identity formed around significant events strung together into a coherent whole that reached into the past and into the future.[87] In that sense, they express a kind of national consciousness. Taken collectively, the pictographs in winter counts mark the progression of time and the collectivity of the community while simultaneously functioning as a textual site wherein the community imagines itself as stable and continuous. The structure of the narrative, an outward spiral from a singular initial pictograph which begins the cycle, reflects both a cyclic, calendric sense of time and an expansive sense of dynamic yet contained movement within a space marked textually by the edges of the buffalo hide and spatially by the edges of the tribal territory.

Despite their differences, Plains winter counts, with their singular narrative beginnings and novel pictographic conventions, are linked by an almost imperceptible continuity to earlier indigenous forms of writing rooted in the Northeastern Woodlands. This continuity may be deduced from their shared territorial and cultural origins and traced via formal similarities. For example, in both Woodlands and Plains records, individual warriors would be depicted according to unique facial markings and regalia, respectively, in such a way that they could be reliably identified. Conversely, prisoners would be stripped of individual markers of identification in Woodland records hailing back to Lafitau's time and in Plains records as recent as the late nineteenth century. Such similarities suggest a connection to and continuity between Plains pictography and the birch-bark writing common in the areas in which many Plains peoples originated.

Time and the disruption brought about by European colonialism limit our ability to understand exactly how these systems of writing functioned prior to contact, although inference and recovery remain viable methods of study. Because these forms of writing were widespread, and much noted, when Europeans arrived, the colonial archive remains an important resource for such inquiry. At the same time, it is itself a product of this process, for this archive emerges out of, and is shaped by, colonial conflict. The arrival of Europeans brought about immense disruption and social reorganization in the lives of all the peoples living in the Northeastern Woodlands, and those changes are reflected in pictographic documents. Likewise, the writing of Europeans during early and later periods is marked by the encounter with indigenous forms of writing. In *New Voyages to North America*, for example, Baron Louis-Armand de Lahontan claims authority for himself and his narrative by including invented examples of pictography.[88] De Lahontan's "savage hieroglyphs" are not accurate examples of indigenous script.[89] Nonetheless, Lahontan's appropriation and transculturation of "savage hieroglyphs" as a self-authenticating move depends on the existence, and widespread knowledge, of indigenous hieroglyphs in the first place.[90] While the fake pictographic passages in his text are not authentically indigenous, neither are they exclusively European or alphabetic. Rather, they constitute an example of North American colonial semiosis, a "colonial text" which is marked by a dialogue between distinct forms of writing, narrative, and representation. Lahontan adapts certain conventions from Woodlands pictography, such as the representation of individuals according to their unique tattoos and the depiction of prisoners without identifying marks. However, he transforms these pictographs in a way that reflects the recovery and renaissance of classic Greek iconography in Europe. Lahontan represents prisoners as anonymous and identical Greek nudes, simultaneously adapting and transforming the textual logic of Woodlands pictography. His pictographs represent, then, a site of semiotic interaction and cross-cultural transformation. In early colonial records, this sense of dialogue and reciprocity is more readily apparent than in later American literature produced in the context of a fully entrenched colonial project. Nonetheless, indigenous forms of writing remain present and embedded in later American literature in ways that become apparent when our reading of such literature is informed by and situated within this framework.

Colonial Continuities: From Lahontan to Longfellow

Henry Wadsworth Longfellow's *The Song of Hiawatha* is one of the most popular and best-known publications of the American Renaissance.[91] Published in 1855, the poem became an immediate success. It sold more than thirty thousand copies in the first six months and was performed on stages across the nation, recited by schoolchildren, and translated into numerous foreign languages.[92] While Longfellow's trochaic tetrameter inspired comparisons to a Finnish epic, the *Kalevala*, Longfellow names the ethnographic publications of Henry Rowe Schoolcraft as his most important source.[93] Like many other writers of the period, Longfellow set out to articulate a particularly American aesthetic that could convey and promote a distinct national identity. To that end, he appropriated the language, culture, and writing of indigenous groups, particularly the Ojibwe, as found in the work of the Indian agent and ethnographer Henry Rowe Schoolcraft. Longfellow's *The Song of Hiawatha*, which takes a number of liberties with his source material, tells the story of Hiawatha and his marriage to Minnehaha, interspersed with the lore of the "Ojibways" along with "other curious Indian legends."[94] It concludes with Hiawatha welcoming white missionaries to the area and instructing his community to "Listen to their words of wisdom, / Listen to the truth they tell you" before departing forever westward.[95] Casting the newcomers as his "guests," to whom he voluntarily transfers ownership of his personal "lodge," Hiawatha becomes a figure of transition from indigenous to settler authority, a move he authorizes. This analysis traces how Longfellow's vision of American literature and national identity depends on the appropriation of indigenity, focusing particularly on how this transition is enabled by the simultaneous deployment and disavowal of Woodlands "pictography."

Longfellow's representation of Ojibwe writing has been linked to a small passage on that subject in Schoolcraft's *History, Condition, and Prospects of the Indian Tribes of the United States*, but it is equally indebted to the Ojibwe writer Kah-ge-ga-gah-bowh, or George Copway, and his depiction of specific Ojibwe scriptural signs in *The Traditional History and Characteristic Sketches of the Ojibway Nation*.[96] While Longfellow openly acknowledges his debt to Schoolcraft, he does not extend the same courtesy to Copway. Indeed, the differences in Longfellow's intertextual relationship to his sources mirror and enable his construction of a national epic based on the simultaneous appropriation and erasure of indigenous culture.

This analysis focuses on the fourteenth chapter of *The Song of Hiawatha*, entitled "Pictography." The chapter, located almost exactly at the center of the poem, signals and enables the transition from an American Indian to a settler culture that the Hiawatha figure facilitates. It is also the site of a significant revision of Longfellow's sources, because here Ojibwe writing is the invention of a single individual, Hiawatha, rather than a longstanding tradition practiced by many indigenous Woodlands tribes: "Thus it was that Hiawatha / In his wisdom, taught the people / All the mysteries of painting, / All the art of Picture-Writing."[97] All other native people in Longfellow's poem are located outside of, and prior to, any kind of literacy.

In contrast, Schoolcraft describes a geographically and historically expansive tradition of indigenous writing in the area known "by travellers [sic] and writers from the earliest times," one that extended "at the era of discovery, among most of the tribes, situated between the latitudes of Florida, and Hudson's Bay, although they have been considered as more particularly characteristic of the tribes of the Algonquin type."[98] Schoolcraft notes that the use of such writing has decreased considerably, so that now "pictures and symbols of this kind are to be found only on the unreclaimed borders of the great area west of the Alleghanies [sic] and the Lakes, in the wide prairies of the west or along the Missouri and the upper Mississippi."[99] Yet even hundreds of years after European settlement, such indigenous forms of writing were apparently well known and still in use. It is thus a significant and intentional revision by Longfellow, who read Schoolcraft's words, to represent Ojibwe writing as uniquely the invention of a single individual.

The writing that Longfellow's Hiawatha invents, ostensibly to preserve the memories of his people, casts the transition to alphabetic settler culture as an ascent to literacy in which indigenous people and their writing naturally and willingly give way to settlers. This representation was, of course, in stark contrast to the reality of military struggle which readers knew only too well. The nineteenth century was marked by its "Indian wars," and ethnologists such as Schoolcraft—and, for that matter, Mallery—came to their material as agents of the military and of the colonial state. Schoolcraft was an Indian agent who played a crucial role in dispossessing the Ojibwe, and Mallery was a colonel in the U.S. Army. Schoolcraft and Mallery documented indigenous forms of writing in the service of an expansionist nation, and Longfellow made those materials the basis of a national identity by simultaneously claiming, appropriating, and erasing indigenous literacy.

This dynamic is particularly evident in Longfellow's textual relation to Copway's work. This relationship is never acknowledged, but it can be detected in Longfellow's description of certain pictographs, which bears a striking relationship to specific pictographs included in "Their Language and Writings," the tenth chapter of Copway's The Traditional History and Characteristic Sketches of the Ojibway Nation. One can literally match Longfellow's description of pictographs for "earth," "sky," "daytime," "nighttime," "sunrise," "sunset," "noontide," and "rain and cloudy weather" with the corresponding pictographs in Copway's overview of "over two hundred figures in general use for all the purposes of correspondence."[100]

Thus, the following lines in Longfellow's poem:

For the earth he drew a straight line,
For the sky a bow above it;
White the space between for daytime,
Filled with little stars for night-time

corresponds directly to the pictographs from Copway's book in figure 3:

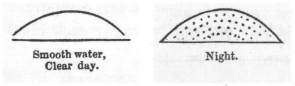

And these lines in Longfellow's book:

> On the left a point for sunrise,
> On the right a point for sunset,
> On the top a point for noontide, ·

Corresponds to the pictographs in Copway's text in figure 4:

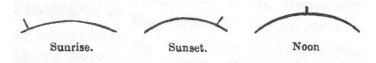

Finally, these lines in Longfellow's poem correspond to the pictographs in Copway's book in figure 5:

> And for rain and cloudy weather
> Waving lines descending from it.

Indeed, every single pictograph that Longfellow describes can also be found in Copway's overview, including signs for "life" and "death" and for "Great Spirit." Longfellow's description of this particular sign as "an egg, with points projecting / To the four winds of the heavens" perfectly describes Copway's pictograph (see figure 6). Furthermore, Copway annotates this pictograph to mean "Great Spirit" and "everywhere," a connection Longfellow reproduces by linking "Everywhere" with "the Great Spirit."[101]

These correspondences are so striking that they are unlikely to be coincidental, even though Longfellow never acknowledged Copway's influence.[102]

**Great Spirit,
every where.**

3, 4, 5, 6. Ojibwe pictographs from *The Traditional History
and Characteristic Sketches of the Ojibway Nation* by
George Copway (Kah-Ge-Ga-Gah-Bowh). WHi-66975.
Courtesy of the Wisconsin Historical Society.

The only other possible explanation would be that Longfellow had consulted another source and that the pictographs in both were identical due to the conventionalized nature of Ojibwe pictographs. However, given the close correspondence between Longfellow's description of Ojibwe pictographs and Copway's representation of those same pictographs, it seems likely that Copway himself was Longfellow's source. Copway published his book in 1850, five years before *The Song of Hiawatha*, so the material would have been available to Longfellow. Furthermore, the poet invited the Ojibwe writer and lecturer to his home in Cambridge for "tea and conversation" in February 1849, evidence that he knew of Copway six years before Longfellow published *The Song of Hiawatha*.[103]

Ojibwe pictographs used for a variety of purposes thus make their way first into Copway's text and then, translated into alphabetic script, into Longfellow's. The issue of translation is central and makes an interesting contrast to Longfellow's use of Ojibwe words, several of which also appear in Copway's book. Longfellow retains the Ojibwe words, transcribed alphabetically, to give his poem authenticity and to set the poem linguistically apart from British English. The Ojibwe words provide Longfellow with a marker of Americanism that is indigenous and yet translatable. The pictographs, on the other hand, are erased as part of the process of translation. Like Ojibwe words, they serve as markers of indigenous difference, but in the process of being translated they become alphabetic script. Not only are the pictographs themselves erased, but so is the American Indian writer who made them available to Longfellow and the cultural context in which they are more than disembodied and fetishized abstractions.

In the context of Ojbwe culture, as Copway explains, these pictographs are used for religious purposes, to transmit "tradition from one generation to another," and for mundane correspondence for "an Indian well versed in these [pictographs] can send a communication to another Indian, and by them make himself as well understood as a pale face can by letter."[104] In Longfellow's poem, however, Hiawatha complains that the Ojibwe do not have the means to send messages across distance: "We cannot speak when absent / Cannot send our voices from us / To the friends that dwell afar off; / Cannot send a secret message."[105] Hence, indigenous people are defined by their distance from literacy in a poem that imagines itself as speaking for, and to, a settler population defined by its widespread literacy. Longfellow casts himself as the poet of the people and *The Song of Hiawatha* as immediate and accessible to a population imagined as literate. This is done, in part, by representing indigenous people and their writing detached from contexts in which they can be anything but self-referential, and in the process of translation, they are simultaneously appropriated, translated, erased, and displaced.

Like the Ojibwe words scattered throughout Longfellow's poem, indigenous graphic signs become a means of constructing and authenticating a uniquely American culture, in distinction to England.[106] Positioned between the British colonial power from which they had separated and the indigenous people they were still fighting to displace, citizens of the United States faced a vexing question of how to constitute and legitimate a national identity. Claiming an American settler indigeneity became one way to resolve such tensions. Native people were thus cast as the symbolic ancestors of the settler nation and the citizens of the United States as the legitimate heirs to the people they displaced.[107] In order to naturalize and justify colonial dispossession and displacement, what was an ongoing military struggle was recast as a temporal progression.[108]

The Song of Hiawatha thus reflects notions of writing similar to those articulated by Taylor, but Longfellow makes a crucial revision by making "pictography" the invention of a single individual as well as the bridge between indigenous and settler culture and temporality. In this way, indigenous people can be represented as pre-literate even as Longfellow appropriates their writing as evidence of American authenticity. Pictography lends itself particularly well to Longfellow's populist project because it can be figured as immediate and accessible in the same way that Longfellow's meter and narrative aimed to be.[109] This populism is quintessentially colonial, as the broad appeal and consumption of Longfellow's poem is linked to its representation of conquest. Indeed, colonial displacement is not only naturalized but also celebrated in the poem, which offers a palatable vision of a national identity rooted in a conquest that is welcomed and enabled by the epic poem's indigenous hero, Hiawatha.

The meeting between Longfellow and Copway could have initiated a North American parallel to Sahagún's work. However, Longfellow's project was different, and so was the context, because the colonial project was well advanced, and native people were weary of sharing such materials. Copway himself explains in his text that native experiences with settlers had caused them to keep their writings secret and hide them in carefully sealed containers buried in the ground in locations known only by the initiated.[110] Such practices may explain the lack of extant documents more generally because Plains people also guarded many of their documents carefully and buried them with their guardians when there were no descendants to pass them down to.[111] Much more important, however, is the fact that Longfellow's project was a nationalist rather than a philological one. This is why Longfellow not only erases Copway's pictographs and fails to credit Copway, but also "disappears" the entire tradition of pictographic writing which Copway describes and to which Schoolcraft alludes.

Instead, Longfellow makes pictography idiosyncratic, temporally unique, and the genius and short-lived invention of a single individual. Making Hiawatha the sole inventor of pictographic script allows Longfellow to invoke multiple and even contradictory colonial tropes such as indigeneity without writing and pictographic indigeneity as a forerunner to alphabetic settlement. Pictography then becomes a necessary step in the transition to alphabetic settler culture rather than a challenge to discourses which claimed writing exclusively for Euro-American culture. Pictography becomes, ironically, a marker of primitivism *and* of the absence of indigenous writing in Longfellow's poem in a way that foreshadows not only Taylor but also Ignace J. Gelb's simultaneous invocation and dismissal of indigenous American forms of writing.

Like Lahontan centuries before him, Longfellow uses indigenous pictography that depends on settlers' knowledge of such writing from "the earliest travellers and writers" to Longfellow's own era. Such continuity suggests a remarkable persistence in the production and prevalence of pictography in the region, despite centuries of colonial onslaught. It also reveals continuities between early colonial texts, such as Lahontan's, and later American literature such as Longfellow's. Both authors use indigenous writing as an authenticating device, even as both texts reflect a colonial process of appropriation, erasure, and replacement. In Lahontan's case, Greek-style nudes in classic poses displace indigenous glyphs, whereas Longfellow replaces Ojibwe graphic signs with alphabetic script. But even though "pictography," in *The Song of Hiawatha*, is only conjured up in order to illustrate its own displacement, it remains an animating and enabling presence behind the alphabetic words.

While the disruptions of colonialism made American literature predominantly alphabetic, the realization that alphabetic script is only one kind of American writing has important implications. In relation to Longfellow's poem, for example, we might see Ojibwe script as a silent and absent referent, silenced and displaced because of the colonial history out of which it emerged and on which depended the national project that Longfellow's poem so embodied. To a greater extent than we have realized, indigenous forms of writing have persisted not only within native communities, but also were embedded in alphabetic texts such as *The Song of Hiawatha*.

Colonial struggles inflected ideas about writing which became a contested space where different forms of literacy came into contact and, at times, inter-animated each other. Many of the pictographic narratives that are now extant came out of sites of conflict like the military prison at Fort Marion in Florida where Plains warriors produced narratives about their captivity.[112] In such texts, a neglected yet important part of nineteenth-century American literature, we can trace how Cheyenne and Kiowa men adapted pictographic conventions to new media such as paper and ink, and to new circumstances such as captivity, in the process creating a dialogue between traditional and new forms of pictography and between pictographic, syllabic, and alphabetic ways to record narrative.

Likewise, the Potawatami writer Simon Pokagon's *A Red Man's Rebuke* (1893) was printed on birch bark, linking the traditional medium of Algonquin writing with alphabetic script and modern print technology.[113] Pokagon, whose tribe had struggled against federal relocation, wrote this searing critique of the colonial legacy just three years after the massacre at Wounded Knee and sold it at the Columbian exposition in Chicago in 1893. His decision to print the text on birch bark can be seen as a stunning, if subtle, assertion of Native American literary legacies that disrupts the fair's celebration of Anglo-American superiority while foregrounding separate, but compatible, traditions of literacy.

Such texts deserve far more attention from American literary scholars working with an understanding of indigenous literary traditions. Analyses that trace the multiple antecedents and contexts of such work have the potential to radically recast our understanding of American literature and of textuality more broadly. The next chapter focuses on a peace council between French and Haudenosaunee people in what is now Canada and explores the literary implications of that event.

CHAPTER TWO

Negotiating Peace,
Negotiating Literacies

The Undetermined
Encounter and Early American
Literature

It is July 5, 1645. A large canoe carrying three Haudenosaunee men and a French captive approaches Trois Rivières, a small settlement on the banks of the St. Lawrence River.[1] French settlers and indigenous refugees begin to gather along the water.[2] Located downriver from Quebec, Trois Rivières is the smallest of three colonial settlements in an area where the French have only a tenuous foothold. The crowd awaits the approaching boat with anxiety. While their relations with the neighboring Huron are friendly, the French are weary from a decade of fur trade wars with the mighty people they call "Iroquois," who live farther south and west.[3]

Suddenly, those gathered along the shore recognize one of the passengers. Guillaume Cousture, a young man taken captive south of Lake Ontario and presumed dead, has been brought back alive.[4] As the settlers rush to welcome Guillaume, a tall and stately man stands up in the front of the vessel and addresses them.[5] He is Kiotseaeton, a well-known Haudenosaunee orator and diplomat with great prestige. He has come to negotiate for peace. His body is covered with the kinds of beaded strings and belts that the French call "*porcelaine.*" Among the Haudenosaunee, such beaded belts, which native peoples throughout the region call wampum, are central to diplomacy. Exchanged during peace negotiations, these strings and belts of wampum serve, according to a Jesuit missionary in the area, "the same use that writing and contracts have with us" (*Jesuit Relations*, 40:165).[6]

From the stern, Kiotseaeton calls out to the crowd before him in his own language. The envoy beside him, a Haudenosaunee man recently released from captivity by the French colonists, translates his words into broken

French, which a Jesuit missionary named Barthélemy Vimont records as follows in *The Jesuit Relations* of that year:

> Mes Freres, i'ay quitté mon pais pour vous venir voir, me voila enfin arriué sur vos terres, on m'a dit à mon depart que ie venois chercher la mort, & que ie ne verrois iamais plus ma patrie; mais ie me suis volontairement exposé pour le bien de la paix: ie viens donc entrer dans les desseins des François, des Huron & des Alguonquins, ie viens pour vous communiquer les pensées the tout mon pays. (*Jesuit Relations*, 246–48)

> ❧

> My Brothers, I have left my country to come and see you, now I have finally arrived in your lands, they told me when I was leaving that I was going to find death, & that I would never again see my homeland; but I have voluntarily exposed myself for the sake of peace: I come therefore to enter into the designs of the French, the Huron and the Algonquin, I come to communicate to you the thoughts of my whole country.

The wampum that Kiotseaeton has brought to this encounter represents the thoughts and, indeed, the words authorized by the tribal body on whose behalf he speaks and negotiates. This wampum is part of a narrative and documentary tradition that the Haudenosaunee have used for generations.[7] To this encounter the French bring their own mystic and powerful media for materializing words: pen, ink, and paper.

After Kiotseaeton's greeting at the water's edge, the French respond with a celebratory cannon discharge as a sign of welcome. They are ready to join in peace negotiations with the "The People of the Longhouse." As everyone waits for the French governor to arrive, the Haudenosaunee envoys spend the next few days feasting with the French, the Huron, the Montagnais, and the other native people gathered for the council, attempting to build bridges across the linguistic and cultural chasms that separate them. The stakes are high. In the years since the French arrived in northeastern America in the early 1600s, they have engaged with the Haudenosaunee intermittently, in both war and peace. Hostilities over the fur trade have alternated with brief periods of peaceful coexistence and exchange.[8] Will they now be able to negotiate a lasting peace?

On the arrival of the French governor, called Onontio by the Haudenosaunee, the parties join each other in a council that follows not European but Haudenosaunee forms of diplomacy.[9] Thus, Kiotseaeton has not only come to "enter into the designs of the French, the Huron and the Algonquin"

7. Engraving of a council at which a speaker is holding a wampum belt. From *Moeurs des sauvages amériquains, comparées aux moeurs des premiers temps* by Joseph-François Lafitau. Courtesy of Special Collections, Knight Library, University of Oregon.

(*Jesuit Relations*, 248). He has also come to bring them into the political and narrative designs of the Haudenosaunee.

In the days that follow, those assembled join in peace negotiations that weave together these peoples and their documentary traditions (see figures 7–8). Encounters such as these attempted—indeed, needed—to create "a multicultural nomos, a normative universe of different peoples 'held together by the force of interpretive commitments.' "[10] While attempting to inscribe the French into their narrative traditions, the Haudenosaunee modify aspects of their traditional rituals and create new, shared forms of diplomacy and communication. The French, in turn, struggle to make sense of, adapt to, and record these proceedings, and their early records remain indelibly marked by their efforts to translate and assimilate Haudenosaunee modes of textuality.

This peace council exemplifies a dialogic attempt by French and Haudenosaunee delegates to both enroll and inscribe each other in their respective textual systems. In the process, they modify existing modes of documentation and struggle with experiments in writing adequate for and rooted in the encounter of radically different textual traditions. The Jesuit missionary

Barthélemy Vimont attempts to capture the proceedings on paper.[11] He watches as Kiotseaeton hands over and explains the meaning of the wampum that he has brought with him. These strings and belts, according to Kiotseaeton, carry the words of his people. With the wampum belts in hand, the Haudenosaunee diplomat delivers his words and his gift: He has brought back a prisoner raised from the presumed dead. He now offers up his own body to link together himself, a Frenchman, and an Algonquin with a wampum belt that Vimont considers "extraordinarily beautiful" (*Jesuit Relations*, 260). Vimont relates his own and Kiotseaeton's efforts with fascination and frustration:

> Voilà ce qui se passa en cette assemblèe, chacun auoua que cèt home estoit pathetique & eloquent, ie n'ay recuilly que quelques pieces comme decousues tirèes [de la] bouche de l'interprete, quie ne parloit qu'a bastons rompus, & non dans la suite que gardoit ce Barbare. (*Jesuit Relations*, 264)
>
> ❧
>
> Here is what happened at this meeting, everyone recognized that this man was moving & eloquent, I gathered but a few bits coming like disjointed heaps out of the mouth of the interpreter, who spoke only in broken fragments, and not in the order maintained by this Barbarian.

What, this chapter asks, is "this Barbarian" doing? What does it mean when Vimont later writes that Kiotseaeton hangs his words (the wampum) from a cord stretched between two poles in the center of the meeting space? How do radically different narrative and textual traditions organize these proceedings and the way they are recorded? How does all this "make sense"?

Making Sense of the Textual Encounter:
The *Jesuit Relations* and Colonial Dialogization

This council in 1645 represents one of the earliest and most detailed European records of Haudenosaunee diplomatic rites and the literacy that supported them; the alphabetic text remains indelibly linked with the Haudenosaunee textual and narrative traditions that organized it.[12] The records of the negotiation, thus, represent an opportunity for a dialogic literary study of the early textual inter-animation between indigenous and settler communities through a comparative textual study of wampum and "Pen-and-Ink Work," as one Haudenosaunee speaker described alphabetic writing.[13] Such a project brings to the fore issues of cultural and textual incommensurability.

The Indians giving a Talk to Colonel Bouquet in a Conference at a Council Fire, near his Camp on the Banks of Muskingum in North America, in Oct. 1764.

8. Engraving of a council at which a Native diplomat is speaking on a wampum belt, from *An Historical Account of the Expedition against the Ohio Indians* by William Smith. Courtesy of the Beinecke Library, Yale University.

Given their radical difference, should wampum and script both be considered writing? This project uses the term "Pen-and-Ink Work" to defamiliarize alphabetic script, while also using the term "writing" for both alphabetic script and wampum, to claim the authority of that term for both forms of inscription. The term "Pen-and-Ink Work" displaces the hegemonic power of the word "writing" (too easily equated solely with alphabetism) and marks alphabetic script as one of many kinds of writing at play in the conflict between Europe and the Americas. The existence of such a term reveals the presence of multiple and distinct literacies, each of which was strange and illegible outside its own cultural context. Simultaneously, the word foregrounds the often forgotten materiality of "Pen-and-Ink Work" and sets it alongside wampum to argue that, while French alphabetic script and Haudenosaunee wampum are radically different media, in the context of this and other early negotiations they served similar purposes. They recorded events and made words of agreement material and binding.[14]

On July 12, after the French governor has arrived and peace negotiations have begun, Vimont attends the council and sets out to record the proceedings. If colonialism is organized by the effort to abstract resources from the colony and deliver them to the metropolis, then a similar logic guided much literary production in early colonial America, where the writing of Europeans was almost always intended for a European context. However, in this passage from the *Jesuit Relations*, the desire to take words from one context and send them into another engenders a crisis of representation, as the textual logic of wampum collides with that of French script and resists easy translation. Consequently, the French colonial text is marked throughout by the terms and textual logic of wampum.

An important desire and mission in Vimont's text, similar to many other early colonial and ethnographic writings, is to capture and comprehend the indigenous presence and discourse. Vimont repeatedly claims to represent "what happened" and asserts the ability of the record to represent and reproduce the proceedings with phrases such as "This is what he said" and "This is what happened." As other scholars have argued, colonial texts became, for Europeans, a site of imaginary possession and containment.[15] This focus on textual assimilation also marks Vimont's text, which omits the words of the French governor, Kiotseaeton's interlocutor and negotiating partner. While the actual negotiation entailed a dialogue between Kiotseaeton and the French governor, Vimont's narrative stages a one-sided monologue by Kiotseaeton. Such omission suggests that what is at stake in the text is not recording "everything that happened" but, rather, capturing, converting, and assimilating Kiotseaeton's discourse into the Jesuit record. Just the same, Vimont repeatedly expresses frustration at his inability to adequately record, translate, and transmit the complex council proceedings —a frustration that simultaneously expresses thwarted colonial desires.

The space between that desire and that frustration creates a process of inter-animation between Haudenosaunee and European modes of communication and representation. As the European colonial project advances, this undetermined state of linguistic and semiotic dialogue becomes increasingly difficult to trace. In the eighteenth century and nineteenth century, for example, weakened native peoples negotiated with increasingly powerful British, and then American, governments. However, this peace council represents an earlier moment in colonial relations when neither party (nor its documentary system) had established hegemony.[16]

In the *Jesuit Relations*, this balance of power manifests itself as fractures and tensions in the narrative. At one point, for example, the famous Isaac le Joques, who endured several rounds of Haudenosaunee captivity before he was killed in 1646, contradicts Kiotseaeton's version of events:

> Le quinziéme fut pour témoigner qu'ils auoient toujours eu enuie de ramener de Pere le Ioques & P. Bessani, que c'estoit leur pensée, que le P. le Ioques leur fut dérobé, qu'ils auoient donné le P. Bressani aux Holandois, pour ce qu'il l'auoit desiré, s'ill eust eu patience ie l'aurois ramené, que scay-je maintenant où il est? peut-estre est il mort, peut-estre est-il noyé, nostre dessein n'estoit pas de le faire mourir. Si François Marguerie & Thomas Godefroy, adjourstoit-il, fussent restez en notre pays, ils feroient mariez maintenant, & nous ne ferious plue qu'une Nation, & moy ie ferois des votres. Le P. le Ioques entendant ce discourse, nous dit en sousriant, le bucher estoit preparé si Dieu ne m'eut fauué, cent fois ils m'ont osté la vie, ce bon home dit tout ce qu'il veut, le P. Bressani nous dit le mesme à son retour. (*Jesuit Relations*, 262)

🎐

> The fifteenth [wampum string] was to testify that they had always desired to bring back Father le Ioques and Father Bressani, that they thought Father le Ioques had been abducted or escaped, that they had given Father Bressani to the Dutch, because he wanted it, that if he had had patience I would have brought him back, how do I know now where he is? Maybe he died, maybe he drowned, it was not our intention to kill him. If François Marguerie & Thomas Godefroy, he added, had stayed in our country, they would be married now, & we would be but one nation, & and I would be one of you. Father le Ioques, having listened to this discourse, said with a smile, the stake was ready if God had not saved me, they would have taken my life a hundred times, this good man says anything he pleases, Father Bressani told us the same when he returned.

Here, Vimont's record juxtaposes two contradictory statements without narratively resolving the contradiction. Competing claims by Kiotseaeton and le Joques are represented in the text as an argument, a dialogue, a discrepancy in versions of "what happened," which the text leaves apparent even as it obviously sides with le Joques. However, the narrative voice, with its unstable points of view, undermines this textual allegiance. In this passage, Vimont flips back and forth from the third person plural "they" to the first person singular "I." These conflicting voices and narrative points of view reveal the absence of an authoritative and coherent colonial narrative.

Furthermore, Vimont repeatedly foregrounds discrepancies between the proceedings and his own record, marking the inability of the text to adequately represent and assimilate indigenous voices into his writing. Markers of omission are left to indicate when the Haudenosaunee orator's discourse has been erased. For instance, Vimont writes at one point that Kiotseaeston named each of the tribes but doesn't record this list in the *Relations*. Moments of such indirect speech (and silence) can be seen as markers of a discourse that is in the process of being assimilated and yet resists translation. Likewise, Vimont at times paraphrases Kiotseaeton rather than quoting him directly. Such moments represent Kiotseaeton's "voice" and words as absent from the text in a different way. While the narrative can be paraphrased, the words themselves are actually located in the wampum rather than in the Jesuit record. They remain beyond capture, translation, and transcription. In the move toward English translation, supplied by Ruben Gold Thwaites's *Jesuit Relations*, quotation marks seemingly indicate transcription, the presence of speech; however, such quotations are not part of Vimont's original text and thus represent not Kiotseaeton's speech but, rather, the continuing process of textualization of native discourse.

Vimont, on the other hand, explicitly comments on the gaps between Kiotseaeton's discourse and his own record, drawing attention to the disjunctions between the speaker (Kiotseaeton), the writer (Vimont himself), and an anonymous interpreter between them. There are numerous references in the text to Kiotseaeton's eloquence and wit, but because of the linguistic barrier between speaker and writer, Vimont cannot record the lyricism of Kiotseaeton's discourse. Instead, Vimont criticizes the interpreter, thus highlighting the discontinuity between speaker, interpreter, and writer in his account of "what happened":

> Voilà ce qui se passa en cette assemblèe, chacun auoua que cèt home estoit pathetique & eloquent, ie n'ay recuilly que quelques pieces comme decousues tirèes [de la] bouche de l'interprete, quie ne parloit qu'a bastons rompus, & non dans la suite que gardoit ce Barbare. (*Jesuit Relations*, 264)

🦋

> Here is what happened at the meeting, everyone admitted that this man was moving & eloquent, I gathered but a few bits like disjointed heaps in the mouth of the interpreter, who spoke only in broken fragments, and not in the order maintained by this Barbarian.

"Here is what happened" can then be read in two different ways. First, as a claim to representation, these words follow a detailed description of Kiotseaeton's speeches as he elaborates the meaning of each wampum belt. On closer inspection, however, "Here is what happened" marks a crisis of representation if it is read instead in reference to the passage that follows, where Vimont explains his inability to understand and represent the speech act of "this Barbarian." In this case, "what happened" was a failure of translation and transcription. As Vimont relates it, he gathers bits here and there, which he describes as disjointed heaps, fragments that are not adequately translated. Vimont understands enough from those around him to realize that Kiotseaeton's oratory is moving, eloquent, and carefully organized. It is the verbal equivalent of the wampum belts themselves, well-organized, beautiful, and coherent wholes. However, as words travel from Kiotseaeton's mouth to the translator's ears, from the translator's mouth to Vimont's ears, and then onto the page, they become broken and disconnected. Vimont's phrasing, itself a proliferating heap of disjointed and repetitive adjectives, describes a process of meaning and coherence breaking down as it encounters the limits of translatability.

The words that have come apart in the process of translation will be reassembled again in the process of transcription. The passage quoted earlier constitutes a marker in the text of that process and the violence it entails. It also draws our attention to something quite remarkable: In describing these events, Vimont inadvertently conceptualizes Kiotseaeton's words according to the logic of wampum. While, "decousues" can be translated as "disjointed," another meaning of the word is "unstitched." Vimont's diction here registers a sense that Kiotseaeton's speech is parallel to the wampum belts; indeed, the process of translation and transcription breaks up this speech act as if the belts themselves had been torn apart, unstitched, so that the beads, detached from their proper context, become a meaningless heap.

In fact, throughout Vimont's record of the peace negotiations of 1645, he reproduces what turn out to be Haudenosaunee conceptions of textuality:

Les Iroquois firent planter deux perches, & tirer une corde de l'un à l'autre pour y pendre & attacher les paroles qu'ils nous deuoient porter, c'est à dire, les presens qu'ils nous vouloient faire, lesquels consistoient en dix-sept collier de pourcelaine, dont une partie estoir sur leurs corps. (*Jesuit Relations*, 252)

❧

The Iroquois had two poles planted, & a cord tied from one to the other in order to tie & hang the words that they were to bring us, that is to say, the presents that they wanted to give us, which consisted of seventeen porcelain collars, some of which were on their bodies.[17]

Not only does Vimont use the term "words" to refer to the wampum, rather than saying "beads" or "belts" or "strings" of wampum; he also naturalizes the act of hanging words, in the material form of wampum, from a pole. Surely, such a concept would be rather foreign to his interlocutor(s), the reverend back in France and the reading community within which the *Jesuit Relations* circulated. This statement is accompanied in the text by minimal explanation of the relationship between words and presents in Haudenosaunee culture.

In fact, French and other colonial negotiators had to attain some level of Haudenosaunee literacy to function in these contexts. In other, early records of treaty councils, European negotiators accept this conception of contract writing, as Vimont does in his prose: "Le Gouuerneur respondit aux presens des Iroquois, par quatorze presens qui auoient tous leurs significations, & qui portoient leurs parolles (The governor replied to the presents of the Iroquois by fourteen gifts, all of which had their own meanings and which carried their own words)" (*Jesuit Relations*, 266). Here, and throughout this passage, Vimont's writing is marked by the presence of Haudenosaunee modes of communication and representation: Wampum can carry words to which one replies.

New Kinds of Writing: The Encounter of Haudenosaunee and French Literacies

Not only is Vimont's writing marked by the presence of Haudenosaunee conceptions of literacy, his attempt to capture the proceedings also gives rise to experiments in translation and transcription that amount to a new kind of writing rooted in this particular exchange. When Kiotseaeton hands over the second collar of wampum, he chides the French for sending back Tokhrahenehiaron, an Haudenosaunee prisoner, without a protective escort. Tokhrahenehiaron's journey back home was fraught with danger, Kiotseaeton explains as he acts out the obstacles faced by the lone traveler. It was dangerous for a man to navigate a canoe alone against the currents and rapids of the river, which is why Kiotseaeton personally brought Guillaume back to the French settlement at the risk of his own life. This, Vimont notes, is what the second wampum belt "said" (*disoit*). Vimont's use of the word "said" reflects Haudenosaunee conceptions of textuality, according to which wampum speaks, and simultaneously reveals how these notions intersect with European ideas about writing as recorded speech, where a printed page might "say" something to a reader. This passage marks Vimont's increasing adaptation and naturalization of Haudenosaunee terminology, made possible, perhaps, by such similarities. Ironically, linguistic rather than textual disjunctures present the greatest challenge to Vimont and lead him to experiment with ways of writing that can account for the scene unfolding before him.

When Kiotseaeton begins to act out the obstacles that Tokhrahenehiaron had to overcome on his way home, Vimont switches from transcription to description: "Celuy que vous auez renouyé a eu toutes les peines du monde en son voyage, il commença à les exprimer (He whom you sent back has had all the difficulties in the world on his trip, he began to express them)" (*Jesuit Relations*, 254). The first part of the sentence ("He whom you sent back has had all the difficulties in the world on his trip") refers to a speech act by Kiotseaeton, while the second part ("he began to express them") refers to the diplomat's gestures and movement. Kiotseaeton probably added gestures to his spoken words at this point to compensate for the linguistic barriers among the various groups. In fact, sign language commonly functioned as a lingua franca in intertribal trade and peace negotiations. At first, Vimont simply describes these gestures without assigning meaning to them: "Il faisoit mille gestes, il regardoit le Ciel, il enuisageoit le Soleil, il froittoit les bras (He made a thousand gestures, he looked at the sky, he gazed at the sun, he rubbed his arms)" (*Jesuit Relations*, 252). This shift in Vimont's text points to the limited capacity of alphabetic writing to represent a *foreign* spoken language as the Jesuit dispenses with the translator and begins to transcribe gestures, rather than sounds, into the alphabetic text. What follows in Vimont's text is a careful description of Kiotseaeton's gestures and movement, which eventually transitions into an attempt to transcribe meaning directly:

> Il prenoit un batton, le mettoit sur sa tette comme un paquet, puis le portoit d'un bout de la place à l'autre, representant ce qu'auoit fait ce prissonnier dans les faults & dans de courrant d'eau. . . . Il cherchoit contre une Pierre, il reculoit plus qu'il n'auançoit dans son canot, ne le pouuant soutenir seul contre les courans d'eau, il perdoit courage, & puis reprenoit ses forces. (*Jesuit Relations*, 254)
>
> ❧
>
> He took a stick, put it on his head like a package, then he carried it from one end of the space to the other, representing what this prisoner had done in the crevices & in the water's current. . . . He came against a rock, he lost more

ground than he gained in his canoe, overpowered by the current, he lost courage, & then regained his strength.

As Vimont records the narration of the second wampum belt, he begins with a careful description of Kiotseaeton's gestures (such as rubbing his arms and placing a bundle of sticks on his head) but eventually attempts to record meaning directly: "He lost courage, and then regained his strength" (*Jesuit Relations*, 254). Alphabetic script here records gestures and then concepts rather than spoken words. Thus, the written words that follow refer not to sounds but to gestures and, beyond that, to ideas such as courage and strength. The sliding movement in this segment of the *Jesuit Relations* between description, transcription, and translation (Vimont's account of what Kiotseaeton said, did, and meant) progresses as Vimont experiments with novel ways to write that are adequate for, and rooted in, this encounter. The text reveals a dizzying narrative progression from Haudenosaunee community words, recorded in wampum, to Kiotseaeton's gesture words transcribed by Vimont into alphabetically written words which translate meaning into French so the printed page can speak directly to the French reader. These slippages arise from the impossibility of transcribing the spoken word, given the linguistic barriers between the writer and Kiotseaeton. Vimont responds by attempting to transcribe, first, gesture words and finally concepts, using graphic signs (French alphabetic script) that simultaneously translate. Discrete segments of the sentence represented by French words actually attempt a simultaneous transcription and translation of indigenous gesture language.

The concept of "courage" ➤ Kiotseaeton's gesture ➤ the French printed word "courage"

This progression is dependent on experimental, fluid, and creative adaptations of known and foreign ways to record and transmit meaning on the part of both the French and the Haudenosaunee. Although they resemble other kinds of alphabetic writing, the printed words on this page function semasiographically—or, to use a more familiar term, pictographically. They transcribe gestures and ideas, not sounds. Hence, this passage in the *Jesuit Relations* is simultaneously alphabetic and ideographic writing, because the printed graphic signs on these pages, like "courage," attempt to record Haudenosaunee concepts, not spoken French words. According to classic theories of writing, which have defined it narrowly as the transcription of sound, this passage is not "real writing," despite its familiar appearance. It is something much more complicated: A kind of hybrid cross-cultural pictographic writing, a slippery chain of transcription and translation in which the graphic sign we think of as a printed French word performs two functions at once. On the page, words like "courage" are both pictographic transcriptions of Haudenosaunee concepts communicated without recourse to verbal language and phonographic translations of those concepts into French. This passage in the *Jesuit Relations* represents a moment in which the conventional meaning and use of the French written word is modified in such a way as to destabilize classic Western notions of what writing is and does.

If, as Myra Jehlen argues, "translation is the Achilles' heel of the colonizing culture," where potentially "the monologue of imperial authority—the empire's sole right to authorize—breaks down into dialogue," then this moment of translation—or, rather, its crisis of representation—exemplifies colonial dialogization.[18] As Mikhail Bahktin argues, a "word, discourse, language or culture undergoes 'dialogization' when it becomes relativized, de-privileged, aware of competing definitions for the same things."[19] In the *Jesuit Relations*, Vimont's attempt to produce an authoritative, coherent colonial record that captures and translates a foreign discourse is subverted by the dialogization within his text. Thus, this segment of the *Jesuit Relations* marks itself as an imperfect record of a collective narrative act that is in excess of what can be assimilated and translated. In this conjuncture between Haudenosaunee and French conceptions of writing, we see a novel linking of wampum and words, body and gesture, and alphabetic script. Importantly, these connections between speaker, spoken and material word, body, and text reflect the conventions of wampum rather than script.

The Bead Embodied the Word: Haudenosaunee Literacy in Practice

While wampum is commonly known as a form of currency—"Indian money" —this function emerged mainly as a consequence of colonial exchange and was never primary for the Haudenosaunee.[20] European market economies incorporated native peoples into early capitalist exchange as fur traders, allies, and consumers in part by shrewdly exploiting the high value native peoples placed on wampum.[21] Economic analyses of wampum teach us little, however, about what it meant to native people, particularly before the arrival of Europeans. This section describes how wampum was used by the

Haudenosaunee prior to and in the early centuries of European contact, focusing particularly on how it functioned as a form of literacy—that is, as a communicative and archival medium that facilitated, organized, and recorded social relations. At the time of the council in 1645, wampum was central to Haudenosaunee diplomacy (particularly peacemaking) and archival production; its use was deeply embedded in, and extended throughout, Haudenosaunee culture.

On a material level, early post-contact wampum belts and strings consisted of sinew that held together deep purple and white shells called *quahog*, with holes drilled at each end, in graphic patterns or specific sequences. Its earliest use remains controversial, but archeologists have found wampum throughout the eastern parts of the U.S. that date as far back as the Archaic period.[22] For generations before and after the arrival of Europeans, the Haudenosaunee conceptualized wampum as a medium of communication that materialized and embodied words. As such, it was capable of carrying the words of a speaker to an interlocutor, just as Europeans understood ink and paper as capable of carrying words from one location to another. With wampum, however, the word was spoken into and then back out of the beaded string or belt, which was conceptualized to function as a kind of tape recorder.[23] As Michael Foster explains it, a "speaker performs a speech act which roughly translates as 'reading the message into the wampum.' "[24] The words were spoken into the wampum in the presence of a messenger who memorized them and repeated them at his destination. But the Haudenosaunee considered the wampum, rather than the messenger, as the repository of the words: "Words spoken over wampum became *embodied* in the beads."[25]

In a diplomatic context, exchange of wampum represented acceptance of a message or proposal; refusal of wampum represented rejection. As it was used in Woodlands diplomacy, wampum functioned as the medium that materialized the oral word and made it contractual, just as a signature on legal papers materializes consent and makes it binding. For the Haudenosaunee, however, the agreement rested beyond the written, or beaded, document in the reciprocal and active relationship between parties continually enacting its terms.[26] Records of events had no relevance or power in and of themselves; they had relevance and power only as they were embedded in a matrix of social relations and communications.[27]

Exchange of wampum bound participants in mutual and reciprocal relationships which had to be actively maintained. A concluding note in Vimont's record reveals that the French and Haudenosaunee understood the process and the relationship between words, records, and social obligations quite differently. In the final paragraph of Vimont's dispatch, he characterizes the negotiations as "concluë pour les François & bien auancée pour Sauuages (concluded for the French and well-advanced for the savages)" (Jesuit Relations, 304). For the French, an agreement once made and sealed by a document concluded the matter. For the Haudenosaunee, however, exchange of wampum marked the beginning of an ongoing relationship that had to be affirmed continuously to be meaningful.

Throughout French treaty records, Haudenosaunee diplomats conducted negotiations according to specific ritual structures, particularly those adapted from the interrelated Haudenosaunee Condolence Council and the Epic of the Peacemaker. These narratives, in fact, are absent texts or master narratives that structured the exchange between the Haudenosaunee and the French, between wampum and "Pen-and-Ink Work." Wampum strings were (and still are) symbolically exchanged at set periods throughout the Condolence Council; such exchanges form one of the founding rituals of the Haudenosaunee Confederacy. According to Haudenosaunee mythology and history, this sacred founding ritual was introduced to the Haudenosaunee by a prophet known reverentially as "the Peacemaker" and can be seen as the "chartering myth of the Five Nations."[28] Because these cultural master narratives will be unfamiliar to many readers, the following sections outline them in some detail to tease out how the Haudenosaunee conceptualize the textuality of wampum and how this, in turn, shapes Vimont's text.

The Epic of the Peacemaker:
The Story and Vision of a Peacemaker

The legendary Deganawidah, or Peacemaker, helped to end a period of violent intertribal turmoil by establishing the Great Peace and the Haudenosaunee League of Nations, a Confederacy of Five Nations consisting of the linguistically and culturally related Onondaga, Oneida, Seneca, Cayuga, and Mohawk nations (see map 1).[29] Before the formation of the League, these groups had been locked in internal warfare and blood feuds. At some undetermined point before the arrival of Europeans, these Haudenosaunee groups came together to heal intertribal divisions and to lay the ritual and political foundations on which their confederacy has rested.[30]

This process began when Deganawidah helped heal Hiawatha (or Ayon-

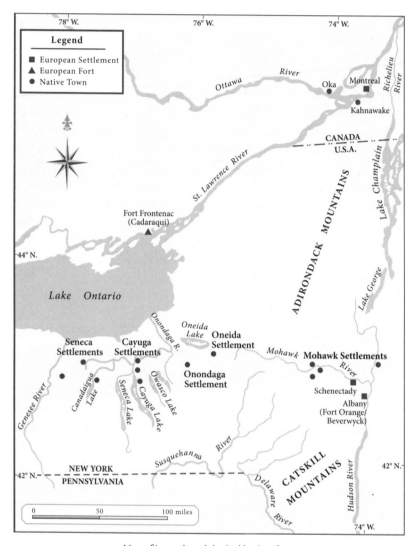

Map of Iroquoia as it looked in the 1670s

watha), a man who had lost his family and was wandering the woods in grief.[31] The Peacemaker strung shells together and then, as he consoled Hiawatha, handed him strings of shells while repeating a series of ceremonial teachings that eventually became the foundation for the rituals of the Condolence Council. Hiawatha became the Peacemaker's collaborator in the difficult task of organizing the Haudenosaunee into a unified political league, and together they accomplished a peaceful social revolution. The

Condolence Council became the core of this new social order that mitigated retaliation and war. "When men accept it," the Peacemaker said of his message, "they will stop killing, and bloodshed will cease from the land."[32] In this process, wampum helped heal grief and restore reason in the aftermath of war and loss. It was, in fact, foundational to establishing and maintaining the social fabric of Haudenosaunee society.[33]

The Peacemaker and Hiawatha eventually carried the Great Law to the various chiefs of the surrounding settlements and brokered peace over the course of a number of years. The Haudenosaunee imagined this peace in metaphoric terms as the planting of a great tree of peace with the expansive potential for its four white roots to extend in the cardinal directions and eventually reach all peoples.[34] They thus conceptualized the basis on which their confederacy was founded as a growing, multicultural community linked together in solidarity under the sheltering branches of the great tree of peace, as a new social order organized by a commitment to communication, solidarity, and reciprocity. This social order was maintained, in part, through continuous ritual reenactments of the Condolence Council.

As many scholars have noted, the protocol and the metaphoric language of the condolence ritual permeate the records of Haudenosaunee diplomatic negotiations with the French, the Dutch, and, finally, the English. Organizing peace and trade councils with Europeans according to these principles affirmed the authority of Haudenosaunee society while simultaneously attempting to enroll Europeans into their social order.

The Condolence Council Ceremony

The Peacemaker's ritual healing of Hiawatha evolved over time into the ritualized Condolence Council that is still in use today.[35] The rituals of the Condolence Council "comprised an institution of vital importance for maintaining the integrity and efficient functioning of the Iroquois state."[36] This foundational and sacred ritual extended outside the confederacy and prescribed the forms of Haudenosaunee diplomacy with neighboring nations, as well as European powers. It became a way for the Haudenosaunee to enroll European and other Native groups, ceremonially and literally, in their own social and political order. The Condolence Council "consists of an elaborate interweaving of . . . five prescribed texts, administered in this period of a 'mutual embrace.' "[37] At least two of these five rituals occur in recognizable forms in the 1645 French-Haudenosaunee encounter recorded by Vimont. This and later peace and treaty councils can then be conceived as complicated interweavings of intercultural texts and ways to make the word material.

Reading the "text" of this encounter, then, means reading the account in the *Jesuit Relations* in conjunction with the epic of the Peacemaker and the Condolence Council.[38] In this section, I trace several situationally specific adaptations that shaped the encounter of 1645 and reveal how the Haudenosaunee master narrative derived from the Condolence Council also changed as a consequence of the encounter to become the template for later peace and treaty negotiations.

The Condolence Ceremony traditionally begins with what is known as a "Welcome at Wood's Edge." Visitors from "clear-minded" villages—those who have not sustained personal loss and have come to console and comfort the bereaved—declare their presence and peaceful intentions at the "Wood's Edge," the point where cleared land around the settlement of the mourning village meets the forest. This part of the ceremony derives from the custom of strangers making their presence and peaceful intentions known before entering a village. At this temporal and geographic junction, a wampum string is offered to clear the mourning villagers' eyes; a second string is offered to clear their ears; and a third and final string removes obstructions from their throats. In other words, wampum heals and clears the organs of speech and perception.[39] Kiotseaeton seems to perform this same ceremonial cleansing with the first three wampum strings that he gives to the French at the council in 1645. This process restores the faculties of seeing, hearing, and speaking that have been impaired by the shock of death. Grief is thus conceptualized as an obstruction to communication, which must be alleviated prior to negotiation. Kiotseaeton and the French governor themselves become symbolic and metaphorical organs of communication: Calling himself the "mouth" of the Haudenosaunee, Kiotseaeton asks the French governor to be the "ear" of the French (*Jesuit Relations*, 252).

However, these three wampum strings are not the first to be used in the ceremony. The proceedings are initiated with an invitational string, sent even before the parties meet, by the mourning village. The name of this string literally means "that which stretches a person's arm."[40] The invitational string leads the recipients "by the arm" to the Wood's Edge, where the hosts welcome them and lead them to the council.[41] Wampum, then, functions not only as a medium that negotiates space, grief, and obstructions to communication but also as an agent of diplomacy. It does not simply record information but organizes and enables communication, which, in the case of the Haudenosaunee-French negotiations, entailed the construction of an interethnic community of shared signs. Haudenosaunee diplomats may have chosen to adapt the form of the Condolence Ceremony for diplomatic negotiations with colonists not only because of the need to negotiate peace between formerly warring parties, but also because of the need to facilitate communication itself. Given the cultural and linguistic barriers, mutual understanding was a central problem that the Condolence Ceremony and wampum specifically addressed and attempted to negotiate.

In the episode I retold at the beginning of this chapter, we can recognize Kiotseaeton's modification of the Condolence Ceremony's conventions in his cautious call to the settlers at "Water's Edge." In Vimont's account, another modification of the ceremony becomes apparent. When Kiotseaeton has finished his speech, a shot is fired from the boat, and the fort replies by firing a cannon shot as a sign of celebration and welcome. In a subsequent council, three canon shots are likewise fired to clear away the atmosphere of war ("le mauuais air de la guerre") and celebrate the joy of peace (*Jesuit Relations*, 268). Such cannon shots suggest the invention of new, shared rituals specifically rooted in the relationship between Haudenosaunee and French people; cannon shots became figuratively and metaphorically new and recognizable forms of initiating diplomatic proceedings.

The next part of the Condolence Council, following the welcome, is the "Requickening," a ritual in which the deceased is mourned and a new member of the Chief's Council is selected to replace the lost one, ensuring continuity of the social fabric. The Haudenosaunee conceptualized the incorporation of the French and British according to this framework. All French governors were given the title "Onontio," meaning "the Frenchman who was responsible for maintaining the French colonies' treaty obligations toward the Indians." Later, governors of Pennsylvania were given the hereditary title "Onas," which meant "Pen" in reference to the treaty negotiated between the Haudenosaunee and Pennsylvania's first governor, William Penn, in 1682.[42]

The fact that the Haudenosaunee organized peace negotiations around the rituals of the Condolence Ceremony indicates that they viewed these negotiations as matters of life and death, crucial to the survival of their community. Clearly, the ceremony was seen by the Haudenosaunee as a powerful text that the League could use to counteract the destruction and death that attended the arrival of Europeans.[43] The emotional effect on the colonists of Cousture's reappearance may have been calculated in part to relate this significance and sense of mystic, even sacred, power to the French.

The return of Cousture played on the powerful symbolism of resurrection, or requickening. In addition, the return of a captive hostage constituted an opening gift in efforts to build trust despite a history of war. In fact, gifts of condolence were central to the healing ceremony and to the establishment of social bonds in general. The Haudenosaunee considered solidarity and reciprocity, shared suffering and shared resources, as necessary for the establishment and maintenance of diplomatic and social ties.[44] Indigenous diplomats absolutely insisted on the ritual exchange of gifts before negotiations could commence, while Europeans often expressed impatience with this requirement and either failed or refused to understand this element of diplomatic protocol. The gift economy into which the Haudenosaunee attempted to enroll the Europeans conflicted with the money economy that the newcomers had brought with them. The simultaneous uses of wampum as a diplomatic and narrative device for the Haudenosaunee, and as monetary currency for the Europeans, testify to these conflicting economies of meaning.

For the Haudenosaunee, the words used in negotiations were inextricably linked to gifts and a gift economy. In fact, the gift and the word were considered inseparable.[45] For example, Vimont writes, "Ie n'ay que faire de reïterer si souuent que les paroles d'importance en ce pays-cy sont des presens (I do not need to reiterate that important words in this country are presents)" (*Jesuit Relations*, 280). Not only were words considered gifts, but without attending gifts (usually wampum), words were meaningless. The wampum belts used in diplomatic negotiations were produced by the tribal community and testified that the words of the envoy were backed up by the community, that he was carrying the words of the tribal council. Haudenosaunee leaders often remarked, "You may know our words are of no weight unless accompanied with wampum."[46] With such remarks, the Haudenosaunee warned and educated the French that only wampum, not spoken words, could represent the thoughts of the community at a bargaining session.

The wampum belts used in treaty negotiations were produced by the tribal community and proved that the words of the envoy were supported by the community, that messengers carried the words of the tribal council. This early encounter between the French and the Haudenosaunee, then, illuminates how the Haudenosaunee theorized wampum within human negotiations as instantiating a powerful, healing, and sacred linkage between words and human beings. While there is no invitational string initiating the council in 1645, the captive Guillaume Cousture, who has been brought figuratively back to life, functions as the gift or wampum string that initiates the healing process and makes the meeting possible. Perhaps, the earlier French release of Tokhrahenehiaron, the Haudenosaunee captive whose return Kiotseaeton describes with such dramatic flair, could have functioned similarly so that, in this context, the bodies of captives functioned as the mutual invitational wampum strings that led negotiators by the arm to the peace council.

At a follow-up meeting ten days later, five Haudenosaunee envoys who have arrived for the council once again deliver a short speech on the bank of the river—what we might call the Water's Edge segment of the adapted Condolence or Peace Council. This time, however, the envoy speaking at the Water's Edge does not carry wampum: "Ie n'ay point de voix, ne m'escoutez pas ie ne parle point, ie n'ay en main qu'vn auiron pour vous ramener vn François, qui a dans sa bouche la parole de tout noitre pays (I have no voice at all, do not listen to me I do not speak at all, all I have in my hand is an oar to bring you a Frenchman, who has in his mouth the word of our entire country)" (*Jesuit Relations*, 280). The wampum words are carried this time by a French captive, Isaac le Joques, "auquel les Iroquois auoient confié leurs presens, c'est à dire leurs paroles . . . composez de porcelaine (in whom the Iroquois had confided their presents, that is to say their words . . . composed of porcelaine)" (*Jesuit Relations*, 280). This equating of "presents" with words "composed of porcelaine" signals an internalization of the logic of wampum literacy by which beaded strings and belts are words that can be confided.

As le Joques proceeds to relate the messages stored in and carried by the wampum in a textual matrix that now includes his own body, he and Vimont both conceptualize the speech as coming from the wampum: "The first [wampum string] *said* that. . . . The second *said* that" (*Jesuit Relations*, 280).[47] Such scenes constitute apparently successful attempts by the Haudenosaunee to invest the Frenchman with their words and enroll him in their textual community by linking his body to their wampum. This effort is represented, in turn, by the French in indigenous terms: It is the wampum, not le Joques, that speaks.

During the initial meeting of the council, recorded by Vimont on July 12, something equally remarkable happens as Kiotseaeton brings out the tenth wampum string:

Le dixiéme fut donné pour nous lier tous ensemble tres-estroittement,[48] il prit un François enlaça son bras dans le sien un Algonquin de l'autre, & s'estant ainsi lié auec eux, voila le næud[49] qui nous attache inseparablement, rien ne nous pourra des-vnir. Ce colier estoit estraordinairement beau, quand la foudre tomberoit fur nous elle ne pourroit nous separer. (*Jesuit Relations*, 260)

🐾

The tenth was given to link us all together very closely, he [Kiotseaeton] hugged a Frenchman with one arm & an Algonquin with the other, & being thus linked himself with them, [he said] here is the knot that binds us inseparably, nothing can dis-unite us. This collar being extraordinarily beautiful, even if lightning should strike us it would not be able to separate us.

I have translated *enlaça* (of *enlacer*) as hugged because this translation seems to flow best in the context. Other, more accurate translations, however, are interlace, intertwine, thread. In fact, Kiotseaeton is "lacing," or interweaving, the three men into a kind of bodily equivalent of the wampum —they are themselves part of the text. In this situation, wampum is the textual medium that weaves together people in political covenants, as parts of a shared design of reciprocity and peaceful coexistence. It is worth remembering here the etymology of "text" and "textuality": They are rooted in the Latin word "*textere*," which literally means "that which is woven."[50]

Like Vimont, Kiotseaeton points out the extraordinary beauty of the wampum to suggest to the French that it indicates a special strength to overcome any assault on the alliance represented and authenticated by the wampum—even a force as strong as lightning. The wampum is itself an actor with agency and power to secure the alliance, in part because its beauty is a result of the efforts and resolve of the community that produced it, the community Kiotseaeton represents, and perhaps also the metaphors or semiotic logic that organizes it.[51] Vimont's choice of words thus registers an internalization of Haudenosaunee conceptions of the contract and of wampum textuality while foregrounding the reciprocity and exchange inherent in Haudenosaunee theories of the textual.

Haudenosaunee and European Conceptions of Textuality

At this point, we can glean the outlines of an Haudenosaunee theory of textuality that perhaps Vimont himself sensed ever so vaguely, one that becomes clearer when wampum is understood in its cultural context. First, we have learned from the story of the Peacemaker, from the Condolence Ceremony, and from the peace council of 1645 that wampum can be theorized as a form of textuality that facilitates the process of communication. This would be particularly important in negotiations between aggrieved parties such as former enemies, where grief and anger could impede the process. In cross-cultural negotiations, the ability of wampum to facilitate communication became important in new ways. In the contact situation, the Haudenosaunee may have used wampum to counteract what we might call "cultural interference" in communication between two very different groups of peoples who shared neither language nor culture.

Wampum also functioned as a narrative device, which organized proceedings, speeches, and the recounting of key historical events such as the founding of the League. Haudenosaunee diplomats like Kiotseaeton were great storytellers, as Vimont notes.[52] Indeed, only the best storytellers were sent to forge multicultural alliances, and like Kiotseaeton they frequently used wampum to organize the narrative.[53] In negotiations with Europeans, Haudenosaunee orators used wampum to facilitate the creation of a shared symbolic and interpretive community. With each wampum string, Kiotseaeton told a different "installment" of a story inspired by and adapted from one of the great "meta-texts" of Haudenosaunee culture. Stories were told not only to establish a shared communicative ground and to educate Europeans about the norms of behavior expected by treaty partners, but also because stories provided a space in which to imagine a shared world.

Wampum is also an archival record. For example, the founding of the Haudenosaunee League of Nations is documented in the Hiawatha Belt, and the Dust Fan Belt records the League's constitution. The Haudenosaunee continue to maintain certain belts that record treaty agreements, and tribal leaders have traveled to both North American and European capitals to present these belts as documentary evidence of rights secured by treaties.[54] In 1988, for example, an Haudenosaunee diplomat made a special presentation before the United Nations Human Rights Commission's Working Group on Indigenous Populations in Geneva. As evidence of the longstanding sovereign status of the Haudenosaunee, the diplomat explicated the Guswentah or Tekeni Teiohate, also known as the Two Row Wampum Treaty.[55] On the belt, two dark rows are embedded in three lighter rows which

symbolize vessels,
traveling down the same river together.
One will be for the Original People, their laws, their customs,

and the other for the European people and their laws and customs.
We will each travel the river together,
but each in our own boat.
And neither of us will try to steer the others' vessel.[56]

In this belt, the Haudenosaunee recorded an early agreement with European settlers to be "like brothers" rather than "like father and son"—metaphoric language that means to interact as distinct, equal, and sovereign nations.

As evident in this belt, with its dark and light rows, wampum designs were not pictographic in nature. Wanting clearer correspondence between wampum design and message, European participants in treaty councils promoted explicit symbolism on belt designs.[57] During the eighteenth century, English negotiators such as William Penn encouraged the production of wampum belts where symbols corresponded to the signified in a pictographic fashion.[58] As indigenous people using wampum came to realize that Europeans did not share their ability to reproduce the full and exact meaning of a given belt without the supplementary use of an alphabetic record, they began to request that notes be attached to the belts. These modifications represent changes to wampum textuality as a result of the confrontation with European forms of literacy. Indeed, we might think of such notes, along with the use of wampum as money and Penn's use of "pictographic" designs on wampum belts, as examples of the colonial dialogization of wampum.[59]

Importantly, the use of wampum does not mean that the Haudenosaunee were unfamiliar with pictographic records. Like other Woodlands peoples, they used a system of pictographic writing on birch bark. Farther west, the Ojibwe made pictographic birch-bark records of treaties.[60] Why, then, did wampum come to play such an important archival role in Haudenosaunee treaty negotiations? One answer probably rests with its nature as a healing medium that facilitated communication. It may be that large wampum belts were a relatively recent phenomenon rooted in the history of the establishment of the Haudenosaunee League of Nations, which linked the wampum form with a particular kind of state formation. The concurrent existence of wampum and birch-bark records in the Northeastern Woodlands reveals that the use of wampum for certain documentary functions was a choice based on the qualities of wampum rather than the lack of other textual forms like pictography. What distinguished wampum from other records, such as pictographic birch-bark records, was its unique power derived in part from the Condolence Council. The death of a tribal leader or a family member was ameliorated by the selection of a "replacement" who would step into and fulfill the role and obligations of the departed member of the community. Wampum played a crucial role in this process of ensuring the stability and continuity of society. We can gain further insight into the logic which linked wampum and the social fabric by considering how important agreements with a large amount of information were collectively stored and maintained in and by the tribal body.[61] Designated people served as the keepers of specific wampum records, but a much larger number of people might be responsible for remembering the exact wording of a particular, smaller segment of the agreement related to a specific belt. Thus, individual members of the tribal body would be linked to particular parts of a given belt, creating a parallel correspondence between the belt as a whole and the community as a whole. Only together, and in dialogue, were the two coherent.

Whereas alphabetic writing is distinguished by its capacity to be detached from the body and to circulate far beyond the original community of writers and readers, wampum was never meant to be separated from the context in which it was produced, the tribal body which guaranteed its meaning, and the agreement it recorded. This is almost antithetical to the logic of print, which is meant to facilitate reproduction and circulation and makes possible detachment from original context. The link between wampum and the tribal body is crucial to understanding how wampum functioned as a record and how the Haudenosaunee understood the interrelation of text, memory, society, wampum, and the body.

Because of the linkage between message and body, and because it is not representational, wampum has often been considered a mnemonic aid by philologists and other scholars of writing. For example, Jack Goody distinguishes wampum from writing because wampum belts are "not transcriptions of language, but rather a figurative shorthand, a mnemonic, which attempts to recall or prompt linguistic statements rather than to reproduce them."[62] However, wampum appears to have been neither "figurative" nor mnemonic. Furthermore, the distinction between "writing" and "mnemonics," can be rather fuzzy when put under analytic pressure and is often a question of function rather than essence.[63] For example, the words "mnemonics versus writing" on an index card might function as a mnemonic aid for me during an oral presentation. The words refer to my notes and my argument, which are stored not only in this chapter, but also in my memory, in my body. Outside of this matrix, they are meaningless and cannot be "deciphered" properly by other readers, even if they understand alphabetic writing.

The confrontation with alternative literacies can bring into focus underlying assumptions about writing which are rooted specifically in Western, alphabetic culture. For example, David Murray notes that "clearly there is an important difference between the ability to repeat based on mnemonic structures grounded in common knowledge, memory and a shared context, and what Derrrida describes as iterability, the way in which the statement can be separated from the context which apparently guaranteed it its meaning."[64]

This "iterability" is usually cited as evidence of the unique nature of alphabetic writing. Separation of writers and written documents became increasingly common during the colonial era, as documents circulated between the metropolis and distant colonies. In classic scholarship, the ability of a text to circulate independently of the writer and detached from its original context became a defining characteristic of "real writing," in distinction to mnemonic devices. However, as Mary Carruthers has shown, alphabetic writing in medieval Europe functioned mnemonically until the invention of print, the Age of Discovery, and other historical developments brought about dramatic changes in the use and function of writing, including greater circulation of texts detached from writers and authors.[65] Yet such medieval texts are not now considered mnemonic because we still understand the code and context that make them "iterable." This is partially because the context that gives alphabetic script, or Pen-and-Ink Work, its iterability remains intact and has been extended across the globe as a consequence of the history of colonialism. For many Western scholars, alphabetic script is so familiar and transparent as a code that it becomes naturalized and nearly invisible.

Textual analysis of intercultural conflict not only confronts us with the difficulty of studying texts that are part of non-alphabetic semiotic systems but also draws into question the assumed "iterability" of alphabetic writing. After all, Vimont's texts would not have been iterable among the Haudenosauneé in 1645. Indeed, iterability depends on an intact relationship between text and context and is never inherent in any given form of writing which may lose its iterability if the link to its cultural context is ruptured or severed.[66] Furthermore, as we see in his record of this French-Haudenosaunee peace council, cross-cultural negotiations bring into focus the limitations of many scholarly assumptions about writing. Linguistic transcription becomes difficult, and notions such as iterability become increasingly problematic, when the context is an intercultural and inter-linguistic encounter. Alphabetic script could not record Kiotseaeton's discourse without a number of modifications and adaptations by Vimont.

Negotiations organized around distinct kinds of writing provide windows onto the reciprocity between different textual systems and literary traditions as they confronted each other in early colonial America. The Haudenosaunee observed and evaluated European forms of literacy as carefully as their transatlantic counterparts observed them. At a treaty council in 1765, for example, an Onondaga man praised the durability of messages put down on paper. However, he and others expressed concern that written articles of agreement could be used to deceive, when, for example, indigenous people signed falsely translated documents. A British missionary reported that the Seneca had told them that "some of the Indians were afraid of *writing any letters* because those letters would speak for a great many years afterwards."[67] Throughout the colonial era, the Haudenosaunee criticized what they perceived to be a practice of placing undue weight on written words, particularly when human beings contradicted written records.[68] For example, there are numerous examples of Haudenosaunee individuals objecting to the use by European colonizers of written documents—which were illegible to the Haudenosaunee—to transfer land. At a meeting between Haudenosaunee deputies and Maryland and Virginia commissioners in 1744, the great Canassatego protested one such land transfer and added that native people had been "liable to many other inconveniences since the English came among us, and particularly from that Pen-and-Ink Work that is going on at the table."[69] In short, the Haudenosaunee were critical of the often celebrated ability of Western letters to separate written words, speaker, and context.

While Europeans valued signed contracts as concrete symbols of agreement, these documents were meaningless to the Haudenosaunee if the terms were not continually honored by communities who kept their words "alive" through their actions and through a reciprocal relationship. Conversely, while the Haudenosaunee prized wampum as the authoritative records of agreement, and have maintained them as such to the present day, Europeans and Euro-Americans have not always honored agreements recorded in wampum. Clearly, neither medium is inherently superior to the other. The iterability of wampum and alphabetic script depends on and reflects the relative power of the communities that use these records rather than the documentary "value" of either form.

Taking seriously the internal logic of both wampum and alphabetic script, rather than arguing for the superiority of either, seems the more useful pursuit for scholars interested in a literary study of reciprocity and dialogism in colonial America. In 1645, on the banks of the St. Lawrence River, wampum and Pen-and-Ink Work were alternative literacies confronting each other in a space of cross-cultural conflict in which neither was hegemonic. Hence, this negotiation offers a new perspective not only on early colonial America but also on how we understand textuality and the literary implications of coloniality. This and other records of early peace negotiations present us with the possibility of studying the inter-animation of truly different literacies.

Conclusion: Wampum and Treaty Negotiations
as and in American Literature

Early peace councils and later treaties represent an important site of cultural and literary interaction in colonial America and deserve a more central place in early American literary studies. In fact, published treaties constitute a significant aspect of the colonial press. Reports of treaties were regularly published along with sermons, essays, plays, and personal narratives of exploration, captivity, and other experiences.[70] Recognizing public interest in treaties, Benjamin Franklin published a collection of them from 1736 to 1762, which sold in both the U.S. and Britain.[71] Yet literary scholars have paid only scant attention to this genre of early American literature, and none have taken account of how wampum complemented and interacted with alphabetic records.[72]

An understanding of wampum and the complicated relationship between indigenous and alphabetic forms of literacy also opens up new perspectives on other, more canonical texts from colonial America. Mary Rowlandson's account of captivity, *The Sovereignty and Goodness of God, Together with the Faithfulness of His Promises Displayed; Being a Narrative of the Captivity and Restoration of Mrs. Mary Rowlandson*, for example, contains several references to wampum and to the cultural context which gave it meaning. However, Rowlandson's narrative distinguishes itself from Vimont's in its refusal to recognize and engage wampum as an alternative form of literacy.

Toward the end of her story, in the Twentieth Remove, Rowlandson describes what she calls "a dance" held by her captors the night before her release. There are eight central participants in the event, including her master, Quinnapin, and her mistress, Weetamoo, two leaders of the group that holds her captive.[73] Rowlandson's account focuses in detail on the appearances of these tribal leaders. Quinnapin is wearing "his Holland shirt, with great laces sewed at the tail of it, he had his silver buttons, his white stockings, his garters were hung round with shillings, and he had girdles of wampum upon his head and shoulders," while Weetamoo "had on a kersey coat, and covered with girdles of wampum from the loins upward: Her arms from her elbows to her hands were covered with bracelets; there were handfuls of necklaces about her neck and several sorts of jewels in her ears. She had fine red stockings, and white shoes, her hair powdered and face painted red."[74]

The preponderance of wampum and the formal features of the event suggest that this is a ritual or ceremony rather than a frivolous "dance." The participants are wearing wampum, not unlike Kiotseaeton upon his arrival at Trois Rivières, and they are "throwing out wampum to the standers-by."[75] Weetamoo, Quinnapin, and the other tribal leaders move around a kettle filled with water, from which they drink. The kettle is an important, though ambiguous, metaphor in Woodlands rhetoric, denoting hospitality, kinship, and union when shared, but it can also refer to war and hostility.[76] This event takes place the night before the "council" at which Rowlandson's release will be finalized. The ceremony, with its prevalence and dispersal of wampum, suggests the high status of the "dancers," establishing and affirming it within the community that holds Rowlandson captive.

It is not clear whether Rowlandson herself understood the significance of wampum, but her editor may well have.[77] The use of wampum was not only part of Haudenosaunee society; it was used throughout the Northeastern Woodlands, and Anglophone colonists were well acquainted with wampum as an element in diplomacy and treaty negotiations. Like the French, English colonists and settlers had sealed peace treaties with indigenous people using wampum belts. In New England, native people such as the Nipmunks of Nashaway, the Pawtucket, and the Massachusetts Indians came under the authority of the Massachusetts Bay Colony following the Pequot War. That relationship was formalized in 1644 with, among other things, the presentation of wampum to the colonial legislature.[78] The Nashaway Nipmunks were close neighbors of Lancaster, the town in Massachusetts where Rowlandson lived, and part of the group that attacked her household and held her captive. Thus, wampum was important to her community of captors, and such significance was well known in New England, just as it was in New France.

The representation of wampum as mere finery can be read as a refusal to recognize an alternative system of meaning, one as central to the community of her captors as the Bible was to her own. In that sense, it is paradigmatic of the text at large in its denigration of markers of cultural exchange and its repression of the dialogic potential present in the narrative. Earlier in the text, Rowlandson notes her unwillingness to "condole" with Weetamoo, who loses a young child in the Thirteenth Remove.[79] Rowlandson's references to wampum and her choice of the word "condole" suggests possible knowledge of the meaning of wampum and the rituals associated with it in the culture and society of the native people surrounding the Puritan settlements.[80] Her refusal to "condole" represents an unwillingness to participate in indigenous rituals of mourning. As such, it marks a moment at which Rowlandson pointedly rejects modes of cultural exchange that are not organized by Puritan cultural structures.

In contrast, the willingness of the French to engage in dialogue with native people "fostered a dialogic relationship with the peoples they encountered" that is important for scholars of American colonial literature to recover.[81] Bringing French-language texts into early American literary studies in turn makes it possible to broaden our understanding of the entire body of literature which emerged out of the conflict between European and American peoples. French, and Spanish, was as important in colonial America as English, and French- and Spanish-language texts should be an equally important part of early American studies.

Likewise, indigenous forms of literacy represent an important aspect of early American literature, and moments of intersection between European and indigenous textual forms offer new insights into the continent's literary history. Because treaty negotiations were organized as dialogues and exchanges, they present an important opportunity to move early American literary studies beyond what Myra Jehlen has called the monologic norm of a "Euro-American self-study" and, for that matter, beyond the boundaries of what became the United States.[82] Early exchanges between peoples, narratives, and different conceptions of the materiality of the word present us with an exciting opportunity to appreciate the complexity of colonial literature and to trace colonial semiosis in North America. To make such a shift, we must, like those who first negotiated the enormous transformations instantiated by coloniality, be willing to grapple with unfamiliar texts and narrative forms.

CHAPTER THREE

Writing in the Conflict Zone

Don Felipe Guaman Poma de Ayala's
El primer nueva corónica y buen gobierno

The old man puts down his pen and looks at the thick manuscript before him, almost 1,200 pages of writing and illustrations, done by a hand that has grown thin and frail with age.[1] It is the year 1615, and he is around eighty years old (*Corónica*, 1106).[2] Born shortly after the arrival of the Spanish, this man of the Andes has lived his entire life in the maelstrom of conquest. His knowledge of Spanish language and letters has allowed him to negotiate the violent transformations of his time and world; he has made a living working for and within the colonial power structure as a clerk and translator. At times he has used his literacy and his knowledge of this inter-ethnic world to fight colonial abuses.[3] The manuscript he has just completed contains an indigenous history of the region unlike any other and is ad-dressed directly to the Spanish king, Philip III.[4] It is an audacious act, and he is not humble, this man who calls himself Don Felipe Guaman Poma de Ayala.

Yet he feels again the weight of the project. So much depends on it, and he worries about whether he has been able to do it justice. Foregrounding this doubt, Guaman Poma begins by addressing the king in a manner that is simultaneously respectful and intimate:[5]

> Muchas ueses dudé, S[acra] C[atólica] R[eal] M[agestad], azeptar esta dicha ynpresa y muchas más después de auerla comensado me quise bolber atrás, jusgando por temeria mi entención, no hallando supgeto en mi facultad para acauarla conforme a la que se deuía a unas historias cin esciptura nenguna, no más de por los *quipos* [cordeles con nudos] y rrelaciones de los yndios antigos de muy biejos y biejas sabios testigos de uista, para que dé fe de ellos, y que ualga por ello qualquier sentencia jusgada. (*Corónica*, 8)[6]

✿

Many times I doubted, H[oly] C[atholic] R[oyal] M[ajesty], that you would accept this printed word and then having started I wanted to begin over again, worried that it was beyond my ability to do it as it ought to be done with histories without any writing except for the quipus and relations of the very old, Indian wise men and women testifying what they saw, that credence be given to them, and they are worthy of some fair judgment.[7]

Almost four hundred years later, I look at Guaman Poma's words and feel equally overwhelmed and doubtful. Am I up to the task of engaging a text so difficult? For there is, to this day, no full-length English translation of Guaman Poma's text.[8] Furthermore, his Spanish is archaic, creolized, and idiosyncratic, interspersed with passages in Quechua and Aymara, languages I do not understand. The Andes, and Spanish-language literature, are outside my field of training, yet Guaman Poma's work seems to me to be an important text for any scholar of colonialism, American literature, and American book history. Although Guaman Poma is well known in Latin American studies, his work deserves greater attention from North American literary scholars as well, as a rare indigenous voice in the cacophony of early colonial documents, as an early contribution to textual studies of the colonial encounter, and as an attempt to recast its terms and possibilities.[9]

The manuscript follows printing and typesetting conventions in detail, reflecting the author's knowledge of the European book and his mastery of the form. Carefully paginated for publication, which the author explicitly requests, the text represents an effort to enter into the European world of print. However, El primer nueva corónica y buen gobierno has a more local, formal antecedent as well, one that is important to a full understanding of Guaman Poma's literary achievement—namely, the Andean quipu. Prior to the arrival of Europeans, the Inca and other Andean people used quipus, intricately knotted cords, to record information and narrative. Analysis of Guaman Poma's work reveals that the textual logic of quipus structures his manuscript in significant ways. His chronicle thus emerges out of and is shaped by two distinct literary and textual traditions: the European book and the Andean quipu.[10]

In foregrounding the enormity and difficulty of the task he has taken on, Guaman Poma implicitly asks his reader to recognize the importance of his work and to honor his attempt at cross-cultural communication with a similar effort. Guaman Poma is writing not only for the king of Spain but, indeed, "para todo el mundo (for all the world)."[11] And he is addressing not only Andean history and colonial abuses but also the relationship between power, knowledge, and writing in a textual conflict zone structured by conquest. The term "textual conflict zone" refers to "*material spaces in which disparate cultural modes and conventions of representation* meet, clash, and grapple with each other, often in highly asymmetrical relations of domination and subordination."[12] For Guaman Poma is writing in the aftermath of conquest and must contend with Spanish hegemony, even as he appropriates Spain's discursive apparatus for protest and contestation. Unlike early negotiations between the French and Haudenosaunee, this is not an undetermined, but an over-determined, encounter. In Guaman Poma's lifetime, the highly structured world of the pre-conquest Andes went through large-scale disintegration.[13] Already destabilized by struggles between indigenous groups prior to the arrival of the Spanish, the region was further devastated by conquest and subsequent civil wars. Viceroy Francisco de Toledo executed the last Inca prince, Túpac Amaru, and initiated major resettlements of the native population.

Guaman Poma has negotiated the interethnic strife of the region by moving among many worlds. Claiming descent from both the Inca royal line and the pre-Incaic dynasty of Huánuco, he has acquired Spanish literacy and served the Spanish colonial apparatus for much of his life. He calls himself by both Spanish and Andean names and claims honorific titles in two languages: the Spanish Don and the Andean Auqui (prince). However, he has recently been stripped of all honor and status after a lost legal battle for land in Huamanga, where he grew up and to which he claimed ancestral title.[14] The case culminated in defeat for Guaman Poma, who subsequently endured a painful and humiliating public whipping. Now he has retired to the province of Lucanas to write a manuscript that draws on thirty years of travel in the region.[15] Epic in scope, it is both a petition for personal and collective redress and a counter-history to Spanish chronicles such as José de Acosta's *História natural y moral de las Indias* and Martín de Murúa's *Historia general del Perú*.[16] In it, Guaman Poma will make many claims, including one particularly pertinent to this project: that the Andean people prior to contact possessed a system of writing in the form of knotted cords known as quipus.[17]

Many early records of the encounter between Andean and European peoples refer to these knotted cords, a widely used system of recordkeeping in which Inca and other Andean peoples recorded information such as tax tributes, property rights, genealogy, myths, songs, history, and other narratives. De Acosta's *História* (1590), one of the most widely read Spanish chronicles at the time, notes, "Es increyble lo que en este modo alcaçaron, porque quanto los libros pueden dezir de historias, y leyes, y ceremonias, y cuentas de negocios, todo esso suplen los Quipos tan puntualmente que admira (It is incredible what in this way they can grasp because all that books can say of histories and laws and ceremonies and business accounts, all this the quipus can supply in admirable detail)."[18] Almost four decades earlier, Viceroy Cristóbal Vaca de Castro based a history of the region on the testimonies of *quipucamayoc* from Cuzco reading from their quipus. The resulting Spanish text, the *Discurso sobre la descendencia y gobierno de los Incas* (1542/1608), represents one of the earliest direct transcriptions of historical quipus into alphabetic Spanish script.[19] It is one of a number of texts which lend themselves to studying the intersection between alphabetic and quipu literacy and the ways in which these disparate textual forms interacted and informed each other.

Guaman Poma, however, writes decades later, and his text presents an opportunity to analyze the interaction between alphabetic and quipu forms of literacy after alphabetism has become dominant. This semiotic conflict animates the manuscript in important and understudied ways. Unlike de Acosta and other Spanish chroniclers, Guaman Poma offers an indigenous perspective that is specifically in dialogue with and stands as a counterpoint to colonial narratives while reflecting the contested status of quipus and the politics of writing in the colonial sphere. Guaman Poma explicitly challenges contemporary discourses which justify conquest by casting America's indigenous people as inferior and illiterate. While Guaman Poma's text would be significant for this intervention alone, it also represents an important key to understanding the structures of Andean forms of literacy because the manuscript is informed by the textual logic of quipus. The Spanish brought with them a different and competing system of literacy, and in *El primer nueva corónica y buen gobierno*, Guaman Poma engages this foreign world of alphabetism as he attempts to bring into dialogue European and Andean forms of writing in the pages of his manuscript.

The Challenge of the Quipus

Quipus encode information in strings and knots of various sizes and colors.[20] Spanish colonial records often refer to them as "cordos de nudos (knotted cords)" or "quipus de hilo (string quipus)." Large quipus consist of a central cord, to which a great number of additional, smaller strings may be attached. These cords use a wide variety of colors and knots to store information, although scholars do not yet know precisely how. There are several reasons why the "code of the quipu" has remained even more elusive than the "Maya Code."[21] For one thing, this complex semiotic system is radically different from most records known to scholars of writing. In contrast to paper, parchment, papyrus, and clay (commonly used surfaces for writing), quipus record meaning in three-dimensional space rather than on the surface. Meaning is recorded through colors, types of knots, and the relative positions of those knots on the strings. The manner in which they were read seems to have been nonlinear, simultaneously tactile and visual, and organized according to a decimal principle. Furthermore, quipus were "designed as a closed system with indecipherability and an oral 'key' (known only by the *quipucamayocs*) as positive, and desirable characteristics," enabling strict control of the written sphere by the Inca state.[22]

At the time of conquest, quipus were constructed, maintained, and read by a small class of functionaries called quipucamayoc. The Spanish writer Fernando de Montesino noted that local historians called *amautas* also used quipus "in place of letters" and that a great number of these historical quipus used by amautas existed in Quito and all over Peru.[23] De Murúa, for whom Guaman Poma worked before producing his own narrative, comments extensively on quipus and the broad range of information they contained:

> By these knots they counted the successions of the times and when each Inca ruled, the children he had, if he was good or bad, valiant or cowardly, with whom he was married, what lands he conquered, the buildings he constructed, the service and riches he received, how many years he lived, where he died, what he was fond of; in sum, everything that books teach and show us was got from there.[24]

Indigenous and Spanish sources thus tell us that quipus were used to record and transmit a wide range of information across the region and that they were used across genres to record knowledge that was authoritative and in that sense collective. Today, quipus are sometimes used as private tools by Andean shepherds keeping count of their flocks, but we have no colonial records of private quipu correspondence similar to the pictographic letters and notices used in North America. Likewise, colonial agents in the Andes make no mention of publicly posted quipus that would be comparable to monumental pictography in the Northeastern Woodlands and stelae in Mesoamerica. Rather, quipus seem to have been used exclusively to record,

9. Inca quipu, 1500 A.C. Courtesy of the Museo Larco, Lima, Peru.

preserve, and transmit "official" and authoritative information such as public records (genealogy, tax, and property information); specialized knowledge such as philosophy and astrology; and collective narratives, including songs, myths, and epics (see figure 9).

While quipus were used in the region centuries before the Inca established domination, it was the tenth Inca ruler, Túpac Yupanqui, who instituted the widespread use of quipus for state administration a few generations before the arrival of the Spanish.[25] During the early Spanish colonial period, quipus continued to hold legitimacy in many public forums. Records of court proceedings relating to property represent an important site of alphabetic quipu transcriptions and provide crucial insight into the logic of quipu textuality. From these records we know that two or more quipus were always used simultaneously, in consultation, and always by at least two quipucamayoc. The use of more than one quipu at a time seems to have ensured greater accuracy, as both needed to be in agreement: One eyewitness described two renditions of separate quipus as being "of one tenor."[26] Thus multiple records and their public reading were part of a process of "joining," putting "together into one," or "consolidating" information contained in the records.[27]

Following the arrival of the Spanish, important changes occurred in the use of quipus. First, colonial agents such as Viceroy Cristóbal Vaca de Castro consulted the quipus and transcribed the information directly into Spanish texts such as the *Discurso*. Such transcription constitutes an important site of colonial semiosis that joined together Andean and Spanish texts and forms of writing. As in New France, the earliest phase in the transition to Spanish and alphabetic dominance in this region was marked by the coexistence of both forms of writing and novel experiments in their mutual translatability. For example, the Mercedarian friar Diego de Porres instructed fellow priests to use quipus to transmit biblical teachings by creating quipus that recorded church dogma, including prayers, instructions for Christian behavior, and a Ten Commandments quipu to be posted on the church wall.[28] While it is unclear whether any such biblical quipus were ever produced, since none survive, it seems that Spanish priests did incorporate quipus into Catholic practices such as confession:

> Yo vi vn manojo destos hilos, en que vna India traya escrita vna cófessió general de toda su vida, y por ellos se cófessaua, como yo lo hiziera por papel escrito, y aun preguntè de algunos hilillos que me pareció algo diferentes, y erá ciertas circunstácias que requeria el pecado para cófessarle enteraméte.[29]

> ❧

> I have seen a bunch of these strings, in which an Indian woman brought a written confession of her entire life, and with these she confessed, just as I do by writing on paper, and I even asked about some small threads that seemed different, and they were certain situations that required a sin to be confessed completely.

Early missionaries thus used quipus in conversion efforts; Spanish chroniclers relied on quipus for information about local pre-contact history; and colonial officials initially consulted quipus to determine and manage issues pertaining to property and labor.[30] The use of quipus by Spanish colonial agents instantiated novel intertextual exchanges between indigenous and European textual forms in the Andes, just like in the American Northeast. Each medium recorded and transmitted some version of the knowledge contained in the other, even as that knowledge was necessarily inflected by the process of reinscription and translation, for in that process each medium reshaped and deformed the other in ways we have not yet begun to understand.[31] However, the possibilities suggested by such intertextual exchange were soon foreclosed as Spanish authorities eventually came to regard quipus as a competing writing system and ordered their destruction. The Lima Council of Bishops in 1582–83 issued an edict to ban all quipus except those relating to taxes and property. This campaign of destruction was so successful that even today few quipus survive, and none has been deciphered.[32]

Hence, Guaman Poma's text had to negotiate a political climate in which indigenous records were literally under fire and he himself was being publicly ostracized. He was writing at a historical moment when the transition from quipus to alphabetic script was nearly complete—indeed, the edict to destroy quipus was being implemented while he traveled around the region. It was not a gradual transition from one system to another based on the relative advantages of alphabetism; rather, it was a violent process linked to colonial conquest and administration in which a complete textual system dominant in the region was discredited and forced underground, to be replaced with another textual system in which formal authority would come to reside.

Guaman Poma could not represent quipus as legitimate historical documents in the same ways that de Murúa and de Acosta did, because quipus had become illegal and increasingly discredited. Furthermore, he wrote from a very different subject position. His ethnic identity made his claim to authority far more tenuous than that of Spanish chroniclers. His knowledge of Spanish letters and his identity as a Christian mediated his ethnicity and provided, along with his claim to royal descent, crucial connecting points to his interlocutor. Yet his representation of quipus, in the opening sentence and elsewhere in the manuscript, reveals an unwillingness to concede the possession of writing to Spain and the alphabet alone. Therefore, Guaman Poma simultaneously claims and disavows quipus in his opening sentence, which brings to the fore the topic of quipus and their relationship to writing:

> Having started I wanted to begin over again, worried that it was beyond my ability to do it as it ought to be done with histories without any writing except for the quipus and relations of the very old, Indian wise men and women testifying what they saw, that credence be given to them, and they are worthy of some fair judgment.

While syntactically torturous, the substance of this statement seems straightforward. It appears that Guaman Poma's sources have been the oral testimony of eyewitnesses to the conquest and that he has written his account to give his sources credence, because they deserve the fair hearing that they presumably have not yet received. Indeed, that is how Guaman Poma's "disclaimer" is usually read: that he has written his history based on oral sources *because* the Andeans did not have writing ("*escriptura*").[33] For example, Rolena Adorno notes that Guaman Poma's "task, he suggested, was one of translation from the oral to the written mode; his job was to pass the record from one medium to another, to transpose, not to invent or even interpret." This gesture is necessary, according to Adorno, because Guaman Poma is using the oral testimonies to give his own *Corónica* credence. Adorno translates the passage "unas historias cin escriptura nenguna" as "some narrations which were never written down" and thus suggests that oral testimony and indigenous eyewitness accounts provide Guaman Poma's sole source of authority.[34]

But why, then, does Guaman Poma claim that he wants to lend credence to his sources if they are what provide his credibility? Perhaps his reason was similar to de Acosta's, with whose work he was familiar: the need to validate his history with documentary sources. De Acosta and other Spanish chroniclers resolved this predicament by noting that, while indigenous Americans "had no writing like us," they "did not lack some kinds of letters and books" but had "collections of books and their histories and calendars, many things to see."[35] Pedro Sarmiento de Gamboa, who wrote his own history of the Andes in 1572, noted:

> They would record (and still do) the most remarkable things, in both kind and quantity, on some cords that they call quipu. . . . On the quipu they make certain knots that they recognize, through which and by the use of different colors, they distinguish and record each thing as if with letters. It is remarkable to see the details that they preserve in these cordlets, for which there are masters as there are for writing among us.[36]

Guaman Poma cannot be so bold, however, because he negotiates a very different subject position and historical moment. The ambiguous contradiction, "without any writing, except for the quipus," marks his predicament. While he cannot explicitly claim quipus as his sources or posit their equivalence to alphabetic writing in the aftermath of the Lima edict, he nonetheless retains for quipus the status of historical documentation and, ultimately, "writing." The assertion of functional equivalence between alphabetic writing and quipus is made more explicitly elsewhere in the manuscript, as in an illustration that represents a *chasqui*, a messenger, carrying a small quipu and a letter ("*carta*") in his right hand (*Corónica*, 204; see figure 10).

Later, alongside an illustration of the author consulting with elders, Guaman Poma explicitly links oral accounts with the material record of the

10. Incan runner with quipu. From *El primer nueva corónica y buen gobierno* (1615/1616) by Don Felipe Guaman Poma de Ayala, p. 202 [204]. Copenhagen, Det Kongelige Bibliotek, GKS 2232 4°. Courtesy of Det Kongelige Bibliotek/ The Royal Library of Denmark.

quipu. At the prompting of the author, the elders "muestra los quipos [cordeles con nudos] y le declara y le da rrelaciones los Yngas (show the quipus [knotted cords] and explicate them and give him the history of the Incas)" (*Corónica*, 369). Here the oral account is represented as distinct from, but linked to, the material record, neither of which stands alone. The history of the Incas is recorded in quipus, which are as crucial to the preservation and transmission of that history as the oral account of the elders. This passage in the manuscript supports the interpretation of the opening paragraph as an assertion that elder testimony and quipus both served as key sources for Guaman Poma. The more or less masked ways in which he represents quipus as writing testify to the political climate in which such an assertion was both volatile and an important critique of colonial discourse, which had linked savagery, lack of writing, and the justification of conquest.

In his opening paragraph, Guaman Poma narratively links and contrasts "escriptura" and "quipus" as if they are incommensurable, and, indeed, translators have consistently read "cin escriptura nenguna" to mean "without any writing." However, Guaman Poma may be playing a clever rhetorical trick on his readers. Despite his seeming concession that his people had no written sources, the words "cin escriptura nenguna" are immediately followed by the words "no más por los quipus (except for the quipus)" (Corónica, 8). This subordinate phrase revises the meaning of the sentence significantly. Furthermore, while "escriptura" can be translated broadly as writing, it can also be defined more narrowly as scripture. That is how Guaman Poma consistently uses it in the remainder of the manuscript. In fact, every subsequent reference to "escriptura" links the term to scripture: "escriptura diuina (divine scripture)" or "sagrada escritura (sacred scripture)" (see Corónica, 1, 51, 91, 471, 623, 649, 774, 956, 1087).[37] Conversely, he uses the word "letras," or letters, to refer to alphabetic script ("las letras a, b, c") (Corónica, 926). The consistency with which Guaman Poma uses "escritura" to mean scripture and "letras" to refer to alphabetic letters counteracts what initially seems like a concession that Andean peoples did not possess historical documents and other written sources. Instead, he suggests that they did. This opening passage is the only place in the manuscript where Guaman Poma does not link the term "escriptura" explicitly to biblical scripture, and so it appears that he uses the dual meanings inherent in the term "escriptura" to mask his audacious assertion of an equal narrative authority located in quipus.

Guaman Poma's use of the term "to write" is instructive in this regard. While he uses the term "writing" to refer to alphabetic script, Guaman Poma also links the Spanish term "escriuir" (to write) to quipus. In fact, he repeatedly uses the term "escriuano" in connection with quipus, thus claiming the term "writing" for quipu literacy. Furthermore, he contrasts quipus with letters to deny the superiority of one vis-à-vis the other: "Éstos tenían tanta auilidad, pues que en los cordeles supo tanto, ¿qué me hiciera ci fuera en letra? (The quipus were capable of storing so much information, how could letters have done it any better?)" (Corónica, 361). This question is an audacious challenge to the notion that alphabetism was superior to quipus. Guaman Poma defiantly asserts that quipus were equal, if not superior, to alphabetic script and that writing flourished in the Andes before the arrival of Spanish letters. This passage can then be seen as an impassioned intervention into a debate on quipus, alphabetism, and writing that is still unfolding, and it reveals an acute awareness of the politics of, and the stakes of debates about, literacy. Thus, it is not only the testimony of elders but also this indigenous literary tradition—both the quipus and those who knew how to make and read them—to which Guaman Poma gives credence in the opening lines of his address to the king.

Guaman Poma's careful representation of quipus as a form of writing that is radically different from but equivalent to alphabetic script suggests that he is self-consciously engaging the debate about whether indigenous Americans had writing. At stake in that debate was not only de Acosta's ranking of civilizations according to whether they possessed writing, but also de Las Casas's linkage of the absence of indigenous writing in the Americas to a justification of Spanish rule. Guaman Poma clearly rejects both the legitimacy of the colonial project and the notion that Andean people are incapable of ruling themselves. Indeed, Guaman Poma represents colonial rule as a breakdown in social order. He also rejects the underlying logic of de Las Casas's argument by representing the pre-Hispanic Andes as the home of a highly developed civilization which possessed a written culture.[38]

Notably, Guaman Poma does not represent himself as part of the quipu tradition; nor does he elaborate on how quipus functioned. Perhaps this is a defensive move, as quipus had been outlawed, or maybe he perceived his own authorial standing as closely linked to his identification with Spanish literacy. Guaman Poma explicitly notes his own disconnection from quipus, which he represents as temporal: "porque yo no nací en tienpo de los Yngas para sauer todo que destas cordilleras lo supe y lo fue escriuiendo; adonde estube más tienpos fue aquí (because I was not born in the time of the Incas to know everything about these cords that I found out and went about writing down; where I spent most of my time was here)" (*Corónica*, 860). In this awkwardly phrased passage, Guaman Poma portrays his own efforts to reconnect with the tradition of quipu literacy, driven by a desire for a kind of cultural recovery that might be called proto-postcolonial. He also represents the Spanish conquest, rather than simply time, as the root of disconnection between himself and the quipu literary tradition. Guaman Poma casts himself as a man of Spanish letters—an identity that is as crucial to his authority as is his indigeneity—and locates himself outside quipu literacy while retaining the possibility of reconnection and recovery.

The ambiguous language of Guaman Poma's opening greeting to King Philip III reflects the politics of writing with which he had to contend. Guaman Poma's narrative contests not only European histories of his homeland but also their authority to narrate that history and, by extension, the singular authority of alphabetic script. After the banning of quipus, Guaman Poma uses ambiguous syntax to simultaneously pay homage to and contest European possession of literacy while foregrounding the presence of quipus as alternative sources of knowledge.

The Lost Code of the Quipu

By the 1590s, when Guaman Poma was writing his chronicle, the replacement of quipus with paper documents written in Spanish was virtually complete.[39] Soon, the Spanish also attacked the veracity and legitimacy of quipus, which became not only undecipherable but unrecognizable as writing.[40] Indeed, for centuries thereafter, philologists and scholars of writing would dismiss quipus as nothing more than mnemonic devices. In 1923, L. Leland Locke published the first major study of whether quipus constituted a writing system and concluded that they did not fit contemporary definitions of writing.[41] Other important studies of writing have also categorized quipus as mere mnemonic devices. Ignace J. Gelb, for example, argued that "all the reports about the alleged use of the *quipu* for the recording of chronicles and historical events are plain fantasy."[42] Ironically, alphabetic script in the Andes could have suffered a similar fate had colonial history been inverted. Andean people initially confronted Spanish documents as utterly foreign and perplexing, understanding them as mnemonic devices consisting of paper covered by "ordered lines of abstract shapes" that had to be "interpreted by specialists."[43] Without the survival of people literate in alphabetic script, it, too, might have become a misunderstood relic presumed to be merely mnemonic. This realization should remind us that the legibility of a given writing system is intimately tied to the fate of the culture of which it is a part.

The declining fortunes of the Inca state and the emergence of Spanish hegemony in the region relegated quipus outside the realm of the literary. However, this happened as a consequence of political struggles which, ironically, reflected how quipus were initially seen as comparable forms of literacy by the Spanish colonial regime. An edict banning quipus issued by the bishops in Lima in 1583 marks this struggle and the political climate that Guaman Poma had to negotiate. In the edict, the condemnation of quipus is found under the heading "Libros Profanos y Lascivos (Profane and Lascivious Books)." Hence, quipus are grouped with other books offensive to the church: "libros profanos y lascivos." However, the bishops distinguished quipus from Spanish books also banned by the edict: "y porque en lugar de libros los indios han usado y usan unos como registros hechos de diferentes hilos que ellos llaman quipos, y con estos conservan la memoria de su antigua superstición y ritos y ceremonias y costumbres perversas (and because in place of books the Indians have used and use records made from different strings which they call quipos, and with these they preserve knowledge of their ancient superstitions and rites and ceremonies and perverse customs)."[44] The bishops thus categorized quipus as a form of literature used in the past and in the present to preserve Andean cultural and religious knowledge—instead of and on par with books, despite their radically different form. That is why they had to be destroyed "totalmente." The issue, for the bishops, was one of religious and cultural conversion and acculturation. Quipus, as a kind of book rooted in Andean culture, were ultimately deemed antithetical to missionary and other colonial projects.[45] However, this understanding of quipus as comparable to books, like most of the quipus themselves, was soon lost. Centuries later, scholars still face the quipus as a great conundrum.

One breakthrough in quipu scholarship came in 1978, when Marcia Ascher and Robert Ascher published a study based on careful examination of 191 extant quipus in which they argued that quipus were able to store a great range of information using a mathematical, decimal code.[46] In the past few decades, quipu scholarship has flourished, largely because of the painstaking and meticulous work of scholars who have taken seriously Elizabeth Hill Boone's warning that "our inability to read them should not, however, make us unable to see them as writing systems."[47]

Indeed, Gary Urton argues that "the quipu recording system more closely approximated a form of writing than is usually considered to have been the case."[48] Urton notes the commonplace usage of two quipus and their agreement of content and argues that such close agreement between two separate documents supposedly recording the same information and then rendering it at a later moment would suggest a highly conventionalized system of recording.[49] The Inca empire, Tawantinsuyu, is known to have functioned as a state with a well-developed bureaucracy and a high degree of order and continuity. It is unlikely that such a large and complex state could function on the basis of an idiosyncratic and individualistic mnemonic system of recordkeeping.[50] The last few decades have seen a resurgence of interest in quipus and an accumulation of scholarly insight, allowing us to begin to appreciate their complexity, even though we do not yet understand exactly how quipu literacy functioned in Guaman Poma's time or how to decipher the remaining extant quipus.

In Andean society, numbers served not only a quantitative but also a qualitative purpose, and the mathematical nature of quipus corresponded to what Galen Brokaw has called "a numerical episteme."[51] Andean society was characterized by a high degree of numerical literacy and organized its social and philosophical thought according to an episteme rooted in numbers. The number ten was key in this epistemology, and social groups or villages (called *ayllus*) were organized according to the decimal unit of ten. Guaman Poma's survey of Inca society corresponds to this decimal organization, with its ten "calles." In addition to the decimal-based system of social organization, the number five organized both historical and geographical paradigms in the Andes, as evident in the separation of Cuzco into four parts organized around a "fifth" part, the center. The pair constituted another important numerical unit. A preference for pairs reflected the philosophical notion that singularity signified incompletion and also dangerous imbalance. Pairs represented balance and a completed unit. This philosophy, based on the concept of pairing and the privileging of dualism, pervaded Andean society and thought. Arithmetic, whether addition, subtraction, multiplication, or division, was central to the "art of rectification" by which Andean society sought to maintain balance and equilibrium in moral and social terms.[52] Numbers and their arithmetical manipulation then provides "a process by which indigenous Andean culture shapes the raw, quantitative nature of time, space, and social organization into numerically significant configurations" based on its "ontology of numbers."[53]

In Andean epistemology, numbers can therefore be understood as parallel to words as the privileged signifiers through which reality was understood, represented, and manipulated. Like other kinds of writing, quipus then reflected the privileged forms of representation in Andean society. Indeed, Brokaw has argued that "the Andean ontology of numbers and the conventions of *khipu* textuality developed together dialogically, each informing and influencing the other."[54] The Aschers coined the term "cultural insistence" to explain the ways in which the main ideas, values, and organizational structures of a given culture manifest themselves in material and representational artifacts. They note that cloth was such an important component of Inca culture that it can be seen as "characteristic of Inca insistence in and of itself. At every turning point in the life history of an individual, cloth played a key role."[55] The Aschers argue that portability was equally characteristic of Inca "insistence" and that the most common artifact used to carry things was a piece of strong cloth. The quipu, then, appears to have combined numerous central elements of Andean cultural insistence as a cloth-based, highly portable system of literacy based on an epistemology of numbers.

Thus, quipus can be seen as the perfect writing system for Andean society, capable of expressing far more than numbers even as it used numeracy as an important representational principle. Although we still do not understand exactly how, other recent scholarship suggests that quipus recorded not just numbers but also nouns such as "blanket" and even verbs, "the basic grammatical units necessary for noting specific actions and states of being and for the construction of predicate phrases."[56] Groups conquered by the Inca paid tribute mainly in the form of labor, and transcriptions of Inca tribute quipus suggest "a rich vocabulary of verbs denoting various types of labor service that were to be performed for the state—for example, to make, take, garden, plant, carry."[57] Quipus could register more than one verb, and thus potentially complex sentences, on the same string, as exemplified by this sentence transcribed into Spanish from a quipu: "The gold that they *took*, they *delivered* to Cuzco."[58] Also, quipus were able to record relative chronological relationships, the "syntactical framework that would be needed for narratives detailing relationships of cause and effect, or to identify causality in mythical/historical narrations."[59] While Urton, like other quipu scholars, remains unable to explain exactly how syntax and grammar correspond to knots and colors, he points to the variety of knot types and the broad range and complexity of color and knot combinations and arrangements as the semiotic raw material which made a rich (and conventionalized) semantic vocabulary available to the *quipucamayoc*.

Urton thus argues that quipus recorded full narrative sentences containing subject-verb-object constructions, predicates, and spatial and temporal information: all of the elements of a full writing system.[60] Although radically different from alphabetic script, quipus were similar in their ability to express meaning through an infinite variety of combinations of smaller units, whether they are letters or knots. De Acosta corroborates this hypothesis:

> Y en cada manojo destos tantos ñudos, y ñudicos, y hilillos atados: vnos colorados: otros verdes: otros azules: otros blácos; y finalmente tantas diferéncias, que assi como nosotros de veynte y quarto letras guisandolas en diferentes maneras sacamos tanta infinidad de vocablos, assi estos de sus ñudos, y colores sacauan innumerables significaciones de cosas.[61]

✺

And in each bunch of these [quipus] were so many knots and smaller knots and small threads tied together: some red, others green, others blue, others white, and finally some different. Thus just as we out of twenty-eight letters arranged in different ways produce such infinity of words, so in this way they with their knots and colors produce innumerable meanings of things.

De Acosta draws a direct parallel between the way in which letters of the alphabet and the knots and colors of quipus combine to construct larger units of meaning in their respective semiotic systems. And, importantly, he uses the same verb, "*sacar,*" to refer to both alphabetic and quipu literacy.[62] By using the same verb to describe the relationship between signifiers (arbitrary units such as letters or colored knots) and signified (words and meanings of things), de Acosta posits an equivalence between the function of radically different forms of material records.

While de Acosta at other times makes a clear distinction between alphabetic writing and quipus, he notes that among Andean people, quipus ("ñudos y manojos de cuerdas") were considered entirely reliable written sources for "true testimony and writing (testigos y escritura cierta)."[63] One reason previous generations of scholars might have overlooked the complex nature of quipus is that, in the transfer into Spanish colonial records, linguistic diversity was reduced as colonial administrators recorded only what interested them. Whereas early alphabetic transcriptions of long-lost quipus contain a wealth of verbs such as "to plant," "to make," and "to carry," later Spanish records contain only the verb that interested colonial administrators the most: "to give." What Urton calls the "disappearance of the verbs" simultaneously marks the increasing hegemony of Spanish colonial logic and a corresponding loss in our understanding of the richness of quipu literacy.

Unlike Urton, Guaman Poma may have had access to historical quipus that retained their narrative range, even as the quipus and those who kept them had been forced underground. Furthermore, he was a cultural insider and native speaker with a conscious agenda to "give credence" to Andean culture as a civilization on par with Spain. This project reflects knowledge of the region's history and of its indigenous textual tradition, its many verbs, and their relationships to the strings, knots, and colors of quipus. In fact, Guaman Poma's text does not simply assert the validity of quipus as a form of literacy; it is also marked by the textual logic, the "semiotic conventions," of quipus.[64] The manuscript expresses Andean culture in ways that help us understand quipu textuality, as well as how such indigenous forms of literacy shaped Guaman Poma's narrative and rhetorical strategies.

Recovering the Logic of Quipu Textuality in the *Corónica*

The organization of the *Corónica* reflects both the historical struggles of the region and the multiple textual principles brought into contact and conflict by Spanish conquest. Given our limited understanding of quipu textuality, scholars have been more successful in mapping the presence of Spanish discursive genres and narrative conventions in the manuscript.[65] However, the structural principles of a distinctly Andean poetics can also be discerned by focusing on elements of the text that at first appear to reflect an inadequate grasp of Spanish textual conventions. For example, the Inca biographies have been read as slightly clumsy adaptations of Spanish genres like the royal history, but they show important stylistic divergences, such as the inclusion of information about illegitimate children.[66] These biographies were likely transcribed from quipus, and they are stylistically and substantively similar to Inca biographies in other texts also known to have been transcribed from quipus. As Brokaw has argued, striking similarities in the narrative structure and format of the biographies in Guaman Poma's *Corónica* and in known quipu transcriptions such as the *Discurso* suggest a connection between these two texts. Furthermore, the consistency of the information in these two different texts—the *Corónica* and the *Discurso*—suggests a shared and stable absent documentary source such as a quipu. Brokaw thus makes a convincing case for reading Guaman Poma's biographies as rooted in Andean, rather than Spanish, sources and reflecting Andean textual conventions.[67] Such analysis suggests that elements in Guaman Poma's manuscript that seem unorthodox may best be understood as having Andean, rather than Spanish, formal antecedents. Along the same lines, Jorge Urioste has demonstrated that errors in Guaman Poma's Spanish often reflect the grammar of his native Quechua; analysis of the Quechua passages in the manuscript reveals an impressive command of Quechua linguistic and literary conventions.[68] Passages in the manuscript that seem poorly executed when measured by the standard of European languages and narrative genres may, then, represent moments in which we can glimpse the Andean underpinnings of the manuscript.[69]

The index represents an important case in point. As others have noted, Guaman Poma's index does not correspond to the actual contents of the

Corónica, seemingly indicating a failure to understand the purpose of an index.[70] However, the referent for this particular index may lie beyond the pages of the book, for it seems to be organized by a decimal principle just as quipus were.[71] Brokaw has argued that Guaman Poma's final index is meant not to map the contents of the manuscript but, rather, to inscribe a decimal Andean textual and social logic at the conclusion of the text.[72] This insight highlights the value of a structural analysis of Guaman Poma's text, particularly when developed in dialogue with quipu scholarship. For example, Guaman Poma uses the designation "first" ("primer," "primero," and "primera") as an important organizing principle or marker within the manuscript. The peculiarity with which he uses this designation becomes apparent when compared with Martín de Murúa's manuscript, on which Guaman Poma worked and to which he positioned himself as a corrective. De Murúa appropriately uses the designation "capítulo primero" for first chapters within major segments or parts of the text. In contrast, Guaman Poma uses the "primer" or "first" designation as a way to mark various segments of the manuscript, to announce exposition, and in other ways to organize the text.[73] "Primer" designates first chapters such as "primer capítvlo de los Yngas" in a manner similar to de Murúa but also marks singular elements such as "El primer comienzo de la dicha corónica," "Primer de generación indios," "La primera historia de las reinas," and "Primer capítvlo de palacios" (*Corónica*, 15, 48, 120, 330). There is no "Segundo" or second "capítvlo de palacios."[74] Instead, this "first" chapter is followed by chapters titled "Estatvras," "Regalos," and "Depósitos."

What are we to make of this textual principle, and particularly of the fact that, while it is ubiquitous in the first half of the *Corónica*, the "primer" designation is used only once in the second half, which follows conquest? This contrast is evident when we compare two segments dedicated to the months of the year. The first such segment, located in the first half of the manuscript, begins with "El primero mes, enero" (the first month, January), while the second such segment, located toward the end of the second half, simply begins with "Enero" (January). Perhaps the first half of the manuscript, with its many "primer" designations, corresponds to some aspect of quipu textuality, which Guaman Poma abandons in the second half of the manuscript, after conquest and the Spanish destruction of quipus. We might, then, imagine the first half of the manuscript as a giant quipu superimposed onto a book, where multiple separate segments or chapters are like strings attached to a central quipu cord, with each string marked by the designation "primer." Each chapter then corresponds to an imaginary quipu string which contains information organized by the first, second, third "visita," "inca," and so on. The designation "primer" then marks not only a chapter but also a string on this imaginary quipu. Each element within a given chapter in turn represents subsidiary strings, with the words like knots along the cords. While the entire manuscript is obviously composed in a European textual format, we may nonetheless see one half of the text as corresponding to the form of the Andean quipu and the other half as corresponding to the form of the European book.

The decimal logic of the final table of contents may be seen as a reassertion of quipu textual principles after a period of great social and textual disruption, as Brokaw argues. Or perhaps it is more accurate to see it as a marriage of both Spanish and Andean textual forms brought into uneasy coexistence. The organization of the manuscript thus reflects both the historical and the social contexts of the region and the multiple textual principles brought into contact and conflict by Spanish conquest. Guaman Poma clearly struggles to reconcile these competing forms of literacy. The social and textual rupture brought on by conquest is marked in the manuscript by the division between its two major segments. The first section, "El Primer Nueva Corónica," is a largely historical section that focuses on pre-Columbian history and customs and interweaves it with "European" (biblical) time and history. The second section, "Buen Gobierno," describes the arrival of the Spanish, the period of conquest, and subsequent colonial abuses, along with Guaman Poma's recommendations for reform. Within these two major sections are numerous subsections that range widely in both topic and genre, from the Inca bibliographies to an imagined dialogue with the Spanish king, from ethnographic passages to instructions to the reader.

The division between the time before and the time after conquest creates the manuscript's dualistic structure. This is important because the principle of duality holds a particular significance in relation to quipu textuality and the social order in which it was embedded. Numerous colonial sources tell us that quipus usually functioned in pairs. It was standard practice in the courtroom to have at least two separate quipucamayoc, each working with a different quipu. These dual records were checked against each other to ensure narrative and quantitative accuracy.[75] In the *Corónica*, Guaman Poma depicts a provincial administrator holding two such quipus (*Corónica*, 350; see figure 11).[76]

The use of two interlinked quipus also corresponds to deeper social

11. Incan official with two quipus. From *El primer nueva corónica y buen gobierno* (1615/1616) by Don Felipe Guaman Poma de Ayala, p. 348 [350]. Copenhagen, Det Kongelige Bibliotek, GKS 2232 4°. Courtesy of Det Kongelige Bibliotek/The Royal Library of Denmark.

structures in Andean culture, where society itself was organized around the principle of complementary duality. After the Inca conquered the region, communities were divided into paired halves linked by their tribute obligations. According to Juan de Matienzo, each district was divided into two sectors, "one of which is called hanansaya, and the other hurinsaya."[77] A given district would divide its tribute obligations between these two related halves, each of which would record and track the information with its own quipu. While this dual social structure may have predated the Inca, Frank Salomon argues that it was the Inca empire that brought the *anan–urin* terminology and instituted a corresponding community tribute system.[78] The anan–urin division appears to be linked both to the sacred geography of the Inca and pre-Incaic worlds and to the political and administrative structure of the Andes during Inca and Spanish rule. By the time the Spanish began to make their own tax records, the division had often been incorporated into community names such as Anan Chillo and Urin Chillo.

Such communities were called ayllus or *parcialidades*. The Quechua term "ayllu" refers to a traditional Andean unit of political organization, ranging in size from a small hamlet to a village of several hundred individuals, often related and headed by a chief or noble. As the Inca established dominance in the region, they retained the term for administrative purposes. The Spanish in turn used the term "parcialidad," and both words appear in the colonial literature. In 1571, a longtime servant of the Spanish crown, Juan Polo de Ondegardo, recorded a particular community's tribute calculations, paying careful attention to the ways in which the parcialidad of Sacaca divided its taxes along this anan–urin division.[79] Like other Spanish observers, Polo de Ondegardo noted the use of two quipus, administered by two quipucamayoc. The quipus belonged to and contained the records of each half of the parcialidad. As the two communities came together to divide the tax tribute burden, one quipucamayoc recorded the half due by Anan Sacaca, and another recorded the half due by Urin Sacaca. As the tribute was delivered, it was checked against the records of each community. The two distinct quipus then functioned both individually as community records and collectively as a record of the larger whole of information, the tribute due from the entire parcialidad.

Lydia Fossa proposes that we understand this process not only as one of checks and balances, but also as one of complementarity on a more abstract level. Just as the two communities of Anan and Urin were parts of a larger whole, the parcialidad of Sacaca, so the two quipus recording their taxes together represented a larger whole, a common register. Polo de Ondegardo notes the plurality of the quipus and the sense of unity between them.[80] Extending Fossa's insight, we can theorize that when two social units were linked by their tax obligations, a corresponding complementary relationship linked their quipu records. As the two quipus were brought together, they became part of a larger whole during a process of reconciliation which seems to have been crucial not only to the process of calculating taxes but also to the social structure and to quipu textuality itself. This would explain why Polo de Ondegardo notes the use of two quipus when taxes are being calculated and in legal and historical contexts. Only with both quipus in operation, so to speak, could the larger whole of information and of the social fabric of the related units be reconstructed. The pairing of quipus, then, seems to correspond to a more general preference for balanced dualism in Quechua society. This dualism was part of a cosmological and social philosophy that structured Andean society around principles meant to ensure balance and harmony. Domingo de Santo Tomás, who also observed and wrote about quipus, particularly stresses the notion of "agreement" and even "conciliation" as key to that process in a more abstract sense.[81]

What does this have to do with the *Corónica*? The drive toward reconciliation and the concept of complementary duality, as meta-textual principles rooted in the logic of quipus, link Guaman Poma's text to broader Andean literary and social conventions.[82] In his manuscript, this drive to reconcile dual narratives operates on a number of levels. His division of the manuscript into two sections reflects the quipu convention of dual accounts that functioned as halves of a larger whole and that, in the process of coming together, had to be "consolidated." The first part of Guaman Poma's manuscript describes a somewhat idealized pre-conquest world of order and reason. This section "consolidates" Andean and Christian histories by knotting them together into a larger narrative whole that represents the two formerly separate worlds as distinct strands in a larger narrative and conceptual structure which conquest has now brought together. Importantly, Guaman Poma represents the two worlds as coeval even before each becomes aware of the existence of the other and their destinies become forever intertwined. For example, Guaman Poma's description of the birth of Jesus is embedded within his history of the Inca, in what he calls "Edad de Indios (Age of the Indians)." Guaman Poma locates the birth and crucifixion of Jesus temporally within the reign of the second Inca, Cinche Roca Inca: "Del nacimiento de Nuestro Señor y Saluador del mundo Jesucristo: Nació en tienpo y rreyno *Cinche Roca Ynga* quando fue de edad de ochenta años. Y, en su tienpo de *Cinche Roca Ynga*, padeció mártir y fue crucificado y muerto y sepultado y rresucitó y subió a los cielos y se asentó a la diestra de Dios Padre (Of the birth of our Lord and Savior of the world Jesus Christ: he was born in the time and reign of *Cinche Roca Ynga* when he was of the age of eighty years. And in his time of *Cinche Roca Ynga*, he suffered martyrdom and was crucified and died and was interred and resurrected and ascended to the heavens and sat at the right side of God the Father)" (*Corónica* 90). Similarly, depictions of Jesus, Mary, and Joseph, as well as of the apostle Saint Bartholomew, occur between images of the second and third Inca. In this way, Guaman Poma represents the two worlds and their histories as linked and contemporaneous in both narrative and pictorial terms, even before contact.

The second part of the manuscript describes a post-conquest world of abuse and disorder but again attempts to consolidate that narrative with the possibility of reform and a return to order. In this section, Guaman Poma is not linking separate meta-narratives or reconciling Andean and Spanish narratives of the past. Rather, he is joining together and attempting to bring into accord narratives of abuse and the possibility of reform. The two separate parts of the manuscript complement each other, providing distinct accounts that are held in a tense but dialogic relationship to provide a larger account of "one tenor."

However, Andean and Spanish accounts cannot be in agreement the way that paired quipus traditionally were. In fact, the different histories and epistemologies that Guaman Poma engages are more often in conflict, and this tension cannot be easily resolved. While textual difference between paired quipus was traditionally resolved by a process of reconciliation that erased it, in the *Corónica* Guaman Poma negotiates difference of an entirely different magnitude, and he is in no position to offer clear reconciliation. Indeed, part of his project is to insist on the validity and viability of distinct Andean narrative and textual forms in the face of the Spanish drive to erase that indigenous difference. In place of reconciliation, Guaman Poma insists on a tense and unresolved coexistence that doesn't require the erasure of difference.

The structural division between two different textual regimes, the Inca quipu and the Spanish alphabetic book, is also reflected in Guaman Poma's illustrations (see figure 12). In the "Corónica" section, Guaman Poma visually elaborates the various uses of quipus in Inca times (*Corónica*, 337, 350, 360, 362). In the "Buen Gobierno" section, this visual preponderance of quipus has disappeared. Instead of a *secretario* wielding a quipu (*Corónica*, 360) we see an administrative functionary with pen, paper, and ink writing alphabetic script (*Corónica*, 828). However, the displacement of Andean textuality is incomplete, for traces remain. Guaman Poma refers to this secretario as a *quilcay camayoc*, a term he has previously used to refer to pre-Conquest secretarios who use quipus. The use of an Andean term to describe a scene of alphabetic writing not only claims for Andean literacy an equivalence with alphabetic writing; it also locates the latter within the logic of the former. Likewise, Guaman Poma's illustration of a pre-Conquest secretario wielding two paired quipus (*Corónica*, 350) is linked to a later image of a legal functionary holding a quipu and a book (*Corónica*, 814). In the post-Conquest Andean world, paired quipus have been replaced with a quipu–book pair. These two illustrations express the textual principle of complementary pairs

12. An Incan official with quipu and book. From *El primer nueva corónica y buen gobierno* (1615/1616) by Don Felipe Guaman Poma de Ayala, p. 800 [814]. Copenhagen, Det Kongelige Bibliotek, GKS 2232 4°. Courtesy of Det Kongelige Bibliotek/The Royal Library of Denmark.

and impose its logic onto the book. Taken together, they establish a continuity and a commensurability between quipu and book literacies and visually affirm the kind of post-conquest accommodation and coexistence to which the entire manuscript is committed.

Consolidated into one long narrative, the various parts of the manuscript all reinforce Guaman Poma's main argument: that social order is crumbling, and the way to restore justice and productivity to the region (to the benefit of both its people and the Spanish king) is to institute his recommendations for "buen gobierno."[83] For Guaman Poma, the tradition of consolidating Anan and Urin accounts represents a precedent to the problem of integrating distinct communities and their records, their versions of reality. Furthermore, this precedent offers the conceptual hope that bringing together and into dialogue distinct community records can produce a larger meta-narrative that resolves contradictions within the subordinate accounts. However, in place of the Andean convention of balancing accounts as a philosophical model of resolution, Guaman Poma offers the dialogic as a model of social and textual coexistence, in which the whole is constituted on numerous levels by halves that are sometimes complementary and sometimes in tension.

The attempt to reconcile different and at times radically incongruent dualities remains an important organizing principle in the manuscript, but in decidedly novel ways rooted in Guaman Poma's distinct historical moment and textual predicament. Within the manuscript, various sections represent the distinct worlds and narrative forms that Guaman Poma seeks to consolidate: Andean and Spanish, pre- and post-conquest, textual and pictorial, quipu and alphabetic. According to the Quechua logic of dualism, any singularity is considered "incomplete and implies an imbalanced or even dangerous situation."[84] In contrast, the pair represents a completed unit, a kind of cosmic balance which also reflects a process of rectification necessary to counteract the danger of "one" without its complementary second. From this perspective, the monologue of Spanish sources represented a dangerous singularity which could be balanced only by pairing it with an Andean perspective or narrative.

The principle of dualism and rectification provides another way to understand Guaman Poma's engagement with Spanish texts. Like many of his contemporaries, Guaman Poma reproduces passages from other, well-known texts such as Bartolomé de Las Casas's *Tratado de las doce dudas*, which circulated widely in the area.[85] However, unlike his Spanish counterparts, Guaman Poma suddenly and radically departs from the texts he is reproducing. In her discussion of this textual pattern, Adorno notes that Guaman Poma draws on well-known and recognizable texts, following "historians such as Fernández and Zárate to the letter, then contradicts them flatly," just as he "repeats Las Casas's argument about the injustice of the conquest, then rejects the latter's claim to evangelization as a just title for colonial domination."[86] Adorno explains this unfaithful use of an original text by recourse to a lack on Guaman Poma's part of the "European's reflexive respect for the written word."[87] However, Guaman Poma's invocation of Spanish writers whom he then contradicts "flatly" can also be seen as an effort to bring together and reconcile distinct narratives in accordance with the Andean convention of using multiple quipus. In that sense, Guaman Poma's record insists on a process of checks and balances in which a given record such as *Doce dudas* does not stand alone but must be reconciled with its complementary half: an indigenous perspective.

Of course, Guaman Poma is facing a very different situation than quipu-camayoc reconciling presumably minor differences between two similar records, as accountants might balance minor differences in ledger books. Instead, Guaman Poma brings together distinct literary traditions and perspectives that are often radically at odds with each other. He embodies them on the pages of his manuscript in order to bring them into dialogue and knot them together into a new narrative in which disparate perspectives and claims are reconciled into an admittedly uneasy coexistence. Whether on the micro-level of contemporary narratives such as Guaman Poma's and de Las Casas's version of the conquest and its implications, or on the macro-level of Andean and biblical creation stories, the dual rendering of narratives brought together and reconciled according to the logic of quipu textuality can be seen as an important organizing element in the manuscript.

Traditionally, the use of two quipus seems to have occurred when two distinct yet linked communities brought together separate records that had to be reconciled. It was standard that the pre-eminent community gave its account first. Guaman Poma's manuscript begins with the Christian creation story, which might indicate that he casts Spain as the pre-eminent of the two communities, Spanish and Andean, according to quipu narrative conventions. That would certainly be strategic and appropriate given his interlocutor, the Spanish king, and his representation of himself as a loyal subject of the Pope and Spain. However, throughout the manuscript Guaman Poma refuses to accord Europe primacy vis-à-vis Christianity. He represents the Andean people as more Christian than the Spanish, even before the arrival of missionaries. For example, after describing how the Inca used quipus in the administration of the region, Guaman Poma concludes by asserting their moral superiority as a form of lived, pre-contact Christianity: "Era cristianícimos (They were exceedingly Christian)" (*Corónica*, 361). Hence, Guaman Poma claims Christianity as a third space of reconciliation, a distinct master narrative under which both Spanish and Inca claims can and must be subsumed. In that sense, the convention of the dual quipus provided a precedent for conjoining more than one narrative as a prerequisite for a larger whole to emerge, in narrative and social terms. And perhaps Christianity represented for Guaman Poma not only a utopian rhetorical and spiritual referent, but also that larger community which could emerge only in the painful juncture of Europe and the Americas, conceived as halves of a larger whole, two interlinked provinces under the dominion of the pope.

Unlike that of de Acosta and other European chroniclers, Guaman Poma's challenge is not simply to account for a previously unknown world within the logic of biblical authority. Rather, he must reconcile radically different worldviews, master narratives, and literary traditions from an Andean perspective, and in doing so he turns to both quipus and alphabetic script. Facing the enormous challenge of integrating distinct communities and narratives on a scale never faced by the quipucamayoc, Guaman Poma proposes a quipuesque solution to an unprecedented philosophical and literary problem as he brings together the meta-narratives and forms of the Andean and Spanish worlds within the pages of his manuscript.

While Spanish conquest instantiated cataclysmic changes on an unprecedented scale, Andean people had lived through and negotiated conquest before, when the Inca established dominion over the region. The principle of complementary duality and reconciliation which organized quipu textuality offered a precedent for how to resolve the monumental challenge posed by conquest and difference. As communities reconciled their quipus and narratives, they simultaneously established and maintained social harmony and became part of a larger whole. The conventions of quipu textuality provided a model for the simultaneous processes of ensuring social harmony and arriving at a more comprehensive and cooperative version of reality. In his manuscript, Guaman Poma joins together Spanish and Andean versions of reality, forcing them into dialogue in order to recuperate the "profound rupture of the conquest" and create "the possibility that separate worlds will be legible to each other."[88]

It is not clear whether this is a conscious strategy on Guaman Poma's part; nor is it clear that he succeeds. Guaman Poma is no quipucamayoc, and unlike quipus of the past, his manuscript is not linked to a specific community or another quipu.[89] Detached in both temporal and material terms, the text floats loose in time and space in a manner decidedly antithetical to quipu logic. However, if the quipu drive to reconciliation fails in Guaman Poma's narrative, the process of dialogization succeeds, and we might call it proto-novelistic in its incorporation of different voices, perspectives, and languages.[90]

In using the term "proto-novelistic," I do not mean to suggest that the text is more fiction than fact or history but, rather, that it instantiates what Bakhtin considers the central feature of novelistic discourse: dialogization.

Whereas the quipucamayoc recorded and managed official narratives, they were not authors in the modern sense. In the process of writing his manuscript, Guaman Poma draws on a multiplicity of narrative and rhetorical genres and textual forms and becomes something that did not exist in the pre-Hispanic world of the quipucamayoc: an author. This is a title he claims repeatedly and insistently in the manuscript, where he refers to himself as "autor" sixty-nine times. Thus, his *Corónica* is new not only vis-à-vis Spanish chronicles but also vis-à-vis the old histories contained in quipus. He is neither a quipucamayoc nor an *amauta* but an author. This is one of the ways in which Guaman Poma's manuscript is radically modern, of the new world that emerged out of the violent encounter between Europe and the Americas.⁹¹ Attempting to insert an Andean perspective into early modern Europe, the manuscript offers an intercultural model of modernity. Indeed, the manuscript is narratively oriented toward the future rather than toward the past.⁹² The narrative desire most palpable in the manuscript is the hope that it is still possible to imagine a different future and different terms of engagement. Guaman Poma's claim to the title "autor" marks that orientation. And his recommendation for "buen gobierno" is not a return to Incan rule but a move toward some form of reconciliation and collaboration that can combine the best of Andean and Spanish worlds. Near the end of the manuscript, Guaman Poma proposes the dialogue as a model, one that simultaneously instantiates the logic of dualism and proposes to turn the conflict zone into a zone of, admittedly uneasy, coexistence and commensurability.

Conclusion: Dialogue in the Colonial Conflict Zone

In the past few decades, Latin American scholars have begun to analyze the relationship between quipu and alphabetic textuality in manuscripts like those produced by Guaman Poma and Cristóbal Vaca de Castro.⁹³ On the pages of these texts, the languages and literary forms of Andean and Spanish cultures inter-animate each other in complex ways. Guaman Poma's narrative predicament and desires, however, are radically different from de Castro's, whose *Discurso* consulted quipus in the service of Spanish colonialism. Guaman Poma's *Corónica*, on the other hand, refers to quipus surreptitiously as a de-colonizing move in order to recast the terms of engagement between Europe and the Andes. Quipus were now suppressed and illegal; the Spanish had launched an all-out war on indigenous epistemology. Guaman Poma's narrative act emerges out of this over-determined context in which he, unlike the Haudenosaunee, is a colonial subject. But he is not defeated. His manuscript can be seen as an attempt to create a dialogue between the world of the quipus and the world of the Spanish king to propose as possible a different mode of interaction.

In a section titled "Pregunta Su Magestad," located toward the end of the manuscript, Guaman Poma offers the dialogue as an ideal model for cross-cultural exchange. In this section, Guaman Poma stages an imaginary conversation between himself and Philip III where he serves as a sage adviser to a respectful king. Visually as well as narratively, Guaman Poma represents the two as potentially equal partners against the abuses of renegade colonial administrators. Following the second half of the manuscript, where Guaman Poma describes and condemns such abuses, the section entitled "Pregunta Su Magestad" imagines a series of questions and answers, exchanges between Guaman Poma and the king, about how to reestablish justice in the region. With this imaginary conversation, Guaman Poma posits the dialogic as the ideal mode of interaction and exchange. However, he also insists that a true dialogue must be a collaboration between two equal partners. Thus, while Guaman Poma accepts the authority of Philip III, the king in the imagined dialogue also respects Guaman Poma's authority. This is represented by the king's willingness to ask the questions prompted by the adviser. Narratively, however, this prompting leads to an asymmetry that eventually undermines the dialogic mode. Guaman Poma's imaginary king asks the exact questions suggested to him by Guaman Poma. As the "dialogue" progresses, the author, Guaman Poma, is entirely in charge of the narrative, as evident in the imperative: "Pregunta Su Magestad (Ask, Your Highness)," where the dialogue becomes dictation. This breakdown, however, indicates not necessarily a failed belief in the dialogue as a mode of exchange but, rather, an insistence on the parameters of a true dialogue as the ideal mode of interaction.

In her seminal book-length study of the manuscript, Adorno ultimately concludes that the text is about the impossibility of dialogue and cross-cultural understanding. The despondence in the final account of Guaman Poma's journey to Lima does indeed suggest despair rather than hope. But would Guaman Poma compose a manuscript of more than a thousand pages and carefully paginate it for publication (which he explicitly requests) to make the point that communication is hopeless and futile? The completion of any book-length project would seem to represent a great deal of effort and hope on the part of the writer. Differences in ink color reveal that, after completing the manuscript, Guaman Poma went back to add tiny details on the frontispiece illustration such as cross-hatching on a mat.[94] Such tender efforts suggest a great deal of pride and investment in the potential power of this small yet monumental book. Rather than as a manifestation of despair, might we not see the final sections of the manuscript as an injunction to readers to take seriously the possibility and responsibility of dialogue? Such an exchange cannot be only imaginary or one-sided; it must be a mutual and collaborative venture. This is Guaman Poma's invitation to the Spanish king and to any other reader of this manuscript, which he wrote "para todo el mundo."

Although Guaman Poma traveled to Lima personally to deliver the manuscript to colonial authorities, its destiny after leaving his hands remains unknown. In 1615, Guaman Poma wrote a letter to King Philip III announcing its completion and offering to convey it to Spain. The final lines of text imagine the delivery of the manuscript in "la ciudad de los Reys de Lima (the city of the Kings of Lima)" (Corónica, 1188), but the space left to fill in the names of official recipients is blank. The narrative concludes with the hopeful words "se presentó ante los señores (was presented before these gentlemen)" (Corónica, 1188), followed by a blank space that indicates that the formal presentation of the manuscript did not happen or was not documented as Guaman Poma had envisioned it. Although circumstantial evidence indicates that the Corónica arrived in Lima and even influenced the writing of other chronicles in colonial Peru, the manuscript effectively disappeared after passing from Guaman Poma into the hands of anonymous colonial administrators.[95]

For hundreds of years, Guaman Poma's book languished in obscurity before resurfacing, like Queequeg's coffin, through the vortex of colonial time. In 1908, a Peruvianist named Richard A. Pietschmann stumbled upon the manuscript while working in the archives of the Royal Copenhagen Library and, recognizing its significance, announced his discovery to the scholarly world. This event marked the first step in a process of publication that finally fulfilled Guaman Poma's request. In 1936, the Institut d'Ethnologie of the University of Paris published a photographic facsimile of the entire manuscript. This publication made it possible for scholars everywhere to begin to study Guaman Poma's work, and throughout the twentieth century a critical mass of scholarship on the Corónica began to emerge. Following the publication of a number of articles, book-length studies, critical editions, and partial translations, the Department of Manuscripts and Rare Books of the Royal Danish Library made a digital reproduction of the entire manuscript available on the Internet in 2001 and thus made it possible, finally, "for all the world" to read it.[96] Guaman Poma may not have managed to engage Philip III in the kind of dialogue he hoped to initiate, but the dialogic potential of his epic manuscript remains intact, awaiting the engagement of present and future readers everywhere.

Hence, I read the dialogue between Guaman Poma and the king as simultaneously a failure and a model. While the imagined dialogue marks a kind of failure—the failure of an actual exchange—it also provides a model of the collaborative, the dialogic, which must replace the dictatorial and monologic nature of the colonial conflict zone. Such mutual recognition and understanding require a great deal of work by the reader, as well as by Guaman Poma, who opens the manuscript by foregrounding the difficulty of his project. Perhaps one purpose of Guaman Poma's description of his arduous journey is to share with his readers the magnitude of his own effort and to ask of them that they meet him halfway. According to the metatextual principles of the Andes, the single author, Don Felipe Guaman Poma de Ayala, must not be left standing alone. Only by being joined by a reader can the completed unit required for narrative and cosmic balance emerge. The utopic hope embodied by the logic of complementary duality is also expressed in the decimal order of Guaman Poma's concluding table of contents. In these final pages of the manuscript, Guaman Poma merges European and Andean textual forms. The decimal logic of the Andes and their quipus is expressed in the European form of the table of contents, which conforms to Andean decimal principles. In the same way, the dialogue expresses the Andean logic of complementary duality embodied by the completed pair of the king and the author, a logic which Guaman Poma has managed to translate into a form that can make sense to his European readers. In his epic manuscript, Guaman Poma thus asks us to imagine, at the center of the conflict between Andean and European peoples, not irreconcilable difference but commensurability.

CHAPTER FOUR

Indigenous Literacies, Moby-Dick, and the Promise of Queequeg's Coffin

We call him Ishmael, the enigmatic narrator of Herman Melville's epic novel *Moby-Dick; or, The Whale*, about whom we know only what he tells us. Ishmael is a sailor and a storyteller, a thinker and an observer, the sole survivor of the *Pequod*, and the narrator of the epic story of its demise. He is also a friend of Queequeg, a Polynesian harpooner he meets in the opening chapters of the novel. *Moby-Dick* relays the adventures of this unlikely yet "cozy" pair after setting out from the New England coast and sailing the high seas in search of whales and their precious oil. The novel ends, famously, with the destruction of the ship and the entire multiracial crew. A "romance of adventure," an allegory of Melville's America, a meditation on human nature, an ethnography of the whaling industry, an exposition of the logic of racism—*Moby-Dick* has never been easy to categorize or summarize.[1] It is much more than a story of adventure and disaster, more than the sum of its parts, and much more than the story of a whale. This unwieldy and genre-crossing beast of a book, so immensely rich in its questions and its insights, has captured the imagination of readers and literary critics because it seems to say so much about Melville's world, and our own.

It is not, perhaps, obvious that Melville has anything to say about indigenous literacies, although it is clear that writing and colonial conflict are important themes in many of his books. This final chapter argues that indigenous literacies are in fact central to, and represented as an enabling condition of, *Moby-Dick*. Like his first book, *Typee*, Melville's final novel, *Moby-Dick*, registers and probes the ways in which cultures of literacy confronted each other in a colonial sphere which was much larger than the

United States or even the Americas. This chapter traces the progression in Melville's thought about the meaning of such conflict and argues that, while early work such as *Typee* register the confrontation with indigenous forms of literacy as a threat, his great epic *Moby-Dick* ponders instead interdependence and the possibility of commensurability on both human and literary levels. In that sense, it is, for all its differences, of a piece with Guaman Poma's epic and its concern with the possibilities of literary connection. Like Guaman Poma and, for that matter, Kiotseaeton and Vimont, Melville explores linguistic and cultural exchange between different kinds of writing in the colonial conflict zone. Unfolding largely in locations outside the geographic boundaries of the Americas, *Typee* and *Moby-Dick* also register the global nature of that colonial world.

From the opening pages of *Moby-Dick*, Melville foregrounds the vexed issue of knowledge and its multiple and contradictory sources, with real and invented fragments about whales written throughout the ages and in all corners of the globe. The whale, in *Moby-Dick*, is not only the topic of many written sources but itself a site of inscription, its skin covered with marks that Ishmael compares to ancient hieroglyphs. In his musings on "the mystic-marked whale" and the hieroglyphic marks in his skin, Ishmael links the marks to the "mysterious ciphers on the walls of pyramids" and, simultaneously, to indigenous forms of writing inscribed on the American landscape that Ishmael observed once while sailing down the Mississippi: "I was much struck with a plate representing the old Indian characters chiseled on the famous hieroglyphic palisades on the banks of the Upper Mississippi. . . . Like those mystic rocks, too, the mystic-marked whale remains undecipherable" (*Moby-Dick*, 306).[2]

By using terms such as "characters" and "hieroglyphic," Melville asks his readers to think about these petroglyphic marks as a kind of ancient writing. However, unlike his contemporary Henry Wadsworth Longfellow, Melville does not appropriate these "Indian characters" for his narrative. Rather, the "mystic rocks" observed by his narrator remain "undecipherable" (*Moby-Dick*, 306). They are not easily translated; nor are they pressed into the service of a nationalist narrative. Instead, they stand as markers of alterity and anteriority, testaments to the presence of another literary culture belonging to the continent's original inhabitants. The term "hieroglyphic" frames this indigenous literary culture in relation to an ancient and well-known Egyptian script, one which had been deciphered only a few decades before. Egyptian hieroglyphs had long been considered mysterious and "undecipherable," just like the "hieroglyphic palisades" observed by Melville's narrator. In the 1820s, however, the Frenchman Jean-François Champollion caused a worldwide sensation by deciphering Egyptian hieroglyphic script with the aid of the recently discovered Rosetta Stone. This development represented the overturning of centuries of Western misconceptions about hieroglyphics. Champollion's great achievement lay in his ability to recognize that hieroglyphs were not simply "pictographs" but a writing system that combined logographic and phonographic elements.[3] For Melville, the term "hieroglyphic" could, then, simultaneously invoke both the alterity of non-alphabetic writing from a colonized territory and the recognition that such writing could constitute a different but equally legitimate literary heritage.

Melville explores the implications and ramifications of such possibilities via a colonial context with which he was personally familiar—namely, Polynesia. In *Moby-Dick*, he establishes this link by using the term "hieroglyphic marks" to refer to the symbols engraved by the Polynesian harpooneer Queequeg on his coffin. By carving "hieroglyphic marks" onto the coffin, Queequeg turns it into a text, a "mystical treatise" that becomes an enabling condition of the novel because it saves the life of the narrator. Ishmael survives the wreckage at the cataclysmic conclusion of the narrative by clinging to Queequeg's coffin as it resurfaces from the center of the vortex into which the *Pequod* and its crew have disappeared.

The pictographs on Queequeg's coffin are transcriptions of the Polynesian tattoos on his body. Pondering the mystery of these tattoos, Ishmael notes that Queequeg cannot "read" them. That illiteracy, however, is an assertion made by Ishmael that Queequeg himself never confirms. While Ishmael cannot see Queequeg as a competent reader of his own body and the hieroglyphs he inscribes on his coffin, he may be wrong. Can *we* imagine Queequeg as a literate user of an indigenous system of writing, a reader and writer just like Ishmael? Such an understanding of Queequeg is not only possible but enabled by the text. Indeed, Melville describes these tattoos as "hieroglyphic marks" that are "written" on the "parchment" of the harpooneer's skin. When the crew of the *Pequod* assembles to offer interpretations of the markings on a gold doubloon, Queequeg proves himself as capable a reader as anyone. And Melville is not Ishmael. The contradiction between Ishmael's assertion that Queequeg cannot read the "mystical treatise" that is "written out on his body" and Melville's use of terms such as "written" creates a space in which to imagine the encounter between Ishmael and Queequeg as one between readers and writers.

Of course, Ishmael and Queequeg are both fictional characters, and the notion that a Polynesian native would have a form of writing that could be carved onto a wooden coffin may appear equally fictional. But such a Polynesian script did, in fact, once exist. Today, the only surviving examples are on twenty-five engraved wooden tablets located in museums around the world and named after their current locations, just like the extant Mayan codices. While this Polynesian script remains undeciphered, like Melville's American "hieroglyphic palisades," scholars agree that it "writes what is almost certainly a Polynesian language."[4] Hence, it is possible that during the formative time he spent in Polynesia as a sailor in the early nineteenth century, the young Melville observed remnants of an indigenous system of literacy and, in his subsequent literary production, explored this prospect and its implications. Polynesians not only engraved on wood but also wrote and drew with ink on the "living parchment" of human skin. What would it mean to take seriously the relationship between Melville's alphabetic narrative and such indigenous texts? This kind of analysis reveals that indigenous Polynesian forms of literacy inform the novel in important, though deeply submerged, ways.

If we see Queequeg's coffin as an embodiment of indigenous forms of writing with the potential to resurface, how might we recover that potential? Such a project requires us to implement the method developed in the preceding chapters and allows us to test its applicability beyond the pre-national period. This method begins by taking seriously the possibility that people who inhabited colonized territories had their own cultures of literacy with the capacity to dialogize alphabetic texts. In this chapter, I take Melville's use of the term "writing" as a warrant to initiate such an inquiry into Moby-Dick.

To recapitulate, an "alternative literacies" analysis requires, first of all, some understanding of the internal logic that organizes the non-alphabetic system of inscription at play in a textual encounter—in this particular case, Polynesian tattoos. We can then bring to bear on the alphabetic text the logic of a different system of inscription and consider how the interaction between alphabetic and non-alphabetic forms of literacy, brought into contact and conflict by colonialism, might structure a given piece of literature. While previous chapters focused on texts produced in the context of a still unfolding colonial project, this final chapter explores how the analytical insights gained thus far offer new ways to understand later literature produced in the aftermath of colonial conflict, when alphabetic script was not only hegemonic but often so dominant as to render other forms of writing illegible and all but invisible.

Writing on Wood, Skin, and Paper: Alternative Literacies in Dialogue

While accounts of South Sea journeys abound with references to tattoos, such graphic signs and patterns rarely figure as systems of meaning in their own right. Rather, tattoos generally function as signs of "savagery" that simultaneously fascinate and repulse Western readers and viewers.[5] In *Moby-Dick*, however, Melville represents this ink-on-skin as a kind of writing, "hieroglyphic marks" on Queequeg's skin, which serves as a "living parchment" on which a "mystical treatise" can be "written out" (*Moby-Dick*, 480). Human skin, like parchment and paper, here provides a surface on which graphic marks are made permanent with an ink-like substance and pencil-like tools. This is also the case in earlier work such as *Typee*; in fact, Melville's representations of Polynesian tattoos remain striking for their consistent use of terms associated with writing.

The man who became one of America's great writers first traveled to Polynesia as a young sailor in the early nineteenth century. During that time, he was able to observe regional tattooing cultures before they were seriously affected by colonial interference. Tattooing was and continues to be an important cultural practice on many Polynesian islands, such as Hawai'i, Tahiti, Tonga, and Samoa, although "the tattooing style of the Marquesas Isles was the most elaborate and extensive of any found in Polynesia."[6] Melville spent four weeks living as a "beach bum" in the Taipee Valley in 1842 and some time after that in Nukahiva, one of the centers of Marquesan tattooing, as well as elsewhere in Polynesia. In addition to observations made during this time, Melville used a number of previously published sources, including work by Georg Heinrich von Langsdorff, who wrote about and documented the visual aspects of Polynesian tattooing in the early nineteenth century. Langsdorff's travels began in 1803, and he remains one of the earliest sources available for understanding tattooing in the Marquesas. Etienne Marchand, who had traveled in the region a decade earlier than Langsdorff, provides another important source of information.[7] Like Marchand, Melville compared Polynesian tattoos to hieroglyphics, although Marchand's book is not listed among those owned or borrowed by Melville in Merton Sealts's compendium.[8] The term "hieroglyphics" was used widely in Melville's time, and yet this usage raises the possibility that, just as Egyptian hieroglyphs were once mistakenly seen as imagery rather than script, so Marquesan tattoos might have been more than simple pictures.[9]

A survey of the iconography of this graphic system of inscription reveals that traditional Marquesan tattoos included "naturalistic" images, like fish, calabashes, etc., as well as more abstract designs (see figures 13 and 14). Representational designs conveyed specific and conventionalized meanings. One of the most prominent and common of such designs is a category of motifs known as *ipu*, which means "container," "vase," or "calabash." These terms overlap, as a calabash is a gourd that can be hollowed out for use as a container. The Marquesan word "*hue*" means "calabash," "gourd," "bowl," as well as, on a figurative level, "chief." *Hue* is also part of the name of a number of designs called, variously, "calabash bottom (*hue ao*)," "dirty calabash (*hue epo*)," and "flower calabash (*pua hue*)."[10] Although this is what we might call a naturalistic design, it has often been conventionalized to the point of abstraction so that familiarity with the system of meaning is necessary to recognize the design as related to calabashes.

For example, one variation of the *hue* design consists of concentric circles. This pattern was sometimes associated with the armpit and the underside of the arm, making it visible when a warrior raised his arm to strike at an enemy.[11] This fairly common pattern is relevant to our analysis not only because Melville is likely to have seen it, but also because the image of concentric circles plays a key part in the conclusion of *Moby-Dick*: "And now, concentric circles seized the lone boat itself, and all its crew . . . carried the smallest chip of the Pequod out of sight" (*Moby-Dick*, 572). Here, the moment of impending death for the crew of the *Pequod* is linked to the image of concentric circles, just as the concentric circles of the *hue* design would be associated with impending death for a warrior in battle as he beheld the raised arm of his enemy immediately before being struck. In *Moby-Dick*, the image of concentric circles appears right before the whale brings down the ship, when Ahab raises his arm to throw the harpoon at the whale. Hence, concentric circles in *Moby-Dick* are directly associated with battle, the raised arm of Ahab attempting to strike a lethal blow and the whale, which in turn brings down the ship.

This correspondence could simply be a coincidence, of course, but it is part of a consistent pattern in which images in *Moby-Dick* correspond to images in Marquesan tattooing. In addition to concentric circles, several other key tropes in *Moby-Dick* echo images in the iconography of Polynesian

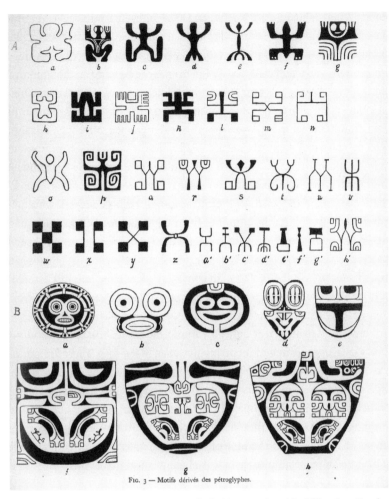

FIG. 3 — Motifs dérivés des pétroglyphes.

13. Abstract Marquesan tattoos. From *Art in the Marquesas* (1922) by Willowdean Handy. WHi-66977. Courtesy of the Wisconsin Historical Society.

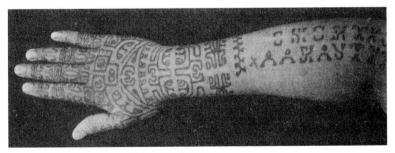

14. A hand with abstract Marquesan tattoo designs. From *Die Marquesaner und ihre Kunst* by Karl von den Steinen. (1925–28). WHi-66979. Courtesy of the Wisconsin Historical Society.

tattoos. When Ishmael first encounters Queequeg, he offers a vague but important description of several tattoos that Queequeg will later transcribe from his body onto the coffin. For example, Ishmael notes that "his very legs were marked, as if a parcel of dark green frogs were running up the trunks of young palms" (*Moby-Dick*, 22). This tattoo is likely an example of what Alfred Gell calls an "anthropomorphic multiplicity motif" in which a human or animal figure is repeated.[12] When running the length of a limb, such a design might be classified as a *kake* motif.[13] Examples of *kake*, which means "to climb" in Marquesan, always have feet and heads and "represent animate beings" that range from turtles and crabs to stylized representations of back-to-back women, a reference to the mythological twin goddesses who, according to legend, brought tattooing from Fiji to Samoa.[14] Had Queequeg been a real person, the "frogs" on his legs would likely be an example of such a multiplicity motif. Given that Queequeg is identified as Polynesian, we can relate this tattoo to a pan-Polynesian context in which one possible referent would be Siamese twins, a prominent element of Polynesian iconography.

Siamese twins would then represent another example of an intertextual link between Melville's text and Polynesian tattooing, for the twin motif appears as a significant and recurring device in *Moby-Dick*. There are multiple twinned figures whose destinies are intertwined in the narrative. The image of Siamese twins more specifically also appears in the text, in chapters such as "The Monkey Rope." In addition, Ishmael refers to himself and Queequeg as a pair of Siamese twins. Because twins are such an important element of Polynesian tattooing iconography, images of twins in *Moby-Dick* can be considered examples of how Melville's novel plays with motifs that correspond to Polynesian tattoo designs.

The motif of multiplication, central to Marquesan cosmology and iconography, constitutes another instance of such linkage, because multiplication is also a narrative element in *Moby-Dick*. As is the case with twins, correspondences can be drawn between images of multiplication in the novel and in Marquesan culture. For example, the story of a mythic hero, Pohu, relates his defeat of a giant caterpillar, which he breaks into small caterpillars and thereby renders harmless. Similarly, at the end of *Moby-Dick*, when the whale is destroyed, a multitude of "unharming sharks" circle around Ishmael as if "with padlocks on their mouths" (*Moby-Dick*, 573). Pohu embodies the ability to combine parts into wholes and vice versa—to break down totalities and to recombine parts into new wholes. Like Pohu, Melville is an author who breaks down discursive formations such as "the

15. An inhabitant of the island of Nukahiwa. From Puteshestvie vokrug svieta v 1803, 4, 5 i 1806 godakh: po poveleniiu ego imperatorskago velichestva Aleksandra Pervago, nakorabliahkh Nadeshde i Neve, pod nachalstvom . . . kapitana . . . Kruzenshterna. 1809–1813. Courtesy of the Slavic and Baltic Division, The New York Public Library, Astor, Lenox and Tilden Foundations.

whale" into their fragments and reveals new perspectives and possibilities through different combinations.[15]

Intersections between Polynesian tattooing and motifs in *Moby-Dick* often mark key narrative or thematic concerns. An important example of a multiplicity motif which relates in significant ways to *Moby-Dick* is the one Gell calls the "checkerboard pattern."[16] When Ishmael describes Queequeg's tattoos, he notes that his chest is covered by a checkered pattern. Such checkerboard designs can be observed in illustrations from the period, such as *An Inhabitant of Nukahiwa* (see figure 15).[17] This motif was called *te vehine na'u*, which, according to Langsdorff, meant "my little wife." This pattern, which looks like abstract squares of black and white, actually represents myriad "little wives" accompanying the wearer as he moves through the world.[18]

In *Moby-Dick*, the description of the "little wife" pattern precedes a passage where Melville uses terms such as "matrimonial" and "bridegroom clasp" to describe Ishmael and Queequeg, who spend the night sleeping together in the same bed. This imagery becomes even more explicit when Ishmael wakes up the next morning with "Queequeg's arm thrown over me in the most loving and affectionate manner. You had almost thought I had been his wife" (*Moby-Dick*, 25).[19] Although only Melville himself might have been able to appreciate this pun, it seems quite possible that Melville was in fact punning on *te vehine na'u.*

Images in the text of *Moby-Dick* thus correspond to images in the pictographic vocabulary of Marquesan tattoos. If we think of Marquesan designs as discrete elements of a larger system of meaning, in which graphic signs represent language, narrative, words, it appears that elements of this code were literally inscribed into the narrative fabric of *Moby-Dick.* Just as the textual logic of wampum became inscribed into the *Jesuit Relations*, so the graphic signs of Marquesan narrative forms appear, transcribed as literary tropes, in the text of Melville's masterpiece—with an important difference. Whereas Vimont's reproduction of wampum textuality seems to have been unconscious, Melville's use of imagery that reproduces Marquesan iconography seems to have been based on a far greater familiarity with and understanding of the relationship between Marquesan graphic signs and their referents than Vimont displayed vis-à-vis wampum.

An "alternative literacies" analysis thus reveals that Melville reproduces significant images from Marquesan pictography as narrative images constructed with alphabetic letters, the components of his native writing system. In such narrative images, we can see the intersection of two distinct graphic systems. As the units of one graphic language, Marquesan tattoos, link up with the images of another graphic language, alphabetic script, the image emerges as the common ground between two radically different forms of writing, displacing translation as the dominant mode of cross-cultural intersection.

Polynesian Hieroglyphs: Tattooing in the Marquesas

If it was radical in Melville's America to imagine writing as a site of cross-cultural commensurability, it was equally radical to conceive of indigenous marks as elements of distinct literary cultures. For Melville, Egyptian hieroglyphics play an important role in the narrative by representing the possibility of such commensurability and legitimacy. For centuries, this Egyptian script had been seen as mysterious, and possibly undecipherable, in Europe. However, its deciphering in the early nineteenth century revealed it to be a fully developed system of writing—both logographic and phonetic—that combined logograms and syllabic signs. It was Champollion's ability to recognize the script's partially phonetic nature that led to his breakthrough in deciphering. This development, in turn, led to a complete revolution in Europe's understanding of the ancient Egyptian script. For Melville, then, hieroglyphics could stand simultaneously for an ancient, mysterious, undeciphered system of writing and for the possibility of its decipherment.[20]

The Rosetta Stone, which made decipherment possible, came to the attention of European philologists as a consequence of the French invasion of Egypt in 1798.[21] The Marquesas, the narrative setting of Melville's first book, *Typee*, had been claimed by the French several times, most recently in 1846. French colonialism, then, linked both territories in a particular way, although Polynesia had been a site of European and American exploration, conquest, and colonialism since the sixteenth century.[22] Melville thus links Polynesia as a colonized territory with other colonized territories, such as Egypt, and by using the term "hieroglyphics" to refer to Polynesian tattoos, he links this system of inscription to a recently deciphered Egyptian system of writing. The colonial conflict is then figured as one not between literate and illiterate peoples but, rather, between different cultures of literacy.

The term "hieroglyphics" also mediates between different, indigenous kinds of writing from the colonial world, because Melville uses it to refer to both Polynesian and Native American forms of inscription. Indigenous writing in North America, a topic of intense interest and debate in Melville's time, as evident in Schoolcraft's and even Longfellow's work, can be seen as a silent referent of the allusion to undeciphered writing systems from conquered territories.[23] Indeed, Melville explicitly links hieroglyphs not only to Polynesian tattoos, but also to Native American petroglyphs.

> These [linear marks] are hieroglyphical; that is, if you call those mysterious ciphers on the walls of pyramids hieroglyphics, then that is the proper word to use in the present connexion. . . . I was much struck with a plate representing the old Indian characters chiseled on the famous hieroglyphic palisades on the banks of the Upper Mississippi. Like those mystic rocks, too, the mystic-marked whale remains undecipherable. (*Moby-Dick*, 306)

In this passage, Ishmael links two different kinds of non-alphabetic writing and calls both (Egyptian hieroglyphs and Native American petroglyphs) "undecipherable." However, Melville insinuates another possibility between himself and his narrator: that Native American petroglyphs represent an equally ancient and important writing system awaiting recognition and decipherment. These petroglyphs are not just etchings in stone; they are "hieroglyphics" like "those mysterious ciphers on the walls of pyramids." The term "hieroglyphic," then, performs a triangulation that links Native American petroglyphs to Polynesian graphic marks via the recently deciphered Egyptian script and posits all three as ancient, legitimate scripts from colonized territories.

This triangulation asserts the literary potential of Polynesian and Native American graphic forms at a moment in nineteenth-century America when indigenous literacy and its forms was a topic of intense interest and philological energy. While Daniel Brinton and Garrick Mallery, among others, documented the breadth of pictographic literacy in North America, philologists such as the eminent John Pickering worked to develop alphabets for Native American languages. These efforts were organized, in part, by a firm belief that whatever forms of writing native people may have possessed, they were inherently inferior to alphabetic literacy. There was probably more at work than simple ethnocentrism, however, for the simultaneous documentation and displacement of indigenous forms of writing had been a central aspect of European colonial effort as far back as the sixteenth century, when Diego de Landa recorded and destroyed Mayan forms of writing in the Yucatan. Colonial projects throughout the continent followed a similar pattern, which we might, via Gordon Sayre, understand as a dialectic of negation and substitution.[24] On the one hand, colonial agents substituted their notion of writing for analogous indigenous practices and then ascribed to colonized peoples the negation of writing, illiteracy. On the other, they attempted to displace or substitute indigenous forms of writing with syllabic or, preferably, alphabetic scripts. Many "Native American alphabets" thus emerged out of the intersection between colonial occupation, philology, and missionary efforts; Pickering had established his reputation in part by developing an alphabet for missionaries working in Hawai'i, making him another point of intersection between writing and colonialism in Polynesia and the United States.

In the 1820s, Pickering had been hard at work on a Cherokee alphabet—reporting directly to President Thomas Jefferson on his progress—when news broke that a Cherokee man named George Guess, or Sequoyah, had developed a syllabic script. In so doing, Sequoyah not only pre-empted

Pickering and other, similarly occupied philologists; he also implicitly challenged the notion that the alphabet was superior to syllabic writing. Sequoyah's script must have corresponded well to the structures of Cherokee language and culture, because it was immensely successful in spreading literacy among the Cherokee.[25]

Although Pickering had proudly reported to Jefferson in 1825 that he was ready to publish an alphabet in which he had "reduced all the sounds of the Cherokee language to a perfect alphabet, nineteen customized characters based on the Roman alphabet, one character for every sound in the Cherokee language," that project was halted once Sequoyah published his syllabary.[26] Rather than attempting to "reduce" his language to the alphabet, Sequoyah had evidently begun his efforts with what the linguist Hans Jensen calls a "picture-script," suggesting that he initially drew on older pictographic conventions indigenous to the area. The success of Sequoyah's syllabary astonished Pickering, most of all because it contradicted a key tenet of contemporary philology: that alphabets were superior to syllabic scripts. Indeed, syllabic writing was, according to prevailing theories, a "grossly imperfect, even savage form of writing," and Pickering initially described Sequoyah's syllabic script as "very unphilosophical" and "quite contrary to our notion of a useful alphabetic system."[27] Although Pickering eventually came to praise Sequoyah's script for its efficiency in spreading literacy among the Cherokee, who embraced it enthusiastically, philologists retained a firm belief in the superiority of alphabetic writing and its corollary, European and Euro-American cultural supremacy.

Melville's invocation of Egyptian script and his linkage of an ancient literary culture with indigenous petroglyphs in North America and tattoos in Polynesia challenge this possessive investment in writing in ways that have yet to be fully appreciated. Egyptian hieroglyphs had been deciphered only decades before Melville published *Moby-Dick*. Today, a number of indigenous American writing systems likewise have been at least partially deciphered, a process that has revealed them to be partially phonetic like Egyptian hieroglyphs. Marquesan tattoos, on the other hand, remain entirely beyond the purview of scholarship on writing. Is it possible, as Melville suggests, that these tattoos were also hieroglyphic in nature, a kind of writing? Was this an uncanny insight on Melville's part or fictional license?

In order to address these questions, we need a better understanding of tattooing in the Marquesas. The Pacific nation consists of a number of small islands, six of which are inhabited. The six islands are divided into two groups: Nukuhiva, 'Ua Pou, and 'Ua Huka in the northwest, and Hiva Oa, Tauhata, and Fatuhiva in the southeast. There are differences in both dialect and tattooing style between these two groups, though there is a history of stylistic exchanges among various areas. The Marquesas are linked in important ways to other Polynesian island nations, including Hawai'i, Tahiti, Tonga, and Samoa, though each island has its own, distinct culture of tattooing. On the Marquesas, Hiva Oa has generally been recognized as the center of tattooing, but Nukuhiva was also an important tattooing center. Although tattooing is an important cultural practice on all of the Polynesia islands, it reached its highest level of complexity in the Marquesas, where Melville had exposure to the practice in its two major centers: Nukuhiva, which is the setting of *Typee*, and Hiva Oa, which is "La Dominica" in chapter 8 of *Omoo*.

Melville spent just under four weeks among the Taipee, but he roamed Polynesia for more than three years and visited both the northeastern and southwestern parts of the Marquesas. Hence, it is not unreasonable to hypothesize that Melville, with his remarkable powers of observation, grasped and communicated an understanding of tattooing as something far more complex than random marking on skin. Can we, removed from that time and context and unable to read the tattoos, nevertheless attempt to understand them as elements in a larger system of inscription? By rhetorically linking them to Egyptian hieroglyphs, Melville seems to ask that we try. Using the method developed in previous chapters, we can begin by sketching the local context in which Marquesan marks on wood and skin "make sense."

Apparently, a great many conventional Marquesan tattoos are linked to larger cultural contexts such as legends and other narratives. This suggests that designs on a body came from a conventionalized code and combined to create narratives that could be "read" by other Marquesans. Tattoos on the body, then, drew on a commonly known code that also appeared on other media, such as wood. Inscriptions on a variety of media would draw from a repertoire of signs capable of producing narrative, though they functioned slightly differently depending on whether they appeared on wood, vases, or skin. For example, bodily tattoos communicated key aspects of an individual's life story, including kinship ties, "great deeds," and mythological allusions with significant personal meaning, whereas writing on a vase might relate to the function or contents of that object. Hertha Wong's expanded notion of autobiography might provide a useful model for understanding narratives that can be simultaneously autobiographical and communal, narrating an individual life and locating it in its social context.[28] Seeing tattoos as a form of autobiography could explain the practice of continually adding tattoos and modifying the designs over the course of a lifetime.[29] These narratives would then be in a continuing state of revision and not fixed, despite their permanence on the skin.

As we have learned from the example of Egyptian hieroglyphs, pictography can be far more complex than immediately apparent. Named for the visual predominance of "pictures," pictographic scripts such as Egyptian and Mayan writing have, when deciphered, proved to be more phonetic than initially apparent to European eyes. Hence, while it is easy to be puzzled by the abstract elements in pictographic writing, it is also easy to be fooled by the naturalistic elements, which, as in the case of Egyptian hieroglyphs, can be phonetic rather than representational. For example, the image of a bird, which Westerners had long assumed represented the idea of a bird, is actually an alphabetic sign corresponding to an "a" sound. Likewise, what resembles a snake stands not for "snake" but for the sound "dj." Should the same apply to the iconography of Marquesan tattoos, the calabash might stand for a phonetic value associated with the word "*hue*," whether it is an alphabetic "h" sound or a syllabic "hu" sound, to give one, admittedly speculative, example.

Just as Egyptian and Mayan hieroglyphs are both combination scripts that mix purely phonetic and logographic elements so that a given script element may refer either to a sound or to an entire word, it is also possible that a calabash design would have functioned either phonetically or logographically, depending on context. If the medium and context determined whether a given sign was read logographically or phonetically, then a calabash design might be read pictographically on a body and phonetically on wood.[30]

The notion of a fully functional script in the middle of the Pacific Ocean may seem farfetched, and yet one is known to exist. On Easter Island, the *rongorongo* script has long puzzled scholars.[31] It remains undeciphered but appears to be phonetic and linked to a Polynesian language.[32] According to oral tradition, the script was brought to Easter Island by the first settler, Hotu Matu'a, who brought sixty-seven inscribed wooden tablets with him from an unknown Polynesian homeland.[33] Twenty-five such tablets remain in existence, though all have been removed from Easter Island (see figure 16). While Easter Islanders have been enlisted in the attempt to decipher the

16. Rongorongo tablet. © Trustees of the British Museum. All rights reserved.

script, the efforts have been fruitless or even misleading, possibly because Easter Islanders in the late nineteenth century were no longer able to read the tablets, may have been protecting the information, or some combination of the two. We do know that missionaries and Easter Islanders struggled over possession and control of the tablets, because missionaries who collected four tablets on Easter Island between 1869 and 1870 represented themselves as intervening in indigenous efforts to destroy them or conceal them from Westerners.

Such struggles echo conflicts between colonial agents and the keepers of indigenous texts throughout the colonial Americas. While the missionaries on Easter Island succeeded in procuring four wooden tablets, efforts to decipher the script engraved on them have remained unsuccessful for more than a century. These efforts have been frustrated by the scarcity of materials, the inability to match signs with linguistic elements, and the same pictographic illusion that long lead decipherers of the Egyptian hieroglyphs astray. Some of the signs look vaguely like people, animals, and other objects and therefore appear deceptively "pictographic" when, in fact, they may be partially or wholly phonetic. For example, an element that looks like a hand appears not only on human figures but also on non-anthropomorphic signs, suggesting that the "hand" functions as a modifier of some sort rather than as a sign for "hand." Konstantin Pozdniakov has suggested that the script consists of fifty-five basic syllabic signs.[34] He has not been able to match the signs with syllables in a language, which may be due to linguistic change in the region or may indicate fundamental errors in current theories about the script.

In addition to linguistic challenges, other key questions remain unanswered. Most scholars agree that the script predates contact with the Western world—but where did it come from? Thor Heyerdahl's famous hypothesis that the Eastern Islanders came from South America has largely been abandoned, and today most scholars agree that they likely came from the West. Could they have come from the Marquesas, which are almost the same distance from Easter Island as South America? As in the Marquesas, full-body tattooing constituted an important social practice on Easter Island, where there is a definite overlap between certain tattoos and script elements such as the ones specialists refer to as "fish hooks" and "vulvas."[35] Is there a common ancestral link between the Marquesas and Easter Island that can provide clues to understanding the ways in which a common code of inscription might link marks on skin and wood? Could the *rongorongo* script and Marquesan tattoos have a common ancestor? Such questions must remain unanswered at this point, for even if a common ancestor existed long ago, material evidence is no longer extant. Furthermore, when the French took possession of the Marquesas again in 1844, they enacted an edict similar to the Spanish *auto-da-fé* in Mesoamerica and the Andes, banning one of the primary indigenous inscription practices—namely, tattooing. This 1844 law seriously disrupted the continuity of Marquesan tattooing in a way that impedes our ability to understand what it might have meant to people on the Marquesas before colonial repression, how it might have developed without interference, and whether Melville grasped a fundamental truth or simply invented the linkage between tattoos and writing as a symbolic device.

We do, however, know that a close link existed between bodily tattoos and wooden inscriptions both in the Marquesas and on Easter Island. Karl von den Steinen's *Die Marquesaner und ihre Kunst* (1925) illustrates the extent to which wood and body designs could be related.[36] While such links lead us no closer to "deciphering" Marquesan designs, it does suggest that Queequeg's coffin, with its text transcribed from tattoos, was based on the existence in Polynesia of a conventionalized system of inscription used on both bodies and wood. Von den Steinen's work, as well as Willowdean Chatterson Handy's *Tattooing in the Marquesas* (1922), indicates that the Marquesans used a limited number of designs with fairly specific meanings and that this was an integral part of Marquesan culture. Melville witnessed the Marquesans using a system of inscription on both bodies and wood and may have perceived a similarity to writing decades before the French outlawed the practice and almost a century before von den Steinen and Handy documented what survived of this practice in the early twentieth century.

The paucity of extant materials that would help us understand pre-contact indigenous literary cultures is a direct legacy of colonial violence. Ironically, the markers of colonial violence are often primary means of understanding the cultural production which that violence disrupted and subsequently rendered nearly invisible. Anthropological work such as Handy's and von den Steinen's, while enabling this project, emerged out of colonial relations. Queequeg and his coffin in *Moby-Dick* mark both the extent and the limits of that colonial legacy of destruction as representatives of a radically different and marginalized but persistent literary culture with the potential to resurface at the center of American literature. Such a moment of possibility stands as a counterpoint to an earlier one in Melville's authorship, where he probes the encounter between colonial and indigenous cultures of literacy from a decidedly different angle that centers on the relationship between writing and violence. Melville's first book, *Typee*, explores the contest over writing and inscription in a colonial context, foregrounding conflict and hostility in ways that reflect the colonial legacy that had made writing a site of struggle rather than of peaceful exchange. In *Typee*, his first major work, conflict appears to be the only possible outcome when different cultures of writing come into contact in the context of colonialism, and the counterpoint to Queequeg is Karky, a menacing tattooist who threatens to disfigure the narrator.

Before Queequeg There Was Karky:
Alternative Literacies in Conflict

While *Moby-Dick* explores the friendship between Queequeg and Ishmael as a site of mutuality where different forms of writing, via the common element of imagery, can function as a meeting ground rather than a battlefield, earlier work such as *Typee* represents the cross-cultural encounter as one in which graphic alterity represents threat. Just as in *Moby-Dick*, where Melville explicitly links Queequeg's tattoos to writing and books by associating them with terms such as "hieroglyphic marks," "written," "parchment," "treatise," and "volume," in *Typee*, Melville refers to tattooing in terms that link it to writing. He compares tattoos to "hieroglyphics" (*Typee*, 8) and refers to the tools of the tattooist as "delicate pencils" (*Typee*, 217).[37] In both works,

Polynesian tattoos thus represent an alternative, if undecipherable, system of literacy in which graphic signs on the surface of human skin convey meaning.

However, the ways in which Melville represents the narrator's encounter with tattoos in *Typee* and *Moby-Dick* differ greatly. In the early chapters of *Typee*, tattooed bodies observed from a distance add exotic flavor and humor to the story. However, that physical and narrative distance is erased when the narrator faces the possibility of being tattooed himself and recoils in horror. Whereas the narrator in *Moby-Dick* moves from initial fright to friendship and respect for Queequeg and his "mystical treatise," the representation of tattoos in *Typee* charts a narrative move from bemused curiosity and ethnographic interest to fear and menace. The crucial moment of transition comes when the narrator encounters a Polynesian tattoo artist who offers, or threatens, to tattoo his face. This scene, and the narrator's thoughts about tattooing, brings to the fore deeper concerns in the story about colonialism and cross-cultural conflict, as well as about the consequences of writing and inscription across cultures.[38]

Published in 1846 with the full title *Typee: A Peep at Polynesian Life*, Melville's first book drew on his experiences as a young sailor in Polynesia, as well as on other colonial accounts and popular genres that ranged from travel and captivity narratives to ethnography and South Seas adventure tales.[39] *Typee* is a semiautobiographical adventure tale about Tom, who jumps ship at Nukuheva on the Marquesas Islands, with another mate, Toby, due to an abusive captain and crew. After traveling across the island, they arrive at the valley of the "Typee people," who are reputedly ferocious cannibals. However, Tom and Toby are treated kindly by the Typee, although the narrator expresses continuous fears of cannibalism. Eventually, the two discover that they are not allowed to leave. At one point, Toby disappears, and the narrator, renamed Tommo by the Typee, wonders whether his friend has escaped the island or been eaten. Nonetheless, he soon settles into a pleasant, labor-free life in which he enjoys the devoted service of the islanders and the company of beautiful and scantily clad native women. Seemingly living an escape fantasy, Tommo re-dubs the place "Happy Valley" and relates his daily life interspersed with descriptions of the natural environment, as well as the culture, religion, government, and customs of the Typee.[40]

However, two events change Tommo's satisfied immersion into Typee life: a meeting with a Typee tattooist named Karky and the discovery that his hosts possess three preserved heads. Fear of being forcibly tattooed and horror at the glimpse of the severed heads revive his earlier preoccupation with Typee cannibalism.[41] He resolves to flee the island and subsequently publishes the narrative when he returns, along with a postscript describing the fate of his lost mate, Toby.

Tattoos appear in the very first chapter of the book, but a passage on tattooing in chapter 30 becomes the pivot both for the plot and for Melville's exploration of the intersection between writing and colonialism. A chance encounter brings Tommo face to face with a working tattooist in a scene initially cast as another example of exotic cultural difference, related, like so many of the chapters that precede it, in ethnographically descriptive terms. Tommo describes the pain endured by the man being tattooed, but the act of tattooing is not represented as an act of violation or coercion. In the Marquesas, tattoos were marks of prestige, and the acquisition of tattoos marked a major rite of passage. Tattoos were created by "tapping," or hammering sharp tools held against the skin and then filling the punctures with ink.[42] The process was both dangerous and painful.

A family would prepare long in advance for the payment of the *tuhuna patu tiki*, the master tattooist. The recipient of tattoos, the *opou*, was aided by younger family members, *ka'ioi*, who cooked, built the special hut, and sometimes received smaller, piecemeal tattoos for free while the opou rested in between the trying sessions. Ka'ioi were usually tattooed on the face first, whereas the tattooing of the opou began at the feet.[43] Thus, a person going through a major tattooing session would have his face tattooed last, whereas a ka'ioi, who was lucky to get as much tattooing as he could for free, would get his tattoos first and foremost on the face. Tommo's encounter with Karky might partially draw on the tradition of offering free tattoos to ka'ioi. The process of tattooing was expensive. Only wealthy families could afford the expense, and only for their firstborn. In this context, it would be generous, not menacing, for a tattooist such as Karky to offer Tommo a free tattoo. Karky's refusal to be satisfied with the hand might be understood as a refusal to "waste" a free tattoo on an extremity and, perhaps, even as an effort to communicate to Tommo why the face would be the preferred site for a starter tattoo. Given the detailed knowledge of tattooing that Melville shows in *Typee* and in his subsequent novel, *Omoo*, it is possible that he witnessed such scenes and imaginatively inhabited a ka'ioi's subject position.[44]

Melville's narrator, however, neither understands nor appreciates this Polynesian tradition. When Karky proposes to tattoo Tommo, he recoils in horror.[45] Yet this is not initially a scene of violence. What Tommo chances upon is an old man having his tattoos touched up by Karky, whom the narrator describes as an "artist." However, once the tattooist offers to apply the pencil to Tommo's own skin—to turn the pen on the writer, so to speak— Tommo's reaction is one of unmitigated dread. Instead of an ethnographic curiosity, cross-cultural tattooing is figured as violence and menace.[46] This shift, which is caused by the reversal of Tommo's position from observer to observed, reflects the relationship between writing and power. This is a moment of reversal in more than one way: Not only is the colonial gaze returned, but the pen is also turned on the colonial writer. In that moment, Tommo is confronted with the potential loss of control over the direction of, as well as the monopoly on, inscription.

This moment then reverses the colonial gaze and threatens to turn Tommo into a text rather than a writer, an object rather than a subject. While Tommo is willing to receive a tattoo on his arm, where he might easily hide it, the thought of a tattoo on his face fills him with dread. Significantly, it is not the pain of tattooing that most frightens Tommo but, rather, the representational consequences. A tattoo on his face would forever mark him with the cultural difference of the Typee, something that carries consequences in Western culture and society to which he still hopes to return. "This incident opened my eyes to a new danger; and I now felt convinced that in some luckless hour I should be disfigured in such a manner as never more to have the *face* to return to my countrymen, even should an opportunity offer. . . . What object he would have made of me!" (*Typee*, 219).

In this chapter of the book, Tommo identifies three interrelated consequences of such cross-cultural inscription. First, it will mark him for life in a way that will affect his status among his own countrymen and compromise his whiteness; second, it will make "an object" of him; and third, it will "convert" him into Typee society and identity. In the West, facial tattoos would forever alter his social identity, identifying him with a colonized people and making him an object rather than a subject. Among the Typee, a tattooed face would function similarly, indicating his assimilation into their society, a "conversion" and assimilation that would link his identity and destiny to theirs. In short, a facial tattoo would change Tommo's identity and cost him the most important privilege of whiteness: being unmarked.[47] It is this inscription into Typee identity, this compromise of his whiteness, and this objectification that make Karky's offer to tattoo his face so unsettling. After the encounter, the narrator's desire to escape from the valley revives "with additional force," particularly because the entire Typee society begins to pressure him to submit to tattooing (*Typee*, 220).

Throughout most of the narrative, Tommo is preoccupied with the threat of cannibalism, but it is his encounter with a tattoo artist that first reignites his desire to leave the island. The reasons cited by Tommo elucidate Melville's linkages between writing, cross-cultural inscription, and racialization. The scene brings into focus deep anxieties about what it means to write on, and about, bodies in the context of colonial conflict. As Samuel Otter has argued, Tommo's description of the consequences of receiving Polynesian tattoos on his face directly echoes the logic of racial inscription imposed on colonized peoples in Western writings and in U.S. society.[48]

Tommo's encounter with Karky follows a number of chapters that reproduce conventional genres of colonial writing, such as exploration narratives and ethnographic description.[49] These are chapters in which Tommo—and Melville—inscribe the Typee into Western literary modes. Thus, this section of the narrative contrasts the narrator's seemingly innocuous inscription of the Typee into colonial literature and its economy of signs with the terrifying possibility that the Typee will inscribe him into their social, literary, and hermeneutic systems.[50] In fact, the preceding chapters are far from harmless description; they reflect Melville's assimilation of the real Taipi people into a colonial system of meaning in which they are offered up for consumption by his audience.[51] The chapters on native life and the chapter on tattooing each represent modes of inscription of the "other" during the cross-cultural encounter, and the apparent violence of Karky's pen mirrors the hidden violence of the Western writer's pen.

In *Typee*, Melville thus contrasts two kinds of literacies and two systems of inscription. There is the invisible (because naturalized) alphabetic literacy that Melville brings to the encounter, with which he inscribes the Typee into his narrative and through which he transmits the story to his readers. Contrasted with this ink-on-paper literacy is the hyper-visible ink-on-skin literacy of the Typee, the tattooing with which they mark themselves and threaten to mark the narrator. The tattooing scene in chapter 30 encapsulates the conflicts and contradictions of the colonial encounter, making it a narrative site that exposes the interface between inscription practices on the Marquesas and in the United States.

Although *Typee* reverses (and thus obscures) the historical direction of colonial force and inscription, the book does probe the relationship between writing and violence in a way that reflects historical links between whiteness, inscription, and colonial power. Karky is such a frightening figure to the narrator because he threatens to disrupt the monopoly on writing and inscription on which his whiteness depends. In *Moby-Dick*, however, Melville divorces the anxiety of inscription from the possibility of indigenous literacy.[52] To some extent, these differences reflect stages in the colonial project historically and narratively. In *Typee*, Melville explores the anxieties of a cross-cultural encounter whose outcome is uncertain and the capacity of colonial genres such as ethnography to manage that conflict. The narrator's exchange with a Polynesian tattooist, represented as a writer on bodies, generates a great deal of anxiety and marks a moment in which the narrator's monopoly on inscription is momentarily disturbed. Unlike the narrator in *Typee*, however, Ishmael in *Moby-Dick* never negotiates the threat of cross-cultural inscription that appears to be at the crux of the anxiety associated with tattooing in *Typee*. Furthermore, he encounters Queequeg on U.S. soil, where Queequeg is already enrolled in the colonial sphere. It is from this vantage point, then, that Melville explores the dialogic potential of the colonial encounter and represents writing as a potential meeting ground rather than a battleground. In contrast to his early work in *Typee*, the more mature Melville in *Moby-Dick* proposes an alternative to the colonial paradigm that organized his first book, one in which writing can be imagined as a site not of struggle but of mutuality and connection.

"The Potluck of Both Worlds": Queequeg and Ishmael

While *Moby-Dick* is rich in allusions to many forms of mutuality, the imagery of marriage in Queequeg's and Ishmael's first meeting is among the most striking. Ishmael's and Queequeg's relationship represents, on the one hand, the trajectory from initial culture shock to something well beyond accommodation: mutual respect, a linking together of their destinies and futures, an ability to see each other as human beings. Significantly, this relationship is figured as one that does not require the erasure of difference; rather, it rests on a sharing of each other's cultures and circumstances. Not only do they share Peter Coffin's wedding bed; they also share a "social smoke," Queequeg shares his "thirty dollars in silver," and Ishmael pays homage to Yojo, Queequeg's idol. This last act is important because otherwise the sharing of silver might simply represent Ishmael's ability to appropriate Queequeg's resources.[53] Instead, the two characters establish a relationship organized by some degree of mutual respect that can be seen as Melville's model for cross-cultural relations.

The relationship between Queequeg and Ishmael is foregrounded in early chapters of the novel as the two decide to join their fates and fortunes by going on the same whaling voyage. This relationship, where compatibility displaces incommensurability, represents Melville's assertion that mutuality is central to the human condition. Whether conceived as a "joint-stock world in all meridians," in which Presbyterians and pagans are equally "cracked about the head, and sadly need mending," or in deeply intimate terms ranging from matrimonial to maternal imagery like the umbilical "monkey rope," such mutuality has important implications for Melville's representations of the colonial world in *Moby-Dick*. The relationship between Ishmael and Queequeg has at its core the simple, and profound, postulation that "savages" are human beings, equally "cracked about the head"; equally compassionate, civilized, and savage; and equally capable readers and writers. The last point is significant, alternately threatening in *Typee* or redeeming in *Moby-Dick*, because the presence or absence of writing has played such a significant role in the colonial imaginary as a marker that distinguishes "white" people from their colonial others.

Ishmael and his relationship with Queequeg thus represent an important alternative to the logic of conflict rooted in fundamental difference, which is embodied in part by Captain Ahab. One of the most frequent adjectives applied to Ahab in scholarly literature is "monomaniacal." In narrative terms, Ahab represents dictation and monologue rather than dialogue. While he is paired with the Parsee and Pip, among others, his primary relationship is arguably with the whale. This relationship is rooted in the quest for domination and ultimately organized around destruction. The singularity of Ahab's thought stands in contrast to the cooperation and exchange that characterize Queequeg's and Ishmael's relationship. Comparing the relationship between Ishmael and Queequeg with the relationship between Ahab and Moby-Dick raises the question of what, beyond himself, that whale represents. There is no single answer to the question, as the whale in *Moby-Dick* is a multivalent textual presence. I do, however, want to dwell briefly on one particular connotation that bears on my argument here: the whale as an "original inhabitant" of the ocean.

Indeed, the violent struggle between the whale and Ahab can be seen as symbolic of a conflict between original inhabitants of the ocean/the Americas and those who try to extract its resources and enact domination, even to the point of destruction.[54] The struggle between the indigenous people of the Americas and European colonists expressed itself in part as a struggle over writing. The hieroglyphic whale is linked explicitly with "the old Indian characters chiseled on the hieroglyphic palisades on the banks of the Upper Mississippi" and Ahab's quest to destroy him is, in part, an effort to eradicate "otherness," be it narrative, ontological, or semiotic.

Together, Ishmael and Queequeg represent an alternative to that destructive struggle. Both characters can be seen as synecdoches for their respective textual cultures, and their relationship stands as a testimony to the possibility of a different dynamic between people and their writing. Queequeg's and Ishmael's narratives, carved on wood and written on paper, are mutually conjoined by their meeting and by a world shaped by colonialism.

Queequeg's coffin, in turn, represents the possibility that non-alphabetic, radically different forms of inscription can be seen as writing, even when they remain undeciphered. Such recognition undermines the distinction between a literate West and a non-literate colonial "other." Melville's persistent allusion to Egyptian hieroglyphs raises the possibility that other non-alphabetic forms of writing from other conquered territories may also someday regain their status as systems of writing. Queequeg's coffin also reveals that decipherment and translation are not prerequisites for seeing indigenous scripts as legitimate literary forms, for gaining a greater understanding of their relationship to alphabetic writing, and for recognizing, at the intersection of indigenous and alphabetic scripts, a vital new center of early American literature.

Conclusion: Indigenous Literacies and the Significance of Queequeg's Coffin

Critics have understood Queequeg and his coffin in a number of ways, most significantly as a means of Ishmael's movement from despair to rebirth. In this sense, the coffin as a symbol of death is converted into a symbol of rebirth for Ishmael. But where does that leave Queequeg and his hieroglyphic text? Is he simply there to serve Ishmael? No doubt, Queequeg is a redeeming and literally lifesaving character. In addition to saving three lives and "melting" Ishmael's despair, he is figured as a sort of midwife, so he can certainly be understood as a conduit of Ishmael's spiritual rebirth. Queequeg then functions as a romanticized and stereotypical noble savage who serves the needs of the narrator—a figure Melville also invokes in *Typee*.[55]

I have argued, however, that Queequeg's coffin can be seen as a text and thus as a synecdoche for indigenous writing, a connection that Melville makes by comparing both Queequeg's tattoos and Native American petroglyphs to hieroglyphics. If we see Queequeg as a representative of "the vanishing primitive," then his coffin can be read as a text that nonetheless survives its maker. In one sense, that is always the promise of writing, that it survives the writer, just as *Moby-Dick* has survived and outlived Melville. Such an interpretation, of course, presupposes my premise: that the coffin is understood as a text, an example of indigenous writing. This could explain Queequeg's decision, once he recovers and no longer needs the coffin, to transfer the tattoos from his own perishable body onto the more permanent medium of wood and to transform the coffin, a symbol of death, into a text, a symbol of immortality. The promise of Queequeg's coffin in this framework would be the prospect that, even as native people faced the genocidal onslaught of colonialism, their writing could survive just as Egyptian hieroglyphs survived.

However, I do not believe that Queequeg represents a "vanishing" collectivity, be it Polynesian, Native American, or conceived more broadly as indigenous. After all, he recovers from his illness, and ultimately he dies no sooner than the rest of the crew. Furthermore, Melville transfigures his coffin into a buoy that saves Ishmael, the narrator. The transformation from coffin to lifebuoy and text is simultaneous and narratively linked to Queequeg's recovery. What does that mean within the narrative logic of *Moby-Dick*? We know that there was a relationship between tattoos and carved glyphs in Polynesia, but what is Melville's purpose in linking this phenomenon to life, death, and writing? What does Queequeg's coffin tell us?

Melville never deciphers the "mystical treatise" engraved by Queequeg; nor does the text of *Moby-Dick* offer clues as to what the text on the coffin might mean. Indeed, while tattooed bodies are compared to books in both *Typee* and *Moby-Dick*, neither narrative represents them as legible to the narrator or the reader.[56] Perhaps that is because Melville spent only a few weeks on the Marquesas. Perhaps he never deciphers—or has his characters decipher—any tattoos because he was not there long enough to learn how a given design might communicate meaning. However, fictional license certainly would have allowed him to elaborate any meaning he pleased.[57] By according Polynesian hieroglyphs the status of undeciphered writing, Melville posits the existence of non-alphabetic forms of writing that retain their alterity and thus remain markers of an indigenous and uncompromised textual presence.

Of course, only Ishmael survives to tell the story, which is transmitted through alphabetic writing. But who is Ishmael? We know merely what he tells us, as Ishmael is the narrative voice throughout the novel proper.[58] The most obvious reference is biblical: As the offspring of Abraham and Hagar in the Old Testament, Ishmael was the product of boundary crossing and mixing across castes.[59] Is Ishmael, in *Moby-Dick*, a racially mixed survivor of the multiracial crew and thus meant to represent an alternative to the logic of racial differentiation—the demographic future of America? Perhaps. But Melville's Ishmael is also the result of a process of travel, inquiry, and cross-cultural encounter; he is not the depressed character of the novel's beginning but, rather, the lone survivor who returns to tell the tale. In one sense, Ishmael, like Guaman Poma, is the result of the story he tells.

The famous opening line of the novel, "Call me Ishmael," leaves open the possibility that this is not the narrator's real name. Could it instead be Queequeg? In the first chapter, the narrator confesses a love for "forbidden seas and . . . barbarous coasts," and in chapter 57 he claims, "I myself am a savage." Given Melville's proclivity to collapse and reverse images of savagery and civilization, we could imagine the barbarous coast as the Atlantic seaboard of North America and the narrator as a Poma-like figure who has mastered the tropes and narrative forms of colonial culture for his own subversive or redeeming purposes.

But perhaps it is the text itself that we should call Ishmael, a text that is the result of cultural and textual boundary crossing. Nuptial embraces and visions of universal brotherhood represent different models of human relationships and human narratives. The interlinkage of different textual traditions, the imagery of marriage and a lifesaving embrace between the narrator and the indigenous text on the coffin represent Melville's search for alternatives to the fatal embrace of colonialism.

Melville's visions of commensurability undermine the very core of colonial logic. The distinction between "civilized" and "savage," between literate and illiterate, is also the distinction between self and other that upholds notions of racial difference. As Albert Memmi has argued, racism is a necessary and enabling condition of colonialism. Its logic is organized around fundamental and irreversible difference.[60] In *Moby-Dick*, as in *Typee*, that logic falls apart the moment the Western writer encounters the supposed contradiction of "writing savages." What is left in its place, emerging out of the space where that logic and the fundamental distinctions that underpin it collapses, is the radical possibility of coeval commensurability also proposed by Guaman Poma centuries earlier.

As a text which survives the wreckage of the *Pequod* along with the narrator, Queequeg's coffin represents indigenous writing and its presence at the center of American literature. Even when such writing is undeciphered or no longer extant, it remains important, its transformative potential intact. In *Moby-Dick*, the alphabetic text and the indigenous narrative inscribed on the coffin are mutually interconnected and enabling. Queequeg's coffin reveals that at the "vital center" of American literature is the intersection between alphabetic and indigenous forms of writing—and the possibility of recovering a sense of shared destiny.

The challenges presented by the non-alphabetic literatures of America's indigenous peoples must not be accepted as an alibi for their exclusion from literary studies. The difficulties such materials pose to scholars point us all toward a new practice that can comprehend the vast and varied literary heritage of the Americas.

This heritage extends back in time to long before the first Europeans arrived. These soldiers, missionaries, adventurers, and settlers found not an empty or illiterate continent, but native people with a great range of literary traditions and practices. We will never be able to fully reconstruct that literary heritage, because colonial agents destroyed so much of it. This fact is an integral element of the literary history of the hemisphere. The colonial archive of the confrontation between European and indigenous peoples in the Americas, and of the subsequent importation of enslaved Africans, is extensive. In contrast, surviving texts by America's indigenous and African peoples confronting the violence of colonization, displacement, and enslavement are far fewer and often present daunting challenges to literary scholars seeking to recover the complex literary heritage of the Americas. Such difficulties are traces of that violence. They do not, however, prevent us from recognizing the radical heterogeneity of American literature. Instead, they challenge us to examine and reject colonial tropes which have organized the field of literary studies for so long and to recast our sense of literature in the Americas to comprehend its dazzling diversity. This means expanding our definition of writing to account for the non-alphabetic literatures of America's indigenous peoples, as well as recasting our methods to suit the heterogeneous, and sometimes disjointed, nature of this archive.

What comes to us through the vortex of colonial time are often mere fragments and traces, torn from the linguistic and cultural contexts that gave them meaning. It is an archive that speaks simultaneously of radical rupture and continuity against all odds, of the magnitude of colonial destruction and cultural persistence. During the past few decades, scholars across the Americas have begun to address this legacy with innovative scholarship that pays attention to previously overlooked sites of literacy and to the intersections between radically different semiotic systems and textual traditions. Much of this work comes from Native American scholars and others working at the fraught intersection between tribal communities and scholarly disciplines, thinkers who, in the process, bring indigenous critiques and ways of knowing to bear on those disciplinary structures.

Indigenous, non-alphabetic texts and literary forms have long been relegated outside the boundaries of American literary studies, beyond the realm of "real writing." This book makes that outside space the center of inquiry. Such a shift casts the encounter and conflict between indigenous and European forms of literacy as foundational to American literature. It also brings to the fore the material and epistemological violence that rendered entire literary traditions invisible and, at times, illegible. The purpose of such a shift is not simply to expand the circle of inclusion but, rather, to begin to undo mechanisms of exclusion and erasure, along with their dehumanizing consequences.

The book begins in 1524 outside Tenochtitlan because that exchange between Spanish friars and Mexica tlamatinime marks a paradigmatic moment in American literature. Out of such exchanges about writing arise a new world literature and a different story about literature in the Americas. The record of such moments has itself been fragmented and scattered, sometimes destroyed forever and at other times inscribed in colonial documents, hidden in imperial archives, lost for centuries before resurfacing, like "The Aztec-Spanish Dialogues of 1524" or like Guaman Poma's El primer nueva corónica y buen gobierno. Such texts alert us to the contingency of colonial erasure and remind us that the possibilities of the dialogic have not been permanently foreclosed. Their recovery brings to light an understudied aspect of America's literary heritage that is about dialogue as well as imposition, about resurgence as well as loss, about survival as well as destruction. It is a difficult and complex project that opens up a vastly expanded and reconfigured archive while aiming to be a transformative, rather than addi-tive, effort. The purpose is not simply to remap the field but to recast the very framework which organizes our inquiry and our sense of what is possible.

It is time to relinquish the colonial trope of people without writing and to untangle from the epistemological framework of imperial Europe our un-derstanding of literacy and writing in the colonial conflict zones. Doing so allows us to re-center the literatures and textual practices that were indige-nous to the Americas while simultaneously de-centering the alphabeticism imported by Europeans. We can then begin to recognize how colonial con-flicts were shaped by alternative literacies that at these early moments of contact were equally strange. The "literature of the undetermined encoun-ter" reminds us of the contingency of the early colonial period. While it has often been cast, anachronistically and artificially, as pre-national, this is not an accurate conception of the period or of its literary dynamics. The colo-nial, the pre-national, and the national period in the Americas overlap in uneven and undertheorized ways marked, to some extent, by the ways in which the alternative literacies of indigenous and settler cultures interact. The postcolonial—which in the Americas remains deferred—could be her-alded, in part, by the restoration to full legal status of indigenous literary forms such as wampum.

That is the trajectory, and those are the stakes, of de-colonizing scholar-ship. It is not surprising, then, that the work before us is daunting and requires the collaborative efforts of many. Literary scholars aligned with that project need to continue the recovery work that has brought out of obscurity long-lost or previously discounted texts and writers. We need to take se-riously non-alphabetic forms of literacy in the Americas and develop meth-ods adequate for understanding their distinct literary histories and textual logics. The diversity of languages and semiotic forms make this, by neces-sity, interdisciplinary work that is not bounded by the limits of scholarly institutions. Such efforts will enable us to trace the ways in which alternative literacies, dominant and subaltern, intersected and dialogized each other in the colonial conflict zone. They can also lead to new ways of understanding the Americas, its literatures, and the textual implications of coloniality.

What did the literary landscape of the Americas look like before and at the point of contact? How did it change as colonial conflict and transformation reshaped indigenous worlds from what is now Santo Domingo to the Andes and across the American hemisphere? The work necessary to answer such questions remains an unfinished project. But this is a time of critical momentum. For scholars engaged in such efforts, method poses an acute problem because of the magnitude of destruction; this book suggests ways to begin to reconstitute some sense of what was scattered by the violent forces of colonial transformation. Fragments and traces provide important pieces in such a puzzle; consequently, fragmented form in this archive is not a deficiency but a symptom of colonial violence. Likewise, "failures" in literary form may represent sites that register previously unrecognized semiotic and literary heterogeneity. In the literature of the over-determined encounter, in the textual conflict zones of colonial literature, we must be carefully attuned to translation and exchange between semiotic and literary forms, as well as languages, to the mutual deformation caused by heterogeneous literacies that mark the limits and possibilities of commensurability.

We are aided in this work by the fact that Europeans were not the only ones who theorized the relationship between textuality and culture. The story of the Peacemaker records a founding moment in the history of the Haudenosaunee League of Nations and, simultaneously, a theory of wampum textuality that can expand our sense of the literary landscape of the Northeastern Woodlands and beyond. In the records of peace negotiations between Haudenosaunee and European emissaries in the early colonial period, we can trace the effort by both parties to make sense of the distinct forms of literacy which shaped the exchange. The history and theories of literature in America must comprehend the full complexity of such exchanges. This requires a change in our understanding of literature, of course, and a willingness to address inadequacies in our training that leave us unable to see and analyze indigenous forms of literacy and their relationships to alphabetic writing. Such efforts, as well, are part of America's literary heritage. In the *Corónica*, Guaman Poma attempts to bring into dialogue the radically different literary worlds of Spain and the Andes and, in the process, change the parameters of colonial exchange. His manuscript represents an important moment in the history of the book, as well as a model for scholars studying colonial dialogization in early American literature.

Across the Americas, European and indigenous peoples in the colonial sphere attempted to make sense of, and educate each other about, the strange new ways to record ideas, words, and meaning that confronted them in the colonial world. Herman Melville's story of the whale registers the confrontation with indigenous writing in the colonial world in subtle ways that become perceptible once we are attuned to the centrality of this dynamic in American literature. Sometimes Europeans and colonial settlers welcomed such exchanges; at other times they actively foreclosed the dialogic potential of a heterogeneous literary sphere. Either way, the confrontation with diverse forms of writing shaped the literature of the Americas in important ways that remain inscribed within both well-known and more obscure texts produced in the colonial conflict zone. Queequeg's coffin has served as leitmotif for this study because it registers the centrality and radical potential of indigenous texts, even those that remain undeciphered, in the literary heritage of the Americas and across the colonial world.

There was little reason to expect, when Guaman Poma's *Corónica* re-emerged from the European archives in 1908, that this recovery would initiate a century of indigenous resurgence. The preceding, and subsequent, decades seemed, if anything, to mark a nadir for America's native people. And yet by the end of the twentieth century, populations had begun to grow, political rights were being reasserted, and a vibrant body of contemporary literature had emerged. The Mashantucket Pequot, namesakes of Ahab's ill-fated ship and targets of one of the first genocidal colonial campaigns in North America, are once again powerful economic and political actors in the American Northeast. Andean people still honor the legacy of quipus, although colonial violence permanently ended their use as the dominant records of a functioning state. Haudenosaunee people continue to maintain an archive of wampum and assert its status as legally binding documents in the United States, in Canada, and at the United Nations, where there is now a Permanent Forum on Indigenous Issues. In defiance of five hundred years of colonial violence, belying the narrative of inevitable disappearance, native people and their texts—alphabetic and non-alphabetic—are still here.

Although it is too late for Guaman Poma to witness such developments, it is not too late for the descendants of colonial conflict to honor his effort to recast the terms of exchange in more equitable and respectful ways. If the colonial trope of people without writing is abandoned, what might emerge in its place? A more capacious sense of American literature and the textual implications of coloniality, to be sure. But the recognition that documents produced and maintained by indigenous peoples are legitimate forms of writing matters beyond the sphere of literary studies. Ultimately, there is far more at stake here—and far more to gain—than new ways of understanding American literature. The future, after all, remains contingent and undetermined.

Introduction

1 The Mexica, or Aztec, settled in the central Valley of Mexico roughly one hundred years before the arrival of the Spanish. By the early sixteenth century, they had achieved dominance in the region through a combination of warfare and strategic alliances. Centered in the city of Tenochtitlan, they controlled a "far-flung empire" as part of the "Triple Alliance (Tenochtitlan, Tlacopan, and Texcoco)." The "Aztec capital of Tenochtitlan became Mexico City" once it was conquered by the Spanish: Cline, "Native Peoples of Colonial Central Mexico," 189.

2 These proceedings were recorded by Fray Bernardino de Sahagún. They were discovered in the secret archive of the Vatican in the early twentieth century. The bilingual text was published in 1924 by Father José Maria Poú y Martí in Spanish and Nahuatl under the title "El libro perdido de las Pláticas o Coloquios de los doce primeros misioneros de México." This imaginative retelling is based on Klor de Alva, "The Aztec-Spanish Dialogues of 1524," 52–193; Mignolo, *The Darker Side of the Renaissance*, 69–122.

3 This is how Mikhail M. Bakhtin describes the social context out of which the novel emerged: see Bakhtin, *The Dialogic Imagination*, 7. Bakhtin argues that modern novelistic discourse is marked by polyglossia and the dialogic relationship of languages: ibid., 82. I invoke Bakhtin because I see this as a useful way to understand the emergence of American literature as rooted in a dialogic relationship between European and indigenous American forms of writing and literary traditions.

4 Mallery, *Picture-Writing of the American Indians*, 2:666. This spelling appears in colonial records but is not preferred by contemporary Mi'kmaq.

5 Ibid., 2:667–71. See also Greenfield, "The Mi'kmaq Hieroglyphic Prayer Book." For another study of Mi'kmaq writing more generally, see Kolodny, *In Search of First Contact*.

6 Of course, there are important exceptions. Those that bear directly on this study are cited in subsequent chapters.

7 The most comprehensive overview of indigenous American forms of writing remains Garrick Mallery's two-volume *Picture-Writing of the American Indians*, which was originally published in 1893 as part of the *Tenth Annual Report of the Bureau of Ethnology to the Secretary of the Smithsonian Institution, 1888–89*. See also Brotherston, *Image of the New World*. A vast body of published materials exists on the many different kinds of indigenous writing on the American continents. Those works are cited in the subsequent chapters as they pertain to my discussion.

8 For an accessible overview of this debate, see Hill Boone, "Introduction."

9 Newman, "Captive on the Literacy Frontier," 31.

10 For one example, see Wong, *Sending My Heart Back across the Years*. Despite her belief in the absence of standard written records among indigenous Americans, Hertha Wong argues for literary attention to indigenous "forms of literacy" such as pictography and offers a model for such scholarship.

11 See Erdrich, *Books and Islands in Ojibwe Country*, 5–6.

12 Brooks, *The Common Pot*, xxi–xxii. In addition to published work on indigenous American literature, Paula Gunn Allen's undergraduate seminar on orality and literacy at the University of California, Los Angeles, and Gerald Vizenor's graduate courses at the University of California, Berkeley, informed my thinking on this topic in important ways.

13 Silko, *Yellow Woman and the Beauty of Spirit*, 155–57.

14 Myra Jehlen, "The Literature of Colonization," 37, explains the absence of Native American texts among the literature of the early colonial period in this way: "The people who already inhabited the North American continent had an old and richly developed oral literature; they did not write." Jehlen here restates a commonly held belief among North American literary scholars that is repeated in major teaching texts. One of the most important anthologies in the field, *The Norton Anthology of American Literature*, concurs that indigenous North America produced great "orature" but no written "littera-tures": Baym et al., *The Norton Anthology of American Literature*, 1:7. For examples of indigenous oral literature in English transcription, see Astrov, *The Winged Serpent*; Bierhorst, *Four Masterworks of American Indian Literature*; Tedlock, *The Popol Vuh*. Werner Sollors and Marc Shell included indigenous pictographic writing with Delaware and English transcription in their American literature anthology, albeit a somewhat problematic example: see Sollors and Shell, *The Multi-Lingual Anthology of American Literature*.

15 Womack, *Red on Red*, 2. Craig Womack is part of a growing cohort of contemporary Native scholars calling for new ways to study Native American literature rooted in indigenous rather than European conceptions of the literary. Brooks's discussion of recent work by Native American writers and scholars on the issue of indigenous literary forms and traditions provides a useful and concise overview of the current state of the field: see Brooks, *The Common Pot*, esp. xxvi–xxxiii. Womack's call for the study of Native American writing "that reaches back to the 1770s in terms of writing in English" has been answered by a growing body of scholarship, such as Hilary Wyss's study of biblical marginalia

and other "marginal" texts by Native Americans in the colonial period: see Wyss, *Writing Indians*.

16 Foucault, *The Archeology of Knowledge*, 26.

17 I am invoking and adapting George Lipsitz's notion of a "possessive invest-ment" in this context to mark the relationship between whiteness and the idea of exclusive possession of writing: see Lipsitz, *The Possessive Investment in Whiteness*.

18 Whitman, "The Spanish Element in Our Nationality," 1146. America, of course, remains more than "our United States," and in this project "America" refers to all of the Americas, although I do not specifically address texts produced in the Caribbean.

19 Smith, *Decolonizing Methodologies*.

20 *The Jesuit Relations*, vol. 40, 1652–1653, 165.

21 Jehlen, "The Literature of Colonization," 49.

22 Only a few generations ago, for example, slave narratives were absent from the American literary canon. Their recovery has brought to light a rich and formerly unknown aspect of the American literary heritage and in the process recon-figured our understanding of the nineteenth century and American literature as a whole. Peace councils and treaty negotiations have a similar potential to recast our understanding of early American literature.

23 See, e.g., Bross and Wyss, *Early Native Literacies in New England*; Cohen and Glover, *Early American Mediascapes*; Hall, *Cultures of Print*.

24 Methodologically, the work in Lockhart, *The Nahuas after the Conquest*, 326–73, has also been very important as a model for how to do dialogic textual studies between two different writing systems.

25 Mignolo, *The Darker Side of the Renaissance*, 336.

26 Ibid., 7.

27 Bakhtin, *The Dialogic Imagination*, 427, argues that "a word, discourse, language or culture undergoes 'dialogization' when it becomes relativized, de-privileged, aware of competing definitions for the same things. Undialogized language is authoritative or absolute."

28 Scholarship on Guaman Poma is cited in chapter 3, as appropriate.

29 Bakhtin, *The Dialogic Imagination*, 427.

30 See Pratt, *Imperial Eyes*. For Mary Louise Pratt on Peru and Guaman Poma's manuscript, see Pratt, "Transculturation and Autoethnography."

31 Brokaw, "Khipu Numeracy and Alphabetic Literacy in the Andes," 276. Brokaw is extending Pratt's notion of "contact zones."

32 See, e.g., Edmonson, *The Ancient Future of the Itza*; Roys, *The Book of Chilam Balam of Chumayel*.

33 George-Kanentiio, "Iroquois at the U.N.," 71.

34 Salomon, *The Cord Keepers*.

35 Gilmore, *Surface and Depth*, 87.

36 Simon Battestini, for example, discusses the inaccuracy of the notion that Afri-cans did not have writing and thus reveal the potential for similar types of studies on the African continent: Battestini, *African Writing and Text*.

37 For a more complete discussion of Queequeg's identity and scholarship on that issue, see chapter 4 of this book.

ONE Writing and Colonial Conflict

1 The literature on Mesoamerican writing is copious. For an accessible overview of the four major Mesoamerican writing systems (Aztec, Zapotec, Mixtec, and Maya), see Marcus, *Mesoamerican Writing Systems*.

2 De Sahagún, *Historia general de las cosas de Nueva España*. For an English translation, see Anderson and Dibble, *General History of the Things of New Spain*.

3 Mignolo, *The Darker Side of the Renaissance*, 188.

4 Alphabetic texts written by indigenous people emerged throughout New Spain. Such texts include the Mayan Books of Chilam Balam and Fernando de Alva Ixtlilxochitl's *Historia de la Nación Chichimeca*, a local history of the Chichimecas written from the perspective of native ruling elites. Jorge Cañizares-Esguerra argues that de Alva Ixlilxocitl's imprint on colonial historiography, transmitted through Torquemada, "through whom it came to dominate the colonial historiography of New Spain," has yet to be fully understood: see Cañizares-Esguerra, *How to Write the History of the New World*, 223–24. For an Andean example of an indigenous alphabetic text, see Yupanqui, *An Inca Account of the Conquest of Peru*. See also Bauer, "Writing as 'Khipu.'"

5 Thwaites, *The Jesuit Relations and Allied Documents*, 67:227.

6 Ibid., 24:83. Such statements corroborate Lisa Brooks's claims to Abenaki traditions of literacy: see Brooks, *The Common Pot*, xx–xxii.

7 Mallery, *Picture-Writing of the American Indians*, 666.

8 Ibid.

9 The willingness of the French to engage in dialogue with native people "fostered a dialogic relationship with the peoples they encountered" that provides an important counterpoint to Puritan cultural separatism: Dorsey, "Going to School with Savages," 413. For a recent study that engages French colonial texts, see Sayre, *Les Sauvages Américains*. James Moore argues that the Jesuits were unique in their willingness to meet native people on their own cultural grounds, as long as it facilitated conversation. The Jesuits successfully adapted indigenous forms of writing into their missionary activities. "The fathers, finding much similarity in the use of picture-writing among those tribes with which they dealt, found it easy to communicate the new religion in this same medium": Moore, *Indian and Jesuit*, 135–36. Although some Jesuits and other Europeans traveling in the area recognized indigenous pictography as comparable to "our letters," many contradictory statements appear throughout the colonial records. Druillettes and Maurault both claim that the hieroglyphic writing they witnessed was unique to each individual user and not part of a conventionalized system, which would make it writing. Likewise, Father Bressani claimed, "They have neither books, nor any writing": Thwaites, *The Jesuit Relations and Allied Documents*, 39:149.

10 Lafitau, *Customs of the American Indians Compared with the Customs of Primitive Times,* 2:36.

11 The adventurer Louis-Armand de Lom d'Acre, Baron de Lahontan, explains this practice in some detail. "When a Party of Savages have routed their enemies in any Place whatever, the Conquerors take care to pull the Bark off the Trees for the height of five or six Foot in all Places where they stop in returning to their own Country; and in honour of their Victory paint certain images with Coal pounded and beat up with Fat and Oyl. These Pictures continue upon the peel'd Tree for ten or twelve Years, as if they were Grav'd, without being defac'd by the Rain": de Lom d'Acre, *New Voyages to North-America,* 2:510–11. Such pictographic postings conveyed detailed and specific information, such as, "A hundred and eight French soldiers set out from Montreal in the first quarter of the month of July and sailed twenty-one days; after which they marched 35 leagues over land and surprised 120 Senecas on the east side of their village, 11 of whom were killed and 50 taken prisoners; the French sustaining the loss of 9 killed and 12 wounded, after a very obstinate engagement": Mallery, *Picture-Writing of the American Indians,* 2:558.

12 Thwaites, *The Jesuit Relations and Allied Documents,* 10:120.

13 Ibid., 10:117. It is impossible to assert with certainty based on this evidence that girls and women were literate. However, the absence of a conjugation for "she" does not necessarily indicate exclusion, because, as in English, it was common at the time to use "he" as a stand-in for both genders.

14 Indeed, direct correspondence between at least one ancient petroglyph from Mi'kmaq and a letter in the current Mi'kmaq alphabet has been established: see Greenfield, "The Mi'kmaq Hieroglyphic Prayer Book," 201.

15 Lafitau, *Customs of the American Indians Compared with the Customs of Primitive Times,* 2:36.

16 See Gelb, *A Study of Writing,* 29; DeFrancis, *Visible Speech,* 47.

17 Some important and influential studies include Cohen, *La grande invention de l'ecriture et son evolution;* Diringer, *The Alphabet;* Diringer, *Writing;* Février, *Histoire de l'écriture;* Jensen, *Sign, Symbol, and Script.*

18 In fact, David Olson has argued that modern hermeneutics and interpretive reading practices arose out of the separation of text and speaker following the invention of print: Olson, *The World on Paper,* 116.

19 Recent and otherwise insightful studies that aim to present a comprehensive theory of writing summarily dismiss "Amerindian pictographs" from the category of writing without consulting or engaging recent scholarship on indigenous writing in the Americas: see, e.g., DeFrancis, *Visible Speech,* 35–47.

20 See, e.g., Sampson, *Writing Systems.* In "Logographic and Semasiographic Writing Systems," J. Marshall Unger and John DeFrancis critique Sampson's use of non-phonetic categories of writing. Their critique, like their work, is deeply rooted in Chinese scholarship and debates and may be appropriate for that context. However, while I find it likely that many forms of writing in the Americas were or are related to language (spoken or gestured), I believe too little is

known at this point to make categorical statements about the nature of all indigenous forms of writing in the Americas. Nor are we able, without taking into account the American context, to make accurate statements about the nature of all writing. DeFrancis's discussion of Native American forms of writing would be far more convincing (and perhaps more nuanced) if he engaged recent scholarship in the field instead of relying on uncritical readings of colonial agents such as Mallery.

21 Moorhouse, *The Triumph of the Alphabet*, 173.

22 Jensen, *Sign, Symbol, and Script*, 47.

23 *Graphikos* derives from *graphein*, which means "to write."

24 For example, a simple but conventionalized representation of a shepherd's staff means "ruler," and a somewhat abstract, conventionalized column is a logogram for Heliopolis, a city near Cairo.

25 For an overview of the history of this decipherment, see Robinson, *Lost Languages*, 104–38. The level of phoneticism in Mesoamerican writing systems remains a subject of debate: see Nicholson, "Phoneticism in the Late Pre-Hispanic Central Mexican Writing System"; Smith, "The Relationship between Mixtec Manuscript Painting and the Mixtec Language."

26 Gelb, *A Study of Writing*, 56–59. Gelb is citing Long, "Maya and Mexican Writing," 31; Schellhas, "Fifty Years of Maya Research."

27 Coe, *Breaking the Maya Code*; Schele, *Maya Glyphs*. For thirteen years, Linda Schele ran an annual weekend workshop on Maya hieroglyphic writing at the University of Texas, Austin: Schele, *The Proceedings of the Maya Hieroglyphic Weekend*.

28 Robinson, *Lost Languages*, 30. Robinson notes that his schema does not posit a historical development from one script to another. He rejects the category of a purely phonetic writing system.

29 Thwaites, *The Jesuit Relations and Allied Documents*, 10:117.

30 Brinton, "On an 'Inscribed Tablet' from Long Island."

31 Olaniayan, *Scars of Conquest/Masks of Resistance*, 4.

32 Spivak, "Subaltern Studies."

33 Taylor, *The History of the Alphabet*. The Age of Discovery brought Europeans into contact with an unprecedented variety of writing systems.

34 Ibid., 1:1–6. Taylor made a fundamental division between "ideograms," which included pictures; pictorial symbols, which expressed abstract ideas; and "phonograms," which included phonetic signs such as logograms (word writing), syllabic signs, and, eventually, alphabetic signs or letters.

35 Ibid., 1:2–4.

36 While many contemporary studies question such notions, they can still be found even in recent and important overviews, such as, "Humankind is defined by language; but civilization is defined by writing": Daniels and Bright, *The World's Writing Systems*, 1.

37 See Fabian, *Time and the Other*. Fabian defines the denial of coevalness as "a persistent and systematic tendency to place the referent(s) of anthropology in a

Time other than the present of the producer of anthropological discourse," ibid., 31. See also Wolf, *Europe and the People without History*.

38 The quotation used as this section's subheading is from Diego de Landa, *Yucatan before and after the Conquest*, 82.

39 This is the main thesis of Mignolo, *The Darker Side of the Renaissance*. Silko, *Yellow Woman and the Beauty of Spirit*, 155, makes the same argument: "Books were and still are weapons in the ongoing struggle for the Americas."

40 Thomas, *Great Books and Book Collectors*, 193.

41 De Landa's book is also a result of dialogues, though less evident than in Sahagún's work, likely with Gaspar Antonio Chi and Nachi Cocom. De Landa's relationship with his informers was complicated and later turned rather hostile: see Gates, "Introduction," iii.

42 De Landa, *Yucatan before and after the Conquest*, 82. De Acosta condemns this act as a destruction of historical sources. De Acosta, *Natural and Moral History of the Indes*.

43 De Landa, *Yucatan before and after the Conquest*, 82. Renato Rosaldo has suggested that colonialism often entails a kind of "imperial nostalgia," an admiration and regretful yearning for what is being destroyed: see Rosaldo, *Culture and Truth*. However, I believe there is more at stake for colonial authors such as de Landa. As William Gates notes in his introduction to de Landa's work, de Landa's fame and immortality, his "position in history," rests on exactly these two related acts: writing a book about the Maya and issuing the order to destroy their books. His knowledge of the Maya stands in place of their own knowledge in the European consciousness, and his authority (as an author and as a ruler of the region) displaces their authority. Later colonial projects in North America would follow similar patterns of cultural negation and displacement. These connected acts of description and destruction—writing reality, as it were—constitute a pattern of colonialism that Gordon Sayre calls the dialectic of negation and substitution. He describes this dialectic as follows: "The colonists substituted their notion of work for analogous but different behaviour among the Indians, then used the difference to ascribe to the 'savages' the negation of work, idleness": Sayre, *Les Sauvages Américains*, 103. Sayre's trope provides a useful tool for understanding the process, embodied by de Landa, of destroying non-alphabetic indigenous writings, replacing them with alphabetic writing and in the process creating the myth of indigenous illiteracy. Thus, colonial agents materially and discursively substituted their notion of writing for analogous indigenous practices and then ascribed to colonized peoples the negation of writing, illiteracy. These processes of conversion and translation, negation and substitution gave particular colonial agents unprecedented control of information on both sides of the Atlantic and thus enormous "authorial" power. In the Americas, indigenous people responded with the counter-production of numerous texts, such as the Popol Vuh and the Books of Chilam Balam, in which the translation from native to alphabetic script was done by and for

indigenous peoples. These texts were sometimes written in Spanish and some-times in alphabetized indigenous languages. Witnessing the pyres of their burning books, native scribes likely deduced that alphabetic writings might be spared where glyphic writing would not; they learned how to code the writing in such a way that it appeared to Europeans as ethnographically valuable material rather than as competing knowledge. Both the Popol Vuh and the Books of the Chilam Balam were "anonymous," collectively written texts. In the opening lines of the Popul Vuh, the anonymous writers claim that they have done a double-take on the Spanish, preserving their own knowledge, "the ancient word" and knowledge that "accounted for everything—and did it, too, as en-lightened beings, in enlightened words," by inscribing and implanting their knowledge in this foreign medium, "amid the preaching of God," amid the reality of military conquest. Contesting the reach of the destruction, they claim the survival of an "original book and ancient writing" that must retreat into hiding in order to survive: Tedlock, *The Popol Vuh*, 71.

44 Cañizares-Esguerra, *How to Write the History of the New World*, 66–67.

45 See Gates, "Introduction," iii. Only fragments of three manuscripts survived. They are named for the three cities in which they are currently housed in mu-seums: Dresden, Madrid, and Paris.

46 Cañizares-Esguerra argues that this represents a sea change from the previous century, when Spanish historians took indigenous historical records seriously as such. For a history of how indigenous records were discredited in part as a process of delegitimizing Spanish scholarship from the period, see Cañizares-Esguerra, *How to Write the History of the New World*, esp. chap. 2.

47 De Las Casas, *In Defense of the Indians*, 30.

48 See Rousseau, *Essay sur l'origine des langues*, 57. Rousseau writes, "Ces Trois maniéres d'écrire répondent assés éxactement aux trois divers états sous lesques on peut considerer les homes rassemblés en nations. La peinture des objects convient aux peuples sauvages; les signes des mots et des propositions aux peuples barbares, et l'alphabet aux peuples policés." Rousseau elaborates these three states immediately preceding the quote. For an English translation of the essay, see Rousseau, "Essay on the Origin of Languages." I have transcribed Rousseau's French-language quote to make it available to the reader. However, I have retained Moran's and Goode's translation because the quote in this particu-lar wording circulates in so much contemporary scholarship on writing.

49 I elaborate on my understanding of the relationship between race, writing, and racialization in Brander Rasmussen, "Attended with Great Inconveniences"; Brander Rasmussen, "Those That Do Violence Must Expect to Suffer." For an overview of American slave codes, see Goodell, *The American Slave Code in Theory and Practice*.

50 John Gonzales suggested this elegant phrasing. I acknowledge this debt with gratitude.

51 Pound, "Hugh Selwyn Mauberley."

52 Bloomfield, *Language*, 283.

53 Gelb, *A Study of Writing*, 12.

54 While Goody, *The Domestication of the Savage Mind*, could be taken as one starting point, Goody and Watt, "The Consequences of Literacy," remains perhaps the most influential (and oft-cited) statement of the ideas of the "literacy thesis." Jack Goody and Ian Watt argue that the emergence of writing in ancient Greece —and, for that matter, in all societies—brought with it cognitive changes that included greater skepticism, the capacity for rational thought, and formal logic. Watt, Goody, and many other early "literacy scholars" modified their ideas in subsequent research. As David Olson notes, the work of the "Toronto School" extends the work of L. Levy-Bruhl, which linked literacy, cognition, and "advanced" cultural and social structures: Olson, *The World on Paper*, 15. The Toronto School generally accounted for these cultural differences in terms of technologies of communication such as print.

55 Todorov, *The Conquest of America*, 81. Asserting that the "three great Amerindian civilizations encountered by the Spaniards are not located on precisely the same level of the *evolution of writing*," Todorov proposes that different gradations in writing technology among the Incas, Mayas, and Aztecs accounted for their varying levels of naiveté—that is, whether and how firmly they believed the Spaniards to be divine. Hence, Todorov postulates relative cognitive differences between Amerindian and European peoples, as well as among the Amerindian groups he discusses, and marshals as evidence the relative presence or absence of writing among different groups. For critiques of Todorov's project, see, e.g., Clendinnen, "Fierce and Unnatural Cruelty"; Greenblatt, *Marvelous Possessions*. Although I have generally used the term "Mexica," I reproduce Todorov's usage of "Aztec" in discussing his work.

56 And it is simply incorrect. Although Diego de Landa boasted that Spanish efforts to supplant indigenous writing were so successful that the Maya people "no longer use any of the characters, especially the young people who have learned ours," James Lockhart has demonstrated how these radically different writing systems continued to coexist in a complementary, overlapping relationship in which alphabetic script replaced not the pictographic but the oral component of indigenous records: de Landa, *Yucatan before and after the Conquest*, 83; Lockhart, *The Nahuas after the Conquest*, 326–73. Lockhart's work provides a model for what a textual study of the reciprocity of colonial encounters might look like in the North, where disparate textual systems also came into contact, at times even on the same page.

57 I am drawing here on Jean-Joseph Goux's work in *Symbolic Economies*. Goux links Marxist and Lacanian theories to explain a general rise in logocentrism that privileged the money form in the economic sphere and the written word in the sphere of signs. What Goux calls the "hegemonic logic of general equivalents" developed on the basis of capitalist modes of production and circulation, and thus structured Western civilization by producing a "dominant symbolic coherence" organized by processes of symbolization, exchange, substitution, and the privileging of universal equivalents in all major spheres of the social: Goux,

Symbolic Economies, 5, 80. This is the context in which the written word emerges as the privileged signifier and general equivalent of sign production. Karl Marx argues that the historical development of the value form originates in the imaginary relationship between two commodities, where one expresses the exchange value of the other. The moment one article of utility becomes an expression or depository of the value of another article of utility, both become commodities. As such, each article acquires a surplus beyond its physical or natural form; this represents the emergence of the value form. In this early, elementary relationship, either commodity can serve as the equivalent form in which the value of the other commodity, the relative form, is expressed. The two commodities are in a specular and mutually exclusive relation in which one commodity expresses its de-materialized value in the body, the matter of the other. For Marx's discussion of value, see Marx, "Capital, Volume One." In economic terms, the historical development toward the money form takes place in the movement from elementary trade relationships, through an extended set of complex relations among numerous commodities such as grain and cloth, to an end stage where one exceptional commodity (e.g., gold) becomes the general equivalent in which the value of all other commodities find expression. This development is one of increasing abstraction, de-materialization, and overvaluation of the equivalent form that in the process monopolizes the representative function—particularly with the gradual abandonment of the gold standard in the first half of the twentieth century. Goux seizes on the parallels of this process to Lacanian psychoanalytic theory, in which a specular relationship with the other becomes the basis for ego-formation: Goux, Symbolic Economies, 13–14. He further argues that a development comparable to that of the money form can be discerned in the history of writing: Goux, Symbolic Economies, 42. Pictography (semasiographic writing) then corresponds to the elementary form of the expression of value. Hieroglyphic writing represents the extended value form because a single figure can serve as the sign for several things, can be multivalent. Syllabic writing (glottographic writing) corresponds to the general equivalent form and alphabetic writing to the money form, the universal equivalent that monopolizes sign production and expresses the value of all other signs: Goux, Symbolic Economies, 42. Although Goux reproduces what I consider a faulty teleology, his work provides a useful analytic framework for understanding how one kind of writing (alphabetic) establishes its normativity through a specular relationship with another kind of writing (pictographic).

58 For Gelb, it is precisely the discussion of writing that is not real that establishes the distinctiveness of "real writing." This process conceptually links the two categories in a system of dependence in which the category "real writing" requires the difference of that which is termed "not real writing" to establish its normativity. A close reading of Gelb's text reveals that specularity and the concept of value are at the crux of the distinction between real and illegitimate writing. "If we believe that the steam engine first started with Watt, then we might also assume that writing began only when men learned to express in

writing notions of linguistic value": Gelb, *A Study of Writing*, 12. The assertion immediately follows that recorded speech is the only writing that "counts." In this key passage, Gelb connects the Industrial Revolution with the operation by which value is expressed in writing. Gelb's definition of writing proceeds in two stages. First, he defines writing as "a system of human intercommunication by means of conventional visible marks," a definition that is not yet organized by a hierarchy of value and is quite broad in scope. However, he then immediately cautions that "what the primitives understood as writing is not the same thing as what we do." The awkward grammar and sentence structure that contrasts the other's understanding (definition) to "our" doing (operationalization) merits close attention. As Gelb has inadvertently argued, the so-called primitives' understanding of writing as a system of human intercommunication is not different in definition from his own understanding of writing—it is "what we do" when we "express in writing notions of linguistic value" that sets apart phonetic writing from all other writing now defined as "not real writing." This is the second, and key, part of his definition of writing that "counts." For Gelb, real writing is distinguished from all other writing, not by its distinctiveness as a system of graphic communication, but by its status as the bearer of value, the standard against which all other semiotic systems are measured. For Gelb, alphabetic writing is superior to other kinds of writing because it is more economic, rapid, and efficient. This preference reflects the logic of capitalism, an economic and social system that emerged concomitantly with colonialism during the same period in which alphabetic writing became a dominant mode of communication and a privileged site for the production of meaning.

59 Houston, "Literacy among the Pre-Columbian Maya."

60 For an introduction to new literacy studies, see Street, "What's 'New' in New Literacy Studies?." I am grateful to Deborah Brandt for bringing this body of scholarship to my attention.

61 Particularly influential for my thinking have been Aveni, "Non-Western Notational Frameworks and the Role of Anthropology in Our Understandings of Literacy; Schousboe and Larsen, *Literacy and Society*, esp. Maurice Bloch, "Literacy and Enlightenment," 15–37, and Michael Harbsmeier, "Writing and the Other: Travellers' Literacy, or Towards an Archaeology of Orality," 197–228.

62 Elizabeth Hill Boone offers a broad definition of writing based on Sampson. Writing, she argues, is "the communication of relatively specific ideas in a conventional manner by means of permanent visible marks" (*Writing Without Words*, 15). I have abandoned Hill Boone and Sampson's requirement that marks be permanent in order to "count," because some writing can fade (i.e., ink) or be erased (i.e., pencil). My definition also accounts for writing systems that are tactile, rather than visual, such as Braille and quipus.

63 In addition to wanting to retain the possibility of reclaiming the term against its history of delegitimization, I also believe the term is helpful for the ways in which it permits us to trouble the distinction between phonographic and semasiographic writing. Not only can "pictographs" be phonographic, but phono-

graphic writing like alphabetic words can function as pictographs, as "images" that are read logographically—an argument I elaborate in chapter 2. Finally, the current use of pictographic symbols like hearts suggest we still have more to learn about how human beings use graphic forms of communication. What is the difference between writing "I love you" and "I ♥ you"? And why would contemporary people use the phrase "I heart you," which employs a slippage between those two constructions in order to say what the phrase "I love you" seemingly communicated just fine? Such questions point to how much we still have to learn about pictographs, their use, their appeal, and their relationship to communication and to other forms of writing, including phonetic scripts.

64 Hill Boone, *Writing Without Words*, 16.

65 On the relationship between Mixtec language and script, see Smith. On Aztec and Mixtec written historical narratives, see Hill Boone, *Stories in Red and Black*. Although I have generally used the term "Mexica," I reproduce Hill Boone's usage of Aztec in my discussion of her work.

66 Hill Boone, "Introduction," 20.

67 Hans Jensen points to this flexibility as one reason that some indigenous writing systems were considered inadequate by agents of colonization. Noting that ideography already existed among the Inuit, this script was found by missionaries to be "inadequate for setting down say, Bible stories, prayers and so forth" because of its relative flexibility: Jensen, *Sign, Symbol, and Script*, 247. Missionaries could not accept such a flexible type of writing for Bible stories when issues of interpretation had proved powerful enough to split Christianity into multiple interpretive communities. Thus, the inadequacy of Inuit writing was that it did not transmit the colonizing culture or allow for tight control of interpretation. Of course, that does not mean it was not an effective kind of writing for the Inuit. They seem to have used writing primarily to leave notices at their dwellings when away on hunts, to inform potential visitors of their whereabouts, and to keep records of hunts: Mallery, *Picture-Writing of the American Indians*, 351–52, 581–82.

68 Often these scripts function in conjunction with an oral performance or exegesis. James Lockhart argues that it was this oral performance, rather than glyphic writing, that alphabetic script replaced in central Mexico in the centuries following the arrival of the Spanish: Lockhart, *The Nahuas after the Conquest*, 335. On the North American Plains, oral performances were also linked to graphic accounts. White Bull's manuscript, which combines pictographic elements and syllabic script, might represent a North American example comparable to Lockhart's discussion. We might, then, see the pictographic elements as rooted in a pictographic script convention and the syllabic elements on the page as standing in for the now absent oral performance. The White Bull manuscript resides at the Chester Fritz Library, University of North Dakota, Grand Forks, Orin G. Libby, no. 183. For an accessible, published version, see Howard, *Lakota Warrior*.

69 Mallery, *Picture-Writing of the American Indians*, 201. Others, including Daniel Brin-

ton, had documented similar forms of writing along the eastern seaboard as far south as Florida and as far west as the Osage.

70 Nicolar, *The Life and Traditions of the Red Man*, 198–99.

71 See Mallery, *Picture-Writing of the American Indians*, 637–48, for discussion of the relationship between selected pictographs and gesture signs. See also Mallery, *Introduction to the Study of Sign Language among the North American Indians as Illustrating the Gesture Speech of Mankind*.

72 Mallery, *Picture-Writing of the American Indians*, 694.

73 This point is underscored by the case of Ojibwe writing, which consisted of two distinct forms. In addition to profane writing on birch bark, called *kekewin*, sacred priest societies such as the Midé used a different kind of writing called *kekinowin*. The latter form of writing recorded idea complexes in the manner of pictography proper. However, the Midé scripts were also a record of speech, in the form of ancient words and verse, in a way that seems to be more phonetic and thus hieroglyphic. No accurate scholarship on this phenomenon exists; nor is it likely to become available, as the Midé records are sacred and kept secret. However, it is worth noting that current scholarship on writing provides few tools to understand scripts that combine phoneticism, mnemonics, and pictography—indeed, these three terms are usually considered distinct and mutually exclusive. Such examples suggest the complexity of indigenous forms of writing in North America and how much we might yet learn about writing by taking seriously these understudied forms.

74 See Jennings et al., "Glossary of Figures of Speech in Iroquois Political Rhetoric."

75 Lafitau, *Customs of the American Indians Compared with the Customs of Primitive Time*, 298.

76 Brinton, "On an 'Inscribed Tablet' from Long Island," 203.

77 Pictographic writing is often contrasted with alphabetic writing, which communicates more specific meaning by combining graphic signs that refer to infinitely small subdivisions of the spoken language. Yet this distinction turns out to be limiting, because pictographic and alphabetic writing are also similar in a number of ways. Both function connotatively, and both use images (literal and figurative) to communicate meaning. Certainly, alphabetic letters can also be combined to make poetry that is rich, economical, and metaphorical. Even alphabetic prose can be highly ambiguous and invite such a multitude of interpretations that literary scholars can ponder them for centuries. On the other hand, pictography can also be entirely devoid of poetry, its imagery strictly utilitarian, as evident in various examples of "instruction" manuals that accompany products sold globally.

78 Lafitau, *Customs of the American Indians Compared with the Customs of Primitive Time*, 114–15 (195–96 in Lafitau, *Moeurs des sauvages*).

79 Marianne Mithun, "Overview of General Characteristics," in Sturtevant, *Handbook of North American Indians*, 17:141, 17:138, cited in Gray and Fiering, *The Language Encounter in the Americas, 1492–1800*, 3.

80 Unfortunately, no sustained studies of a possible relationship between North American Native American languages and writing systems comparable to those done on Mesoamerica exist. Writing specialists such as Gelb and DeFrancis who discuss "Amerindian pictographs" do so without any knowledge of the region's languages. This is unfortunate, not only because it creates the tautology whereby scholars like DeFrancis conclude that such pictography is not phonetic, and therefore not writing, but also because it leaves us without the valuable insights such studies might provide. The relevance of such studies can be deduced from Brinton, "On an 'Inscribed Tablet' from Long Island"; Lafitau, *Moeurs des Sauvages*; and Mallery, *Picture-Writing of the American Indians*, among others.

81 Extant winter counts are rare. The Smithsonian houses those made by Lone Dog, American Horse, The Flame, The Swan, Battiste Good, and Cloud Shield, cited by Mallery, along with a few others. Examples can now be viewed on the Internet at http://wintercounts.si.edu/html_version/html/thewintercounts .html. Published examples of Plains pictography, such as Amos Bad Heart Bull's *A Pictographic History of the Oglala Sioux*, usually hail from the nineteenth century and were produced under rather different circumstances by imprisoned authors responding to requests by white interlocutors. They are generally known as "ledger art" or "Plains Indian sketchbooks": see Dunn, 1877; Earenfight, *A Kiowa's Odyssey*; Peterson, *A Cheyenne Warrior's Graphic Interpretation of His People*; and Peterson, *Plains Indian Art from Fort Marion*, as well as Bad Heart Bull, *A Pictographic History of the Oglala Sioux*, and White Bull's manuscript. For discussions of ledger art and other Plains pictography, see, e.g., Wong, *Sending My Heart Back across the Years*; Dunn, 1878, introduction; O'Brien, *Plains Indian Autobiographies*; Ewers, "Introduction"; Sandoz, "Introduction."

82 In addition to winter counts, tipis and buffalo robes became predominant media on which communities and individuals recorded battles and other events with pictographs: see Ewers, *Murals in the Round*; Wildschut, "A Crow Pictographic Robe"; Wong, *Sending My Heart Back across the Years*. Records of individual achievements came to be known as "bragging skins," while communal histories were called winter counts because years were measured from one winter to the next.

83 One winter count, the Brulé Lakota Battiste Good, begins in the year A.D. 900 but appears to have been retroactively produced by consulting elders: see Mallery, *Picture-Writing of the American Indians*, 268–69.

84 Ibid., 590, 592.

85 Similarly, the graphic sign "9/11" represents a specific date using conventionalized marks (numbers and a slash) while simultaneously marking a complex of experience, meaning, and collective memory in excess of what the signs themselves represent when divorced from cultural context. In order to decipher and interpret correctly the meaning of "9/11," one must possess numerical, cultural, and historical knowledge of the context in which these graphic signs mark, communicate, and interpret human experience with great economy. In

the United States, the destruction of the World Trade Center in New York City on September 11, 2001, marks a watershed in a nation's collective identity and destiny. Conversely, September 11 also marks a key moment in Chilean history and experience as the date in 1973 on which Salvador Allende's democratically elected government was overthrown by Augusto Pinochet's army. If we were to imagine Chilean and U.S. winter counts, 9/11 might be the composite graphic marks signifying 1973 and 2001, respectively.

86 See Mallery, *Picture-Writing of the American Indians*, 271.

87 See ibid., 266.

88 Sayre, *Les Sauvages Américains*, 195–97.

89 Mallery, *Picture-Writing of the American Indians*, 558; Sayre, *Les Sauvages Américains*, 195–98.

90 Sayre, *Les Sauvages Américains*, 197.

91 Longfellow, *The Song of Hiawatha*.

92 See Lockard, "The Universal Hiawatha"; McNally, "The Indian Passion Play"; Trachtenburg, "Singing Hiawatha." Translation testifies to and enables international reception. However, it also targeted domestic immigration populations in the United States.

93 Despite the structural similarities, Waino Nyland argues, the *Kalevala* could not have served as a source for Longfellow: Nyland, "Kalevala as a Reputed Source of Longfellow's *Song of Hiawatha*." In the notes following *The Song of Hiawatha*, Longfellow specifically names Schoolcraft as his source, particularly "*Algic Researches*, Vol. I. p. 134," as well as "*History, Condition, and Prospects of the Indian Tribes of the United States*, Part III. p. 314": as cited in Longfellow, *The Song of Hiawatha*, 299. For these sources in more recent editions, see Schoolcraft, *The American Indians*; Williams, *Schoolcraft's Indian Legends from Algic Researches, the Myth of Hiawatha, Oneónta, the Red Race in America, and Historical and Statistical Information Respecting . . . the Indian Tribes of the United States*.

94 Longfellow, *The Song of Hiawatha*, 299.

95 Ibid., 294.

96 Copway, *The Traditional History and Characteristic Sketches of the Ojibway Nation*.

97 Longfellow, *The Song of Hiawatha*, 197.

98 Schoolcraft, *The American Indians*, 293.

99 Ibid.

100 Copway, *The Traditional History and Characteristic Sketches of the Ojibway Nation*, 134–35.

101 Longfellow, *The Song of Hiawatha*, 190.

102 This intertextual relationship is also noted in Bellin, *The Demon of the Continent*, 180.

103 Williams, *Schoolcraft's Indian Legends from Algic Researches, the Myth of Hiawatha, Oneónta, the Red Race in America, and Historical and Statistical Information Respecting . . . the Indian Tribes of the United States*, xix.

104 Copway, *The Traditional History and Characteristic Sketches of the Ojibway Nation*, 127–34.

105 Longfellow, *The Song of Hiawatha*, 189.
106 Cowan, "Objibwe Vocabulary in Longfellow's *Hiawatha*." For an analysis of how U.S. national culture has constructed itself through appropriations of indigeneity, see Deloria, *Playing Indian*.
107 Numerous scholars have commented on this dynamic in U.S. cultural history: see, e.g., Romero, "Vanishing Americans." For a discussion of this dynamic that centers specifically on Longfellow and Copway, see Bellin, *The Demon of the Continent*, 171–82.
108 We see this dynamic in the nation's literature and in scholarship on writing such as Taylor's. In Longfellow's poem, the two intersect.
109 See also Jackson, "Longfellow's Tradition."
110 Copway, *The Traditional History and Characteristic Sketches of the Ojibway Nation*, 130–31.
111 See the publisher's preface in Bad Heart Bull, *A Pictographic History of the Oglala Sioux*, vii; Wong, *Sending My Heart Back across the Years*, 77. Wong notes that, while indigenous Plains records were often buried with their owners, according to custom, many others may have been destroyed during conflict with the U.S. military that burned twenty Cheyenne villages to the ground in just nine years, between 1865 and 1875.
112 Artists at Fort Marion produced their work specifically for a white audience, as prisoners of war. This context brought about significant changes in the form, such as a move away from older pictographic forms and media toward a freer artistic expression we might call "narrative images" using paper and ink. We also see a new combination of narrative images and syllabic writing in many of the Fort Marion "sketchbooks."
113 Pokagan's work has not attained great standing in American and Native American literary studies thus far. Some critics have questioned his ability to write; others have dismissed him (unfairly, I believe) as "the white man's kind of Indian." Pokagan's use of birch bark can be read as a subversive, critically overlooked move to disrupt the settler culture's possessive identification with literacy. Original copies of several of Pokagan's publications are available for examination at the Beinecke Rare Book and Manuscript Library, Yale University, New Haven. For the only recent, full republication of *The Red Man's Rebuke*, see Walker, *Indian Nation*, 211–20. See also Berliner, "Written in the Birch Bark," for a recent discussion of Pokagan's work, changing assessments of his standing as a writer, and the materiality of the booklet.

TWO Negotiating Literacies

1 This retelling is based on Thwaites, *The Jesuit Relations and Allied Documents*, 27:246–304. The translations are mine, unless noted otherwise. I have generally retained Vimont's terminology and only modernized slightly, noting a few instances where current usage varies enough to potentially cause confusion. *The Jesuit Relations* were first launched by Paul Le Jeune, who was the superior of the

Jesuit missions in New France in 1632. Apart from the *Relation* of 1637, they were published in Paris by Sébastien Cramoisy annually for forty years. Around the turn of the twentieth century, Reuben Gold Thwaites compiled the *Relations* and numerous related documents and published them alongside English translations in a seventy-three-volume set. Hereafter, this volume will be cited parenthetically in the text as *Jesuit Relations*. I have also consulted a number of other sources, most importantly Dennis, *Cultivating a Landscape of Peace*; Marshall, *Word from New France*, 135–55; Richter, *The Ordeal of the Longhouse*; Warkentin, "In Search of 'The Word of the Other,' " 1–27; Williams, *Linking Arms Together*.

2 Trois Rivières was located halfway between Quebec and Montreal. By 1663, there were roughly three thousand French colonists in the area. Quebec accounted for about 65 percent of the total population; Montreal, 20 percent; and Trois Rivières, 15 percent: see Dennis, *Cultivating a Landscape of Peace*, 193; Williams, *Linking Arms Together*, 149.

3 For a history of these complicated interactions, alliances, and wars, see White, *The Middle Ground*. On diplomatic protocol in the Northeastern Woodlands, see Williams, *Linking Arms Together*. On treaty protocol in Pennsylvania in the seventeenth century and eighteenth century, see Merrell, *Into the American Woods*. For a study of a treaty encounter of 1679 that also addresses how to read treaty negotiations cross-culturally, see Richter, *Facing East from Indian Country*, 129–50. For an analysis of the important Lancaster Treaty of 1744, which emphasizes both comparative and cross-cultural issues at play in treaty negotiations while taking account of performance, orality, and print, see Gustafson, *Eloquence Is Power*, 111–39. See also Brown and Vibert, *Reading beyond Words*; Clements, *Native American Verbal Art*, esp. chap. 3.

4 Guillaume Cousture was taken captive in 1642 along with the Jesuit priest Father Isaac le Jogues: see Jogues, *Novum Belgium in American Captivity Narratives*, 95–121. Considered extremely brave, Cousture had been adopted by his Mohawk captors and returned "clothed like a savage," in the words of Marie de l'Incarnation, as cited by Warkentin, "In Search of 'The Word of the Other.' " The other passengers in the canoe included an Haudenosaunee captive recently released by the French and two diplomatic emissaries, one of whom was the renowned diplomat Kiotseaeton.

5 He is described in this way by the Ursuline nun Marie Guyart, Mère Marie de l'Incarnation, in a letter to her son: see Marshall, *Word from New France*, 149. However, it is not clear that she was present at the event. Instead, she may have heard secondhand accounts and seen Vimont's *Relations*, as Warkentin argues.

6 Contradictory statements appear throughout the *Jesuit Relations* regarding whether indigenous people in the Northeast had writing. Many Jesuits noted the proclivity of native students to use pictography and hieroglyphics to "take notes" on missionary teachings. Father Sébastien Râle compares Northeastern pictographs to "our letters" (*Jesuit Relations*, 67:226), noting that a message written by one Abenaki was later read and understood by another, separate group. In an earlier *Relation*, Râle compares wampum to alphabetic script, contrasting the "false writ-

ing of men" in wampum with the "true writing of God" in the Bible but represents both wampum and the Bible as records of words, as writing (*Jesuit Relations*, 15:121). Other Jesuits, such as Father Bressani, write that "they have neither books, nor any writing" (*Jesuit Relations*, 39:149). James Axtell has argued that the success of the Jesuits vis-à-vis Protestant missionaries lay in their adept use of writing among native people "dazzled by the power of print": see Axtell, "The Power of Print in the Eastern Woodlands," 300–309. For a critique of this perspective, see Wogan, "Perceptions of European Literacy in Early Contact Situations," 407–29. English and Dutch sources also represented wampum and writing (particularly written contracts) as equivalent or analogous. For example, a British officer in 1765 characterized wampum as a "kind of record or history": see Stearns, "Ethno-conchology," as cited in Ceci, "The Value of Wampum among the New York Iroquois," 97–107. The Dutch also recorded diplomatic encounters involving wampum: see, e.g., Pearson, *Early Record of the City and County of Albany and Rensealaerswyck*, 1:237, as cited in Dennis, *Cultivating a Landscape of Peace*, 167. More recently, Lois Scozzari has noted that "an integral and intriguing aspect of wampum's use was the sending and receiving of wampum as means of communication . . . designs woven into belts with contrasting color beads, recorded treaties, agreements, important events, and public accounts": Scozzari, "The Significance of Wampum to Seventeenth Century Indians in New England," 61.

7 This is the term that will be used from hereon. For an overview of the formation of the Haudenosaunee League of Nations, see Dennis, *Cultivating a Landscape of Peace*; Fenton, *The Great Law and the Longhouse*; Richter, *The Ordeal of the Longhouse*. On wampum, see Beauchamp, "Wampum and Shell Articles Used by the New York Indians," 166–429; Ceci, "The Value of Wampum among the New York Iroquois," 97–107; Druke, "Iroquois Treaties"; Fenton, *The Great Law and the Longhouse*, esp. chap. 16; Foster, "Another Look at the Function of Wampum in Iroquois–White Councils"; Jennings, *The History and Culture of Iroquois Diplomacy*; Mann, "The Fire at Onondaga"; Martien, *Shell Game*; Revard, "Beads, Wampum, Money, Words, and Old English Riddles"; Slotkin and Schmitt, "Studies in Wampum"; Bruce Trigger, ed., *Handbook of North American Indians*, Vol. 15: *Northeast*; Williams, *Linking Arms Together*.

8 For a concise overview of the desperate situation of the French in general, the Jesuits in particular, and, for that matter, the Huron, who had been devastated by the Haudenosaunee and by disease, see Moore, *Indian and Jesuit*, 1–39.

9 The Haudenosaunee named the French governor Onontio, not as an individual name but as a title for the permanent post. This exemplifies not only the process of mutual renaming, but also the attempt by the Haudenosaunee to locate rotating European "chiefs" within the logic of their own social structure. Native people also renamed each of the major Jesuit missionaries. For example, the Huron called Jérôme Lalemant Achiendassé; Jean de Brébeuf Echon; and Isaac le Joques, Ondessone: see ibid., 68.

10 Williams, *Linking Arms Together*, 51. Williams is citing Cover, "Nomos and Narrative." Mary Louise Pratt coined the term "contact zone" as a space of colonial

encounters marked by coercion, inequality, and conflict. While this is a textual contact zone, is it not (yet) one of coercion and radical inequality. The French are not militarily, demographically, or semiotically dominant in this encounter: Pratt, *Imperial Eyes*, 6–7. I find more appropriate here Myra Jehlen's term "undetermined encounter," which refers to those periods of contingency before one party establishes hegemony, in distinction to the over-determined narrative of conquest: see Jehlen, "Papers of Empire," 57.

11 Barthélemy Vimont worked in the North American missions from 1629 until his return to France in 1659. He was not a major historical figure or *Jesuit Relations* writer like Le Jeune, le Joques, and Lalemant. Vimont wrote the *Relation of 1644* only because his successor, Jérôme Lalemant, had not arrived yet to perform the task. Lalemant was the superior at the Huron mission between 1638 and 1645 (JR, 27:14). In a comparative study of Jesuit writings in North America and Asia, Takao Abé refutes the commonly held notion that the personality of the individual Jesuit writer significantly influenced the content of a given section of the *Jesuit Relations*. In fact, Abé argues that a remarkably consistent pattern characterized the *Jesuit Relations* in both North America and Japan: Abé, "What Determined the Content of Missionary Reports?." This chapter argues that the engagement with Haudenosaunee textuality does make Vimont's account unique.

12 Daniel K. Richter discusses a slightly later record of negotiations between the Mohawk and the English at the famous council at Albany in 1679: Richter, *Facing East from Indian Country*, 129–50. Richter's reading, like mine, takes into account the bicultural nature of diplomatic negotiations: however, Richter, like many other scholars, considers wampum a mnemonic device, not a textual system: ibid., 137.

13 Canassatego, June 26, 1744, Town of Lancaster, quoted in Colden, *The History of the Five Indian Nations of Canada*, 1:120. The occasion for Canassatego's speech was a treaty negotiation between the Six Nations and British colonial administrators. This speech is now included in Mulford et al., *Early American Writings*, 1114.

14 Wampum had other functions, such as bodily ornament, diplomatic gift, medium of exchange, and ritual form of expression, as exemplified in the Haudenosaunee Condolence Ritual.

15 Murray, *Forked Tongues*, 34–38. See also Greenblatt, *Marvelous Possessions*.

16 As Alyssa Mt. Pleasant has noted, alphabetic hegemony is never complete, as wampum retains documentary authority within Haudenosaunee society to the present date. Hence, this kind of analysis need not be limited to the early period: Alyssa Mt. Pleasant, personal conversation with the author, March 6, 2009.

17 I am aware of Ferdinand de Saussure's work on "*paroles* (words)," which he defines as "utterances" and distinguishes from "*langue*," or language: see Bally et al., *Cours de linguistique générale*. However, I have translated "*paroles*" as "words" in accordance with colloquial usage and various dictionaries I consulted (see also JR, 27:314, n. 24).

18 Jehlen, "Papers of Empire," 44.

19 Bakhtin, *The Dialogic Imagination*, 427.

20 While wampum did operate as a medium of exchange among Woodland Indians and European traders, its main functions to native people were never "monetary": Coles, "Wampum Was More than Money"; Fadden, "Beaded History," 4:3, 17–20; Mann, "The Fire at Onondaga"; Slotkin and Schmitt, "Studies in Wampum"; Wilcox, "The Manufacture and Use of Wampum in the Northeast." U. Vincent Wilcox writes, "Wampum did become, strangely enough, true currency among the white colonists," but adds, "In spite of the pressures of this new economic network introduced by the white man, the wampum bead never truly functioned as a monetary unit within Indian society. . . . The monetary connotation which wampum acquired was purely a function of the white economy": Wilcox, "The Manufacture and Use of Wampum in the Northeast," 298–99. For a discussion of gift economies (in distinction to money economies), see Mauss, *The Gift*.

21 William B. Weeden called wampum "the magnet which drew the beaver out of the interior forests": *Indian Money as a Factor in New England Civilization*, 15, as cited in Sturtevant, *Handbook of North American Indians*, 15:422. Europeans quickly moved to control the production of wampum and even used such control over the medium in their struggles with other colonial powers: Ceci, "The First Fiscal Crisis in New York," 97–106. Among colonists, wampum fulfilled the role of currency at a time when a stable medium of exchange was lacking. Massachusetts passed laws to regulate and standardize trade with the beads, and as late as 1693 people could pay their fare for the Brooklyn-Connecticut ferry with either silver coin or wampum. However, by the 1660s, silver coins had become the dominant currency among colonists: Scozzari, "The Significance of Wampum to Seventeenth Century Indians in New England," 65.

22 Mann, "The Fire at Onondaga," 44–47.

23 "Wampum is regarded as a kind of recording device, somewhat in the way we conceive of the function of a tape recorder": Foster, "Another Look at the Function of Wampum in Iroquois-White Councils," 105.

24 Ibid., 104.

25 Wilcox, "The Manufacture and Use of Wampum in the Northeast," 297; emphasis added.

26 Druke, "Iroquois Treaties," 92.

27 Foster, "Another Look at the Function of Wampum in Iroquois-White Councils," 101. Richter makes a similar point when he suggests that the use of the term "always" at the Albany council in 1679 referred to the future rather than the past: Richter, *Facing East from Indian Country*, 145.

28 Dennis, *Cultivating a Landscape of Peace*, 77.

29 This overview is based on Dennis, *Cultivating a Landscape of Peace*; Hale, *The Iroquois Book of Rites*; Hewitt, "The Requickening Address of the Iroquois Condolence Council"; Arthur C. Parker, "The Constitution of the Five Nations," in Parker, *Parker on the Iroquois*, 7–155; Richter, *The Ordeal of the Longhouse*; Wallace, *White Roots of Peace*. For a description and analysis of different versions of the

epic, see William N. Fenton's introduction to Parker, *Parker on the Iroquois*. Thomas E. Sanders and Walter W. Peek also discuss how the story has circulated and been codified in Sanders and Peek, *Literature of the American Indian*. See also Bierhorst, *Four Masterworks of American Indian Literature*.

30 According to Richter, "native traditions and scholarly interpretations point to various eras between A.D. 1400 and A.D. 1600 as the date of the League's founding": Richter, "Ordeals of the Longhouse," 16. Mann and others cite 1451 as a compelling date because "the Great Law tradition mentions a solar eclipse happened while the Peacemaker was lobbying for ratification of the New Constitution. A solar eclipse did indeed occur in Haudenosaunee New York in the year 1451": Mann, "The Fire at Onondaga," 46.

31 This figure is not Henry Wadsworth Longfellow's Hiawatha, a fictional character that conflated a number of sources and narratives, native and European, and bears no relationship to the historical figure I discuss.

32 Cited in Richter, *The Ordeal of the Longhouse*, 32, who in turns quotes Wallace, *White Roots of Peace*, 18.

33 The wampum record of the founding of the Haudenosaunee League is known as the Hiawatha Belt, and the wampum record of the league's constitution is called the Wing or Dust Fan Belt.

34 For a glossary of key metaphors in Haudenosaunee political rhetoric, see Jennings et al., "Glossary of Figures of Speech in Iroquois Political Rhetoric," 115–24.

35 This understanding relies on Richter, *The Ordeal of the Longhouse*; Dennis, *Cultivating a Landscape of Peace*. However, Mann argues that "the Peacemaker" and Hiawatha adapted an ancient condolence ceremony already in place: Mann, "The Fire at Onondaga," 45.

36 Hewitt, "The Requickening Address of the Iroquois Condolence Council," 66.

37 Bierhorst, *Four Masterworks of American Indian Literature*, 12.

38 My description of the ceremony is indebted primarily to the collaboration in 1944 between Chief John Arthur Gibson, a principal speaker for the Onondaga at their ceremonies, and J.N.B. Hewitt. Gibson dictated in Onondaga to Hewitt, who recorded it alphabetically and translated it into English. The text was later revised slightly with the aid of two other federal chiefs: see Hewitt, "The Requickening Address of the Iroquois Condolence Council," 68.

39 Foster, "Another Look at the Function of Wampum in Iroquois-White Councils," 106.

40 Ibid., 104.

41 Ibid., 106.

42 Williams, *Linking Arms Together*, 74.

43 The contemporary indigenous writer and activist Taiaiake Alfred also invokes the power of the condolence ceremony as "an expression of the transformative power inherent in many healing traditions" and the appropriate "metaphorical framework for my own thoughts on the state of Native America and the crucial role of indigenous traditions in alleviating the grief and discontent that permeate our existence": Alfred, *Peace Power Righteousness*, xi.

44 Williams, *Linking Arms Together*, 54.

45 Richter, *The Ordeal of the Longhouse*, 41.

46 Sullivan and Flick, *The Papers of Sir William Johnson*, 9:604, cited in Druke, "Iroquois Treaties," 89.

47 The French word is "*disoit*"; emphasis added.

48 Current usage is "*étroitement.*"

49 Current usage is "*noeud.*" Interestingly, it also has the connotation of "junction" or "crossroad."

50 *Oxford English Dictionary*, online ed., available at http://dictionary.oed.com.

51 Similarly, users of alphabetic script might conceive of some texts as being particularly forceful and enduring because of the beauty of the prose.

52 Joseph-François Lafitau comments on the public role of orators, the qualities that made great orature ("a great capacity, the knowledge of councils, a complete knowledge of all their ancestors' ways, wit, experience and eloquence. . . . They have, withal, a capacity for mimicry; they speak with gestures as much as the voice"), and the social status accorded great orators, particularly among the Haudenosaunee: Lafitau, *Customs of the American Indians Compared with the Customs of Primitive Times*, 297–98.

53 Williams, *Linking Arms Together*, 53, 83.

54 Michael K. Foster recounts a number of instances in which Haudenosaunee representatives protested military conscription in Ottawa during the First World War and appeared in Geneva in 1923–24 to argue before the League of Nations. In 1981, a belt was read before the Canadian governor, and as late as 1988 an Haudenosaunee diplomat presented a wampum belt at the United Nations: Foster, "Another Look at the Function of Wampum in Iroquois-White Councils," 112; Williams, *Linking Arms Together*, 4. See also George-Kanentiio, "Iroquois at the U.N."; McLellan, "Indian Magna Carta Writ in Wampum Belts."

55 The Two Row Wampum Belt, along with the text it records and some background information, can be viewed online at http://www.ganienkeh.net/2row.html (accessed 9/29/2004).

56 The original source cited is Huron Miller, trans., *Turtle* (Native American Center for the Living Arts newspaper, Winter 1980. This rendition of the text is available online at http://www.ganienkeh.net/2row.html (accessed 9/29/2004).

57 Druke, "Iroquois Treaties," 89.

58 Ibid. See also Foster, "Another Look at the Function of Wampum in Iroquois-White Councils," 109.

59 Druke, "Iroquois Treaties," 90. According to Barbara A. Mann, "wampum literacy"—the ability to read wampum in a way more literal than I have suggested— was widespread in the Haudenosaunee community. She claims such literacy only declined as a result of European presence, the "impounding" of wampum by museums, and so on. Indeed, Mann calls wampum illiteracy a twentieth-century phenomenon: Mann, "The Fire at Onondaga," 47. I am not able to evaluate this claim.

60 See, e.g., Mallery, *Picture-Writing of the American Indians*, 256–57.

61 Beauchamp, "Wampum and Shell Articles Used by the New York Indians," 388–89.

62 Goody, *The Interface between the Written and the Oral*, 17, as cited in Murray, *Forked Tongues*, 25.

63 David R. Olson argues that the line between mnemonic devices and writing systems is not "technically defensible": Olson, *The World on Paper*, 99.

64 Murray, *Forked Tongues*, 25.

65 Carruthers, *The Book of Memory*.

66 Interestingly, wampum can be considered "citable" in the sense that a term such as "Two Row" can be used to cite a particular belt and its contents: Alyssa Mt. Pleasant, personal conversation with the author, March 6, 2009.

67 "Journal of the Rev. Samuel Kirkland, November 1764–June 1765," ms., 38, Kirkland Papers, Burke Library, Hamilton College, Clinton, N.Y., cited in Druke, "Iroquois Treaties," 91.

68 For a history of how the written word came to supersede oral testimony in European jurisprudence, see Clanchy, *From Memory to Written Record*.

69 Colden, *The History of the Five Indian Nations*, 141. For a brief, insightful analysis of this particular passage in Canassatego's speech, see Gustafson, *Eloquence Is Power*, 131–32. Sandra M. Gustafson notes that this is a moment in which Canassatego simultaneously contests the superiority of alphabetic script and represents it as a medium that "blocked rather than fostered understanding between the Iroquois and the English": Gustafson, *Eloquence Is Power*, 132.

70 Fifty treaties were published by printers on speculation, and the Lancaster Treaty of 1744 was published repeatedly. Benjamin Franklin printed two hundred extra copies for sale in England, and William Parks of Williamsburg, Virginia, reprinted it with a contemporary account of the Indian ceremony which organized the treaty proceedings: see Gustafson, *Eloquence Is Power*, 119–22; Wroth, "The Indian Treaty as Literature," 750.

71 See Franklin, *Indian Treaties*.

72 Early examples of attempts to read treaties as American literature include Drummond and Moody, "Indian Treaties"; Van Doren, "Introduction"; Wroth. "The Indian Treaty as Literature." For a more recent, literary analysis of early American treaty negotiations, see Gustafson, *Eloquence Is Power*, 111–39. For a comparative, transnational approach to treaties as literature, see Allen, "Postcolonial Theory and the Discourse of Treaties." For an analysis of the relationship between treaties and later Native American literature, see Konkle, *Writing Indian Nations*.

73 Salisbury, *The Sovereignty and Goodness of God*, introduction. Mary Rowlandson was the most famous among many captives in the war between New England settlers and native people. Usually known as King Philip's (or Metacom's) War, for the Wampanoag leader, the war lasted little more than a year, starting in 1675, but cost the lives of Native people and settlers, roughly half of the population on both sides. Thus, it was an incredibly bloody and traumatic period that left many survivors orphaned, widowed, wounded, or facing life as impover-

ished refuges, exiles, or even slaves (in the case of native people who were placed in local servitude or sent to the Caribbean and Bermuda). Rowlandson's captivity lasted three months. Her narrative was first published in 1682; it was immediately a "bestseller" and went through numerous subsequent editions.

74 Ibid., 103. Perhaps Rowlandson's portrayal of wampum as mere finery functions, as Tiffany Potter argues, to represent her captors in terms of European aristocratic fashions abhorred by the Puritans: Potter, "Writing Indigenous Femininity," 153–67. Notably, the two instances in which Rowlandson describes Weetamoo in terms of her finery appear at moments that reveal Weetamoo's status as a war leader participating in planning councils and ceremonies. Potter discusses Rowlandson's representation of Weetamoo's production and use of wampum but links neither wampum nor "condole" to the context I discuss here.

75 Salisbury, *The Sovereignty and Goodness of God*, 103.

76 See Jennings et al., *History and Culture of Iroquois Diplomacy*, 119. The willingness of Rowlandson's captors to share food exemplifies "eating out of the same kettle" as a metaphor of shared circumstances and community. Indeed, much of Rowlandson's suffering comes from her sharing the desperate straits of her captors as they battle hunger and cold. Although Rowlandson accepts the food, she rejects any sense of shared circumstances and community, as is evident in her refusal to "condole" with Weetamoo when Weetamoo mourns her lost child. A kettle is centrally placed during the ceremony, which takes place the night before Rowlandson is ransomed, although its significance is not elaborated by Rowlandson's text.

77 The anonymous editor is generally taken to be Increase Mather, who was the author of several tracts on the region's political history.

78 Salisbury, *The Sovereignty and Goodness of God*, 12.

79 Ibid., 91.

80 Rowlandson's captors were Nipmunks, Narragansetts, and Wampanoags. Wampum figured prominently in diplomacy across much of the colonial world in the Northeast in the seventeenth century and eighteenth: see Williams, *Linking Arms Together*, 51. See also Speck, "Functions of Wampum among the Eastern Algonkian."

81 Dorsey, "Going to School with Savages," 413.

82 Jehlen, "Papers of Empire," 37–40.

THREE Writing in the Conflict Zone

The original title of the manuscript is *El primer nueva corónica y buen gobierno por Don Phelipe Guaman Poma de Aiala*. We do not know exactly when Guaman Poma completed the final, clean draft of the manuscript. While he sent a letter to King Philip III announcing its completion in 1615, the date on the prefatory letter in the manuscript is January 1, 1613. Numerous contemporary editions are available. I have found particularly useful Murra and Adorno, *El primer nueva corónica y buen gobierno por Felipe Guaman Poma de Ayala (Waman Puma)* and the digital Guaman Poma de Ayala, *El primer nueva corónica y buen gobierno*. I cite the digital version because it is easily accessible. Page numbers on it vary slightly from Guaman Poma's own pagination; my citation refers to the digital version, which hereafter is cited parenthetically in the text as *Corónica*. I use the name Felipe Guaman Poma de Ayala. Another variation of his name, as it appears in scholarship, is Waman Puma. Despite the controversy caused by the Naples documents, I will presume until proof of the contrary emerges that Guaman Poma is the author of the *Nueva corónica*. For a discussion of this controversy, see Albó, "La *Nueva corónica y buen gobierno*," 307–48; Cantù, ed., *Guaman Poma y Blas Valera*. For a discussion of the Naples documents, see Hyland, *The Jesuit and the Incas*.

1 According to Guaman Poma, it took him thirty years of travel and writing to produce the manuscript. Rolena Adorno and Ivan Boserup have recently argued that Guaman Poma likely began writing the manuscript after he was exiled to Huamanga on December 18, 1600: Adorno and Boserup, "Gua Poma and the Manuscripts of Fray Martín de Murúa," 220.

2 The manuscript was apparently written between 1587 and 1613.

3 Beyond his own claims in the manuscript, little is known of Guaman Poma's life although recent scholarship has turned up scattered records. For an overview, see Adorno, *Guaman Poma and His Illustrated Chronicle from Colonial Peru*, 13–44. According to Guaman Poma, he learned to read and write Spanish from a half-brother, Martín de Ayala, a mestizo priest. He also tells us that his parents moved from the Huánuco region to Lucanas, where his father served first the Inca and, after conquest, the Spanish king as a *cacique prencipale*: Adorno, "Waman Puma de Ayala."

4 This unprecedented attempt to appeal directly to the king may have been coordinated with increasing tensions between the Spanish king and local creoles over the issue of authority in the region: see Bauer, " 'EnCountering' Colonial Latin American Indian Chronicles."

5 This "opening page" is preceded by a number of prefatory letters, including one from his father, which Guaman Poma corrects to claim the title of prince. On the title page of the original manuscript, it is apparent that Guaman Poma added the title of prince, *prencipe*, to his own name on the bottom left side of the page at some later point. This is evident from the difference in ink color, which reveals the elements of the manuscript that Guaman Poma added later, including minor details as well as pagination. I am grateful to Ivan Boserup and the Royal Danish Library for letting me inspect the original manuscript.

6 "Cordeles con nudos" was inserted by the manuscript facsimile's editor.

7 Unless otherwise noted, all translations are my own.

8 For an abridged translation of Guaman Poma's manuscript, see Frye, *Felipe Guaman Poma de Ayala*. Until 2006, the closest approximation to a translation was Dilke, *Letter to a King*. While that edition is useful in its own right, it is not a scholarly translation. The story of Guaman Poma's manuscript is quite dra-

matic. Lost for almost four centuries, it was discovered in the Royal Copenhagen Library Archives by Richard A. Pietschmann in the first decade of the twentieth century. The manuscript was first published by Paul A. Rivet in Paris in 1936. The first complete version in modern Spanish was published by Luis Bustíos Gálvez in 1956. The manuscript was slated to be returned to Peru in 2008 to mark the one-hundred-year anniversary of its discovery.

9 Scholarly work on Guaman Poma, primarily by Latin American scholars, began in the 1970s and remains a growing body of work. For an overview of early scholarship, see Marsh, "Recent Studies on Guaman Poma de Ayala." For an overview of recent scholarship, see Adorno, *Guaman Poma and His Illustrated Chronicle from Colonial Peru.* For an important, recent article that specifically aims to introduce Guaman Poma's work to a North American audience, see Bauer, " 'EnCountering' Colonial Latin American Indian Chronicles."

10 A great deal of work has been done on the ways in which Guaman Poma engages, replicates, and revises Spanish genres such as the *Crónica de Indias,* as well as the *Relación.* For an exhaustive study of genre in Guaman Poma's manuscript, see Adorno, *Guaman Poma.* Fewer studies have focused on the ways in which Andean textual traditions structure the manuscript: see Brokaw, "Khipu Numeracy and Alphabetic Literacy in the Andes"; Brokaw, "Transcultural Intertextuality and Quipu Literacy in Felipe Guaman Poma de Ayala's *Nueva corónica y buen gobierno*"; Luxton, "The Inca Quipus and Guaman Poma." On the interaction between Spanish and Quechua, see Urioste, "The Spanish and Quechua Voices of Waman Puma." On European and Andean artistic traditions in the manuscript, see Zuidema, "Guaman Poma between the Arts of Europe and the Andes."

11 "Y ací esta *Corónica* es para todo el mundo" (*Corónica,* 1168).

12 Brokaw, "Khipu Numeracy and Alphabetic Literacy in the Andes," 276. Brokaw is extending Mary Louise Pratt's notion of "contact zones": see Pratt, *Imperial Eyes.* For Pratt on Peru and Guaman Poma's manuscript, see Pratt, "Transculturation and Autoethnography."

13 Hemming, *The Conquest of the Incas;* Rowe, "Inca Culture at the Time of the Spanish Conquest"; Stern, *Peru's Indian Peoples and the Challenge of Spanish Conquest.*

14 Guaman Poma claims descent from both the Inca and the Huánuco Yaru Willka dynasty they conquered before the Spanish arrived. The names Waman (falcon) and Puma specifically link him to Huánuco. Guaman Poma gives a great deal of information on his father and his grandfather. Guaman Poma's bicultural name is linked to his ancestral region, as well as services rendered to a Spanish captain (Luis de Ávalos de Ayala). Guaman Poma's name does not appear anywhere in the colonial records except in a court case where he is referred to as "Don Felipe Guaman Poma, who is also known as Lázaro." In the judgment against him, Guaman Poma (a.k.a. Lázaro) is called an "Indian of humble status who, through conniving, calls himself *cacique;* and without being a *cacique* or lord of his people, is nevertheless respected as such": Adorno, "Waman

Puma de Ayala," 14. As Adorno notes, Guaman Poma seems to have been respected as a leader of his people, regardless of whether his claims to specific names and titles were legitimate.

15 Adorno, *Guaman Poma and His Illustrated Chronicle from Colonial Peru*, 29–32.

16 De Acosta, *Historia natural y moral de las Indias*; de Murúa, *Historia general del Perú*. For an English translation, see de Acosta, *Natural and Moral History of the Indies*.

17 Quipus were not the only form of literacy in the area, However, my analysis will not touch on *tocapu* or *quillca*, iconographic systems of inscription. For a discussion of the relation between these two semiotic systems, see Arellano, "Quipu y tocapu."

18 De Acosta, *Historia natural y moral de las Indias*, 410. I have modernized the spelling slightly for clarity.

19 Urteaga, *Discurso sobre la descendencia y gobierno de los Incas*. For an analysis of the relationship between the *Discurso* and Guaman Poma's *Nueva corónica*, as well as the two texts' links to quipus, see Brokaw, "The Poetics of Khipu Historiography."

20 Quipu scholarship is gaining critical momentum. Some major studies that have informed my understanding of quipus are Ascher and Ascher, *Code of the Quipu*; Fossa, "Two Khipu, One Narrative"; Quilter and Urton, *Narrative Threads*; Salomon, *The Cord Keepers*; Salomon, "How an Andean 'Writing without Words' Works"; Urton, "From Knots to Narratives"; Urton, *Signs of the Inca Khipu*; Urton, *The Social Life of Numbers*. Various sources and studies use the terms "quipu," "quipo," "khipu," and "k'ipu." I have followed Guaman Poma's terminology and used "quipu."

21 I am playing here on the titles of two key studies of Amerindian forms of literacy. "Code of the quipu" is part of the title of the Aschers' seminal study of quipus. "The Maya code" is part of the title of Michael Coe's equally important study of Maya pictoglyphs: Coe, *Breaking the Maya Code*.

22 Luxton, "The Inca Quipus and Guaman Poma," 316–17.

23 De Montesinos, *Memorias antiguas historiales y políticas del Perú*, chap. 4, as cited in Hyland, *The Jesuit and the Incas*, 132–33.

24 De Murúa, *Historia general del Perú*, as cited in Brokaw, "The Poetics of Khipu Historiography," 111.

25 Guaman Poma makes the claim that Tupac Yupanqui's administration instituted the widespread use of quipus in the organization and accounting of state resources (*Corónica*, 111). Brokaw reads this section of the *Nueva corónica* as indicating that this was also the time that quipus were adopted for widespread historiographic use: Brokaw, "The Poetics of Khipu Historiography," 137. Quipus have been used in the Andes at least since the period called the "Middle Horizon" (A.D. 600–1,000): see Salomon, "How an Andean 'Writing without Words' Works," 1. On pre-Incaic quipus, see also Mackey et al., *Quipu y yupana*, 19–50.

26 Urton, "From Knots to Narratives," 414.

27 Fossa, "Two Khipu, One Narrative," 461–62. Fossa notes that the Quechua verb "huñuy," which means to join, to put together into one, or to consolidate, was

used in the context of describing such dual quipu use: Fossa, "Two Khipu, One Narrative," 5.

28 Indeed, their main missionary manual required Mercedarian priests to use quipus extensively in missionary efforts: de Porres, "Instrucciones que escribió el P. Fr. Diego de Porres para los sacerdotes que se ocuparan en la doctrina y conversion de los Indios," 4:174–77, as cited in Hyland, The Jesuit and the Incas, 136.

29 De Acosta, Historia natural y moral de las Indias, 411. See also de Murúa, Historia general del Perú, 375.

30 The preponderance of numerical information transmitted from quipus into the colonial records has been taken as evidence that quipus were mainly accounting devices, but it is more likely that this was simply the function that interested the Spanish most.

31 For a recent and ambitious effort to trace such deformations, see, e.g., Lienhard, La voz y su huella. While the entire study is fascinating and important, chapter 5 pertains particularly to Guaman Poma's work.

32 With this action, the Spanish compounded an earlier destructive effort by Atahualpa, an illegitimate brother of the twelfth Inca ruler. After usurping the throne, Atahualpa set out to revise history by burning some historical quipus and killing those quipucamayoc who did not manage to escape to the mountains: see Supno Collapiña, 19–20, as cited in Brokaw, "Khipu Numeracy and Alphabetic Literacy in the Andes," 294. It was in the aftermath of this upheaval that Viceroy de Castro summoned the old quipucamayoc in 1542. Frustrated by the variation in oral accounts of local history, he followed the advice of local elders and sought out the quipucamayoc whose accounts, derived from quipus, were far more consistent.

33 An important exception is Richard Luxton, who argues that Guaman Poma was "consciously attempting a transcription of these knotted cords, or 'quipu-literacy,' into a form understandable to the Spanish": Luxton, "The Inca Quipus and Guaman Poma," 1.

34 Adorno, Guaman Poma, 7.

35 "No teniendo ellos escritura como nosotros . . . no les faltaua algun genero de letras y libros . . . sus librerias, y sus historias, y kalendarios cosa mucho de ver": de Acosta, Historia natural y moral de las Indias, 11, 407–8.

36 De Gamboa, History of the Incas, 57.

37 Note that Guaman Poma uses two spellings, escritura and escriptura, interchangeably.

38 Guaman Poma was acquainted with the writings of Bartolomé de Las Casas (see Adorno, Guaman Poma, 24) but clearly rejects de Las Casas's representation of indigenous Americans as pre-literate. Similarly, Guaman Poma invokes Augustín de Zárate but then refutes his argument that the Andes "ni escritura saben, ni usan, ni aun las pinturas que sirven en lugar de libros en la Nueva-Espana (neither know writing, nor use it, nor have the pictures that serve in place of books in New Spain)" by invoking not only a written but also a pictorial tradition which is both present in and hidden by Guaman Poma's use of Span-

ish pictorial conventions: de Zárate, *Historia del descubrimiento y conquista de la provincial del Perú*, 53, as cited in Lisi, *El Tercer Concilio Limense y la aculturacion de los indígenas sudamericanos*, 316. On the relationship between Guaman Poma and de Zárate, see also Adorno, *Guaman Poma*, 14.

39 Urton, "From Knots to Narratives," 410.

40 Jorge Cañizares-Esguerra has documented and analyzed the transition by which indigenous sources lost their legitimacy as historical documents in Spanish history: Cañizares-Esguerra, *How to Write the History of the New World*, 60–129.

41 Locke, *The Ancient Quipu or Peruvian Knot Record*.

42 Gelb, *A Study of Writing*, 4. Garcilaso Inca was perhaps the first to characterize quipus as mnemonic and accounting devices. Fernando de Montesino claims that because Garcilaso Inca left the Andes when he was only seventeen, he was not familiar with the wider range of *quipus*. Fernando de Montesino, *Memorias antiguas historiales y políticas del Perú*, ed. Jiménez de la Espada (Madrid: Miguel Ginesta, 1882), chap 4, as cited in Hyland, *The Jesuit and the Incas*, 132–33. Montesino, writing in 1644, is specifically refuting Garcilaso Inca's claim that quipus were only mnemonic and accounting devices. Garcilaso Inca is contradicted by two other Andean writers, Guaman Poma and the Jesuit Blas Valera, son of a Spanish father and an Incan mother who lived his life in the Andes. Unlike Guaman Poma and Valera, Garcilaso Inca lived his life in Spain. Garcilaso Inca's dismissal of quipus may reflect his own effort to position himself as a Spanish man of letters speaking from and for the Andes. In fact, a number of indigenous and Spanish writers comment on the use of mnemonic devices, which they distinguish from quipus. For example, when de Acosta discusses the use of mnemonic devices, he refers to pebbles used by individuals to commit Catholic prayers to memory. He clearly distinguishes these pebbles from quipus per se ("fuera destos quipos de hilo [apart from these string quipus]"): de Acosta, *Historia natural y moral de las Indias*, 411. Pedro Sarmiento de Gamboa also discusses a mnemonic device, "a curious invention which was very good and accurate," linked to the oral transmission of information. He does not elaborate on this "curious invention," which he nonetheless distinguishes from "cords called *quipu*": de Gamboa, *History of the Incas*, 41–42. Such accounts reveal that while Andean peoples did use mnemonic devices, they were distinct from quipus. Likewise, Guaman Poma and de Acosta both represent "accounting quipus" as one subset, a specialized form of quipu, rather than as the predominant version. De Acosta also identifies a distinct category of quipus used specifically for processes of calculation and accounting. According to de Acosta, such quipus functioned in combination with grains of maize in a complex system of calculation. Guaman Poma illustrates this particular operation in an image of a "contador y tezorero (bookkeeper and treasurer)" who uses a quipu simultaneously with a grid containing small marks that could be maize or other tokens (*Corónica*, 360).

43 Rappaport, "Object and Alphabet," 284. This perception of alphabetic script tells us much about Andean people's expectations of how systems of literacy

might work, reflecting, perhaps, the structures of literacy with which they were familiar.

44 *Tercer Concilio Limense, 1582–1583*, 103.

45 For a critical edition of the Third Lima Council with commentary, see Lisi, El *Tercer Concilio Limense y la aculturacion de los indígenas sudamericanos*. See also Ugarte, *Historia de la iglesia en el Perú*.

46 Ascher and Ascher, *Code of the Quipu*. Their work built on Leland Locke's study *The Ancient Quipu or Peruvian Knot Record* (1923), which demonstrated the arithmetical content of quipus but concluded that quipus were not analogous to writing. In contrast, the Aschers argued that quipus were capable of storing more than mathematical information, even though they used mathematical principles to do so.

47 Hill Boone, "Introduction," 21.

48 Urton, "From Knots to Narratives," 411. Urton concludes by calling for further research as necessary to bear out "the ideas on the readability of the khipus put forth in this article": ibid., 431.

49 Ibid., 414, cites an eyewitness who notes that the quipus "appear to be of one tenor."

50 Ibid., 294.

51 Brokaw, "*Khipu* Numeracy and Alphabetic Literacy," 285.

52 This section draws on Gary Urton's *The Social Life of Numbers*, which combines ethnographic research on contemporary Andean culture with information culled from colonial documents to posit the existence of this Quechua paradigm: see Urton, *The Social Life of Numbers*, 78–79, 138–72, 183–88, 218–19.

53 Brokaw, "*Khipu* Numeracy and Alphabetic Literacy," 287.

54 Ibid.

55 Ascher and Ascher, *Code of the Quipu*, 45.

56 Urton, "From Knots to Narratives," 427.

57 Ibid., 422.

58 Ibid., 425.

59 Ibid., 426.

60 Ibid., 427. This proposition remains controversial and somewhat speculative.

61 De Acosta, *Historia natural y moral de las Indias*, 410–11.

62 The term "*sacar*" can be translated in a number of ways: to extract, to bring out, to obtain. The key point, however, is de Acosta's use of the same verb to describe the relationship between meaning and arbitrary units, whether they are letters or colored knots. To get this meaning across in the English translation, I use the term "produce."

63 De Acosta, *Historia natural y moral de las Indias*, 411. Indeed, Guaman Poma suggests that quipus constituted a necessary documentary component, without which oral testimony was incomplete.

64 Brokaw, "The Poetics of *Khipu* Historiography," 127.

65 See, e.g., Adorno, *Guaman Poma*; Bauer, " 'EnCountering' Colonial Latin American Indian Chronicles."

66 On the Inca biographies, see also Brokaw, "The Poetics of *Khipu* Historiography"; Julien, "How Inca Decimal Administration Worked." The *Vecita* section in the *Nueva corónica* may also have been based on quipus. Guaman Poma's term "*vecita*" refers to the process of inspections instituted by the Inca, generally known in the Spanish colonial literature as *visitas*. Frank Salomon has argued that Spanish records of visitas also draw on and reproduce quipu knowledge and textual conventions. For this discussion, which also touches on Guaman Poma, see Salomon, *Native Lords of Quito in the Age of the Incas*, 16–18.

67 Brokaw, "The Poetics of *Khipu* Historiography."

68 Urioste, "The Spanish and Quechua Voices of Waman Puma." For a detailed, in-depth analysis of a range of Quechua elements in the manuscript, see Mercedes López-Baralt, "La persistencia de las estructuras simbólicas andinas en los dibujos de Guamán Poma de Ayala."

69 Even elements in the manuscript that seem to reflect European narrative conventions might either be more correctly understood as rooted in Andean textual traditions or might perhaps mark moments in which Guaman Poma successfully marries the two. For example, Bauer notes Guaman Poma's use of a five-part structure in his royal biographies and relates it to Renaissance literary conventions: Bauer, " 'EnCountering' Colonial Latin American Indian Chronicles." However, Brokaw notes that the number five is key in the Quechua "ontology of numbers": Brokaw, "Khipu Numeracy and Alphabetic Literacy in the Andes."

70 To aid readers, Rolena Adorno and John Murra provide a more accurate index at the beginning of their edited version.

71 See Brokaw, "Khipu Numeracy and Alphabetic Literacy in the Andes," 291–92. I find convincing Brokaw's division of the text into ten key sections, indicated by the designation "primer" or "primero." The " 'first chapter' convention" seems to function as a key organizational principle in the text, which would correspond to a meta-textual principle rooted in decimal logic. In his analysis of the structure of the manuscript, Brokaw identifies not only ten key segments or "books," but also seventy chapters, which constitute seven "complete decimal units": ibid., 299. Thus, Brokaw identifies a decimal principle at work on both primary and secondary levels.

72 Ibid., 299.

73 Adorno and Boserup, "Gua Poma and the Manuscripts of Fray Martín de Murúa," 217. The conspicuous use of "first" as an organizing principle sometimes followed by second, third, etc., other times followed by another "first" is striking and suggests that the "first" functions as an important organizing principle regardless of whether it is followed by another "first" or by varying numbers of subsections (second, third, etc.). It is speculative, but possible, to see these "firsts" as referencing an Andean meta-textual principle so that they would correspond on a quipu to strings attached to the central cord.

74 Adorno and Boserup, "Gua Poma and the Manuscripts of Fray Martín de Murúa," 217.

75 Fossa, "Two Khipu, One Narrative," 458.

76 Commenting on this image, Frank Salomon notes that the two quipus have matching end knobs, which possibly suggests they are related: Salomon, *The Cord Keepers*, 144.

77 De Matienzo, *Gobierno del Perú*, 20, as cited and translated in Salomon, *Native Lords of Quito in the Age of the Incas*, 174.

78 See Salomon, *Native Lords of Quito in the Age of the Incas*, 116–42. John Howland Rowe defines an *ayllu* as a kin group which owned a definite territory. For discussion of ayllus in pre-Incaic and modern Andean society, see Rowe, "Inca Culture at the Time of the Spanish Conquest," 253–56.

79 De Ondegardo, *Notables daños de no guarder a los indios sus fueros*. Gary Urton and Lydia Fossa both analyze Polo de Ondegardo's record for insight into how quipus functioned. I rely on their translations.

80 Fossa, "Two Khipu, One Narrative," 457.

81 Ibid., 460.

82 Rolena Adorno has traced the centrality of the anan–urin division in Guaman Poma's images, as well as his attempt to reconcile the contradiction between Andean and Spanish notions of history: Adorno, "The Language of History in Guaman Poma's *Nueva corónica y buen gobierno*," 109–37.

83 Incidentally, Polo de Ondegardo agreed with Guaman Poma and argued in his report that maintaining the native system instituted by the Incas (themselves conquerors and extractors of tribute) would be of greatest benefit to the Spanish, because this system had worked for centuries and made theft impossible due to the dual-records and checks-and-balances process inherent in the quipu system: de Ondegardo, *Notable daño que rresulta de no guardar a estos yndios sus fueros* as cited in Fossa, "Two Khipu, One Narrative," 454.

84 Brokaw, "Khipu Numeracy and Alphabetic Literacy in the Andes," 286. Brokaw is paraphrasing Urton, *The Social Life of Numbers*, 218–19.

85 Adorno, *Guaman Poma*, 24.

86 Ibid., 24–25.

87 Ibid., 24.

88 Ortega, "Transatlantic Translations."

89 Richard Luxton and Juan M. Ossio both suggest that Guaman Poma tries to position himself as, or reclaim a hereditary position as, a quipucamayoc: Luxton, "The Inca Quipus and Guaman Poma"; Ossio, "The Idea of History in Felipe Guaman Poma de Ayala."

90 Adorno, *Guaman Poma*, 33.

91 I am grateful to Henry Turner, who invited me to be part of the Center for Early Modern Studies of the University of Wisconsin, Madison. These discussions prompted me to think about the relationship between modernism and Guaman Poma's work.

92 Adorno, *Guaman Poma*, 33.

93 For a painstaking comparison of correspondences between "manuscript books and khipu structures," see Salomon, *The Cord Keepers*, 185–207.

94 Such details are particularly visible on the original manuscript. I am grateful to Ivan Boserup for permitting me access to Guaman Poma's book at the Royal Library of Copenhagen.

95 Adorno, *Guaman Poma and His Illustrated Chronicle from Colonial Peru*, 17.

96 On the publication history of Guaman Poma's work, see n. 8 of this chapter. For an overview of scholarship on the manuscript, see n. 9 also of this chapter.

FOUR Indigenous Literacies

1 Melville calls it a "romance of adventure" in a letter to Richard Bentley dated June 27, 1850: see Davis and Gilman, *The Letters of Herman Melville*, 108–46.

2 Melville, *Moby-Dick*, 306. Subsequent citations are in parentheses in the text.

3 For an accessible overview of the history of the decipherment of Egyptian hieroglyphics, see Robinson, *Lost Languages*, 51–73. For a discussion of the relationship between the Rosetta Stone and the decipherment of a range of scripts, see Parkinson, *Cracking Codes*.

4 Robinson, *Lost Languages*, 219.

5 Sanborn, *The Sign of the Cannibal*.

6 Gell, *Wrapping in Images*, 163. Two other important sources are Handy, *Tattooing in the Marquesas*; von den Steinen, *Die Marquesaner und ihre Kunst*. Handy is an invaluable source because she was able to interview Marquesan elders who had been tattooed before the ban was enacted.

7 Marchand, *Journal de Bord d'Etienne Marchand*. Handy consulted Marchand, among others, for her study, which was published four decades after the French outlawed tattooing.

8 Sealts, *Melville's Reading*.

9 Irwin, *American Hieroglyphics*.

10 René Dordillon's French-Marquesan dictionary remains the only scholarly source available for consultation: Dordillon, *Grammaire et dicionnaire de la langue des Iles Marquises*. Dordillon translates *ipu* as a small vase or glass. According to Alfred Gell, the term also refers to a category of motifs that includes stylized "calabash" motifs: Gell, *Wrapping in Images*. Dordillon translates several compound words, such as "ipu katu" and "ipu óto as tatouage," a kind of tattoo. The calabash, a key motif with numerous variations, represents not only a bowl or container but also a vessel broadly defined as well as a shell, usually with protective connotations. Such images abound in *Moby-Dick*. The ship is a vessel, a container, a shell; the coffin is also a container, as well as a shell with protective connotations both in its original form as a coffin and in its final form as a lifesaving buoy.

11 This image also has a mythological referent to the story of Kena, which Gell calls "the nearest thing we have to a charter myth of Marquesan tattooing." Even though Kena is only a ka'ioi, this half-mortal and half-supernatural being "cheats" his way to the best tattoos during a ceremony. The quality of his tattoos are linked to heightened erotic as well as physical power. For example, he

becomes irresistible to a woman who had formerly left him and married another man, and he becomes able to shoot lightning from his tattooed armpits: Gell, *Wrapping in Images*, 186–87. The variation of the calabash design in the armpit references Kena's "fire power" as well as his erotic endowment and the social cunning that enables him to obtain the tattoos in the first place. At the same time, it implicitly references a narrative about the power of tattoos, which is linked to "the battlefield" as a literal, erotic, and social space.

12 Such designs include tortoises, crab-like figures, and back-to-back women who may relate to the legendary Siamese twin goddesses: Gell, *Wrapping in Images*, 58–62. Gell notes that "multiplicity motifs are always to some degree anthropomorphic": ibid., 194.

13 Ibid., 193. Gell notes that *kake* means "to climb" and that Dordillon translates it as "curve motifs rising over the loins" when it refers to a tattoo.

14 While the legend of the twin goddesses is not central in the Marquesas, twinned and multiplied figures are prominent motifs in both Marquesan tattooing and carved art: ibid., 181.

15 On the Pohu myth, see ibid., 194–95.

16 Ibid., 194.

17 This image was produced by Wilhelm Gottlieb Tilesius von Tilenau, the expedition artist for A. J. von Krusenstern, who visited the Marquesas in 1804. Tilenau made sketches of a number of Marquesans. These sketches in turn formed the basis of the engravings that illustrated Langsdorff's published account of his voyage: von Krusenstern, *Voyage round the World*; von Langsdorff, *Voyages and Travels in Various Parts of the World*.

18 This pattern represented the protection of affinal alliance relations in the Marquesas. Wives not only represent the web of family relationships in which a given person was embedded, but also organized the social aspect of that person's identity: Gell, *Wrapping in Images*, 194.

19 Melville continues to play with this imagery, which he develops further in chapter 10. There he compares himself and Queequeg to "man and wife" and "some old couples" who "lie and chat over old times till nearly morning." He concludes by describing the two of them as "thus, then, in our hearts' honeymoon, lay I and Queequeg—a cosy, loving pair" (*Moby-Dick*, 53). The affectionate nature of this relationship has received a range of critical attention. See most famously Fiedler, *Love and Death in the American Novel*. For a recent, more complex reading of this relationship, see Bersani, *The Culture of Redemption*.

20 In his study of the influence of hieroglyphics on the American Renaissance, Irwin argues that hieroglyphics in *Moby-Dick* represent the undecipherable and unknowable: Irwin, *American Hieroglyphics*. No doubt, one important concern in *Moby-Dick* is a critique of epistemological certainty embodied, for example, in Ahab. Yet it seems unlikely that hieroglyphics would be symbolic only of the unknowable, given that hieroglyphics had been deciphered only a few decades before the novel's publication, an event that caused great sensation in both Europe and the United States. Melville draws on a wide range of cultural refer-

ences. For a fascinating analysis of the influence of the Egyptian myth of Isis and Osiris on *Moby-Dick*, see Franklin, *The Wake of the Gods*, 53–98. For a study of biblical influences, see Wright, *Melville's Use of the Bible*. For an index of Melville's classical allusions, see Coffler, *Melville's Classical Allusions*. For a compendium of biblical, Shakespearean, Miltonian, and other references, see Maeno, *The Sources of Melville's Quotations*.

21 When Napoleon invaded Egypt in 1798, he brought along scientists and artists to investigate the conquered territory. In 1801, the British claimed key appropriated artifacts as the spoils of war and brought, among other things, the Rosetta Stone to England. Although European efforts to understand Egyptian hieroglyphics, characterized largely by misreading and misinterpretation, began in the early fifteenth century, the arrival of the Rosetta Stone in England initiated an intensified period of interest that culminated in its decipherment.

22 The history of colonial encounters in the Marquesas begins as early as 1595 when the Spanish Captain Mendana landed on the islands. In 1774, Captain James Cook arrived for a short stay, and in 1791 the French established a permanent colonial presence at Nukuheva. During the British-American Wars of 1812, Captain David Porter took possession of the Marquesas for the United States. It became the nation's first colony in 1813. That possession was short-lived, as the British and French continued to struggle over possession of the islands, which were annexed by France in 1844, four years before the publication of Melville's novel. For an overview of this history, see Dening, *Islands and Beaches*; Thomson, *The Marquesas Islands*.

23 Susan Kalter sees many aspects of the novel as referencing Native Americans, focusing particularly on Tashtego as a central figure and linking whales and Indian people: Kalter, "A Student of Savage Thought." Kalter's thesis, while an intriguing reading of Tashtego, differs from mine in collapsing indigeneity so that Queequeg is read as a figural Native American. In contrast, I see Queequeg's Polynesian identity as important in its own right. To me, indigeneity links the two characters without erasing significant cultural differences, while retaining a shared relationship to colonialism as a process of concern to Melville.

24 Sayre, *Les Sauvages Américains*, 103, describes this dialectic as follows: "The colonists substituted their notion of work for analogous but different behaviour among the Indians, then used the difference to ascribe to the 'savages' the negation of work, idleness."

25 The American Board missionary Samuel Austin Worcester reported in the *Panoplist* in 1826 that "young Cherokees travel a great distance to be instructed in this easy method of writing and reading. In three days they are able to commence letter-writing, and return home to teach others": cited in Lepore, *A is for American*, 74.

26 Ibid., 70–79.

27 Ibid., 75.

28 Wong, *Sending My Heart Back across the Years*, 25–87.

29 Gell, *Wrapping in Images*, 166. Social power and position was (at least theoret-
   ically) constituted through genealogy, which was then displayed as a public
   record on skin in the form of tattoos. When chiefs appropriated power by other
   means, genealogy was invoked after the fact to legitimize the power shift.
   Hence, we can imagine that particular aspects of genealogy or kinship ties
   would be emphasized or recast in response to changes in social structures. For a
   discussion of how marriages and kinship ties constituted the "Marquesan
   ego," see ibid., 179. For a general discussion of traditional Marquesan social
   structures, see Maranda, "Marquesan Social Structure."

30 This can also happen with alphabetic script, in which letters such as "b" and "c"
   can function logographically, as has become common in cell-phone text mes-
   saging. There, "c u" can mean "see you," and "b4" can mean "before." In
   addition, alphabetically written words often function logographically, as we
   read the word in one gulp, so to speak, rather than sounding out the letters, just
   as alphabetic script elements regularly combine with logographic signs such as
   "&." With the advent of cyber-communication, it has become common to include "emoticons" in sentences by combining colons and half-parentheses to
   produce a smiley face, for example. The use of emoticons has become so widespread that smiley faces are now available as pictographs in most computer
   programs and on most cell phones: Lisa Photos, personal conversation with the
   author, February 13, 2008.

31 For a history of efforts to decipher this script, see Fischer, *Rongorongo*.

32 Robinson, *Lost Languages*, 219.

33 Ibid., 223.

34 Pozdniakov, "Les bases du déchiffrement de l'écriture de l'île de Pâques."

35 Gell, *Wrapping in Images*, 270–75.

36 See, e.g., von den Steinen, *Die Marquesaner und ihre Kunst*, 3:figs. 7a, 8, 2:205.

37 In line with her general argument's focus on Melville's anxieties regarding
   plagiarism and unacknowledged use of other sources, Elizabeth Renker argues
   that this reference to penmanship signifies the process of copying other writing: Renker, *Strike through the Mask*. Samuel Otter links Melville's indication of
   various tools of writing and engraving to the work and publications of the
   American School of Ethnology: Otter, *Melville's Anatomies*.

38 These concerns are submerged in most of the narrative, but they are related to
   Tommo's preoccupation with cannibalism and the question of whether the
   narrator will be eaten. In the narrative, cannibalism and inscription are connected because they represent modes of incorporation, which is a central issue
   at stake in colonial conflict. Cannibalism and tattoos function as tropes of
   savagery in the narrative, but these tropes are simultaneously self-referential for
   the Western writer and the colonial project of which he is part, with cannibalism
   corresponding to incorporation, and tattoos corresponding to writing. I discuss this correspondence in Birgit Brander Rasmussen, "Re-Imagining Literary
   America." The critical literature on cannibalism in relation to Melville's early
   work is extensive. Particularly useful for my thinking has been Sanborn, *The Sign*

of the Cannibal. Much has also been published on tattoos in Melville. Most influential to my work has been Otter, *Melville's Anatomies.*

39 Melville, *Typee.* Subsequent citations are in parentheses in the text. Important sources, in addition to von Langsdorff and von Krusenstern, include Porter, *Journal of a Cruise Made to the Pacific Ocean;* Stewart, *A Visit to the South Seas.* For a list of books owned and read by Melville, see Sealts, *Melville's Reading.* A number of biographies have been written about Melville: see, e.g., Parker, *Herman Melville.* For two that focus on his time in the Pacific, see Anderson, *Melville in the South Seas;* Heflin, *Herman Melville's Whaling Years.* For an analysis of *Typee* in relation to the genre of American captivity narratives, which were still popular in Melville's time, see Berthold, "Portentous Somethings."

40 For some classic studies that understand *Typee* as critical of Western civilization and colonialism, see, e.g., Anderson, *Melville in the South Seas;* Grejda, *The Common Continent of Men,* 13–27; Herbert, *Marquesan Encounters.* For critiques of Melville's own investment in colonialism, racial difference, and imperialism, see, e.g., Banerjee, "Civilizational Critique in Herman Melville's *Typee, Omoo,* and *Mardi*"; Breitweiser, "False Sympathy in Melville's *Typee*"; Dimock, *Empire for Liberty;* Shueller, "Colonialism and Melville's South Seas Journeys."

41 Fear of cannibalism (and the discovery of the shrunken heads) have rightly been seen as the main reason the narrator wants to escape, but it is the encounter with the tattooist that specifically revives his desire to leave. Thus, I agree with Otter, who argues that it is tattooing, and inscription, which constitutes the greater threat in *Typee:* Otter, *Melville's Anatomies,* 10.

42 After the firstborn, the *opou,* had received these tattoos, the family would throw a celebratory feast. The *tuhuna,* or tattooist, used a range of tools made of bone, tortoise shell, and other materials, as well as an ink made from ground *ama* nut. The tuhuna was assisted by pupils, *ou'a,* who would hold down the opou and keep the skin stretched taut while the tattooist worked: see Handy, *Tattooing in the Marquesas,* 10. For a contemporary description of the traditional tattooing process by a native Polynesian, see Avea, *Tatau.*

43 This sequence was determined by the relative likelihood of inflammation and infection, with the extremities being less likely to become infected. Once infection set in, the process of tattooing would have to be stopped.

44 Melville also describes a feast in great detail. Feasts customarily followed the successful conclusion of an opou's tattooing, so it is possible that Melville, during his stay, observed this sequence of events.

45 John Evelev also notes that the passage focuses on the consequences rather than the pain of being tattooed as the source of terror: Evelev, "Made in the Marquesas," 26.

46 In *Omoo,* Melville returns to the image of a tattooed Westerner from a safer narrative distance with the character Lem Hardy.

47 A number of famous tattooed Westerners made a living by exhibiting themselves as cross-cultural freaks. Evelev argues that Melville takes up von Langsdorff's portrayal of his source, Jean-Babtiste Cabri, as a person whose identity

represents a battleground on which the conflict between civilization and savagery plays out: Evelev, "Made in the Marquesas," 31.

48 For a thorough analysis of the relationship between racializing discourses and practices in the U.S., and novels like *Typee*, see Otter, *Melville's Anatomies*, 1–49.

49 In *Typee*, Melville refers to other well-known narratives, such as those written by Captain Cook and "Stewart, the chaplain of the American sloop of war Vincennes," as well as "Porter's 'Journal of the Cruise of the U.S. Frigate Essex, in the Pacific, during the late War.'" Later, he adds "Wallace, Carteret, Cook or Vancouver" as other writers on the Marquesas. Melville claims not to have read Porter, but according to Anderson, Porter's *Journal of a Cruise Made to the Pacific Ocean* was a major source, along with texts by Stewart, Vincennes, and Ellis: Anderson, *Melville in the South Seas*, 118–19. For a thorough discussion of Melville's vexed relationship to other texts in *Typee*, see Renker, *Strike through the Mask*, 1–23.

50 See also Wardrop, "The Signifier and the Tattoo."

51 A number of critics have discussed the ways in which Melville remains complicit with a colonial project that he also critiques. In *Typee*, Melville participates in and exploits a colonial discourse around cannibalism while he appeals to his audience's "appetite" for such representations. Joyce Sparer Adler asks "who are the real cannibals, the Typees who practice a ritual of eating the flesh of their dead attackers or the aggressor nations who have come to devour the islands?": Adler, "*Typee* and *Omoo*," 245. It seems to me, however, that no actual evidence of cannibalism ever materializes in *Typee*. In fact, the narrative seems to question whether the Taipee are really cannibals. However, the representation of the Taipee as non-cannibals, while it undercuts a colonial stereotype, is actually potentially far more damaging to the Taipee, who had used their reputation as cannibals strategically as a defense against colonial incursions: see Sanborn, *The Sign of the Cannibal*.

52 The relationship between Ahab and the whale represents one narrative site in which Melville continues to explore the struggle to mark and control the direction of inscription and its attendant anxieties: Berninghausen, "Writing on the Body."

53 Giorgio Mariani, citing Louise Owens, argues that "Ishmael's seizure of the coffin should be interpreted as an act of 'white' appropriation of a formerly 'red' space" Mariani, "Chiefly Known by His Rod," 51. I agree with many other critics that Melville remains invested in a white, colonial subjectivity, but I also see him as probing alternatives and exploring other possibilities.

54 This linkage is developed most thoroughly in Kalter, "A Student of Savage Thought."

55 Within the context of my argument, in which Queequeg stands for indigeneity, it is furthermore possible to see him as a synecdoche for indigenous colonized people. For a discussion of how my position differs from Kalter's, see n. 23 of this chapter.

56 This is an instance of how Melville consistently breaks with a Western tradition

of representing the colonial "other" as legible and transparent to Western eyes. Conversely, in a novella like *Benito Cereno*, it is exactly Delano's inability to imagine Babo as capable of "authoring" a complex plot that makes it possible for Babo to fool him for so long. On Melville's ambiguous relationship to the "quest for legibility," see Gilmore, *Surface and Depth*, 87–94.

57 Anderson, *Melville in the South Seas*, demonstrates the great extent to which Melville's fiction often revised and diverged from the autobiographical "raw material" which inspired it. Richard M. Fletcher has analyzed Melville's use of the Marquesan language and demonstrated that Melville generally felt free to invent and improvise: Fletcher, "Melville's Use of Marquesan."

58 Except, obviously, in the important front matter.

59 Although Abraham and Hagar were not necessarily racially differentiated in the way that slaves and masters were in the nineteenth-century United States, they certainly were members of two radically different social classes. At the same time, their identities as master and slave would likely invoke racial difference to Melville's readers.

60 Memmi, *The Colonizer and the Colonized*, 71.

Abé, Takao. "What Determined the Content of Missionary Reports? The Jesuit Relations Compared with the Iberian Jesuit Accounts." *French Colonial History* 3 (2003), 69–83.

Adler, Joyce Sparer. "*Typee* and *Omoo*: Of 'Civilized' War on 'Savage' Peace." *Critical Essays on Herman Melville's Typee*, ed. Milton R. Stern, 244–49. Boston: G. K. Hall, 1982.

Adorno, Rolena. *Guaman Poma: Writing and Resistance in Colonial Peru*. Austin: University of Texas Press, 1986.

——. *Guaman Poma and His Illustrated Chronicle from Colonial Peru: From a Century of Scholarship to a New Era of Reading (Guaman Poma y su crónica ilustrada del Perú colonial: Un siglo de investigaciones hacia una nueva era de lectura)*. Copenhagen: Museum Tusculanum Press, 2001.

——. "The Language of History in Guaman Poma's *Nueva corónica y buen gobierno*." *Oral to Written Expression: Native Andean Chronicles of the Early Colonial Period*, ed. Rolena Adorno, 109–37. Syracuse: Maxwell School of Citizenship and Public Affairs, Syracuse University, 1982.

——. "Waman Puma de Ayala: 'Author and Prince.'" *Latin American Literature and Arts Review* 28 (January–April 1981), 12–24.

Adorno, Rolena, and Ivan Boserup. "Gua Poma and the Manuscripts of Fray Martín de Murúa: Prolegomena to a Critical Edition of the Historia del Perú." *Fund og Forskning i Det Kongelige Biblioteks Samlinger* 44 (2005), 107–258.

Albó, Xavier. "La *Nueva corónica y buen gobierno*: ¿Obra de Guaman Poma o de jesuitas?" *Anthropológica* 16 (1998), 307–48.

Alfred, Taiaiake. *Peace Power Righteousness: An Indigenous Manifesto*. Oxford: Oxford University Press, 1999.

Allen, Chadwick. "Postcolonial Theory and the Discourse of Treaties." *American Quarterly* 52, no. 1 (March 2000), 59–89.

Anderson, Arthur J. O., and Charles E. Dibble, eds. and trans. *General History of the Things of New Spain: Florentine Codex.* Santa Fe: School of American Research, 1950–82.

Anderson, Charles Roberts. *Melville in the South Seas.* New York: Columbia University Press, 1949.

Arellano, Carmen. "Quipu y tocapu: Sistemas de communicación incas." *Los Incas, arte y símbolos,* ed. Franklin Pease G. Y. with Craig Morris, Julian I. Santillana, Ramiro Matos, Paloma Carcedo, Luisa Vetter, Carmen Arellano, Lucy Salazar, and Vuka Roussakis Pease, 215–61. Lima: Banco de Crédito del Perú, 1999.

Ascher, Marcia, and Robert Ascher. *Code of the Quipu: A Study in Media, Mathematics, and Culture.* Ann Arbor: University of Michigan Press, 1981.

Astrov, Margot, ed. *The Winged Serpent: American Indian Prose and Poetry.* Boston: Beacon, 1974.

Avea, Chief Sielu. *Tatau: The Art of the Samoan Tattoo.* Honolulu: Sielu Enterprises, 1994.

Aveni, Anthony F. "Non-Western Notational Frameworks and the Role of Anthropology in Our Understandings of Literacy." *Toward a New Understanding of Literacy,* ed. Merald E. Wrolstad and Dennis F. Fisher, 252–78. New York: Praeger Special Studies, 1986.

Axtell, James. "The Power of Print in the Eastern Woodlands." *William and Mary Quarterly* 44, no. 2 (April 1987), 300–309.

Bad Heart Bull, Amos. *A Pictographic History of the Oglala Sioux,* ed. Helen H. Blish. Lincoln: University of Nebraska Press, 1967.

Bakhtin, Mikhail. *The Dialogic Imagination: Four Essays by M. M. Bakhtin,* ed. Michael Holquist, trans. Caryl Emerson and Michael Holquist. Austin: University of Texas Press, 1981.

Bally, Charles, Albert Sechehaye, and Albert Reidlinger, eds. *Cours de linguistique générale* [Course in general linguistics]. Paris: Payot, 1992.

Banerjee, Mita. "Civilizational Critique in Herman Melville's *Typee, Omoo,* and *Mardi.*" *American Studies* 48 (2003), 207–25.

Battestini, Simon. *African Writing and Text,* trans. Henri G. J. Evans. Ottawa: Legas, 2002.

Bauer, Ralph. " 'EnCountering' Colonial Latin American Indian Chronicles: Felipe Guaman Poma de Ayala's History of the 'New' World." *American Indian Quarterly* 25, no. 2 (Spring 2001), 275–311.

——. "Writing as 'Khipu': Titu Cusi Yupanqui's Account of the Conquest of Peru." *Early American Mediascapes,* ed. Matthew Cohen and Jeffrey Glover. Lincoln: University of Nebraska Press, forthcoming.

Baym, Nina, Wayne Franklin, Ronald Gottesman, Laurence B. Holland, David Kalstone, Arnold Krupat, Fracis Murphy, Hershel Parker, William H. Pritchard, and Patricia B. Wallace. *The Norton Anthology of American Literature,* 2 vols. New York: W. W. Norton, 1994.

Beauchamp, William. "Wampum and Shell Articles Used by the New York Indians," *Bulletin of the New York State Museum* 8, no. 41 (1901).

Bellin, Joshua David. *The Demon of the Continent: Indians and the Shaping of American Literature*. Philadelphia: University of Pennsylvania Press, 2001.

Berliner, Jonathan. "Written in the Birch Bark: The Linguistic-Material Worldmaking of Simon Pokagan." *PMLA* 125, no. 1 (Winter 2010), 73–91.

Berninghausen, Thomas F. "Writing on the Body: The Figure of Authority in *Moby-Dick*." *New Orleans Review* 14, no. 3 (Fall 1987), 5–11.

Bersani, Leo. *The Culture of Redemption*. Cambridge: Harvard University Press, 1990.

Berthold, Michael. *Four Masterworks of American Indian Literature: Quetzalcoatl, The Ritual of Condolence, Cuceb, The Night Chant*. Tucson: University of Arizona Press, 1974.

——. " 'Portentous Somethings': Melville's *Typee* and the Language of Captivity." *New England Quarterly* 60 (1987), 549–67.

Bloomfield, Leonard. *Language*. New York: Holt, Rinehart, and Winston, 1961.

Brander Rasmussen, Birgit. " 'Attended with Great Inconveniences': Slave Literacy and the 1740 South Carolina 'Negro Act.' " *PMLA* 125, no. 1 (2010), 201–3.

——. "Re-Imagining Literary American: Writing and Colonial Encounters in American Literature." Ph.D. diss, University of California, Berkeley, Ann Arbor: UMI Dissertation Services, 2003.

——. " 'Those That Do Violence Must Expect to Suffer': Disrupting Segregationist Fictions of Safety in Charles W. Chesnutt's *The Marrow of Tradition*." *The Aesthetics of Living Jim Crow, and Other Kinds of Racial Division*, ed. Brian Norman and Piper Kendrix Williams, 73–89. Albany: State University of New York Press, 2010.

Breitweiser, Mitchell. "False Sympathy in Melville's *Typee*." *American Quarterly* 34 (1982), 396–417.

Brinton, Daniel G. "On an 'Inscribed Tablet' from Long Island." *Archaeologist* 1, no. 11 (1893), 201–3.

Brokaw, Galen. "Khipu Numeracy and Alphabetic Literacy in the Andes: Felipe Guaman Poma de Ayala's *Nueva corónica y buen gobierno*." *Colonial Latin American Review* 11, no. 2 (2002), 275–303.

——. "The Poetics of Khipu Historiography: Felipe Guaman Poma de Ayala's *Nueva corónica* and the *Relación de los quipucamayos*." *Latin American Research Review* 38, no. 3 (2003), 111–47.

——. "Transcultural Intertextuality and Quipu Literacy in Felipe Guaman Poma de Ayala's *Nueva corónica y buen gobierno*." Ph.D. diss., Indiana University. Ann Arbor: UMI Dissertation Services, 1999.

Brooks, Lisa. *The Common Pot: The Recovery of Native Space in the Northeast*. Minneapolis: University of Minnesota Press, 2008.

Bross, Kristina, and Hilary E. Wyss, eds. *Early Native Literacies in New England: A Documentary and Critical Anthology*. Amherst: University of Massachusetts Press, 2008.

Brotherston, Gordon. *Image of the New World: The American Continent Portrayed in Native Texts*. London: Thames and Hudson, 1979.

Brown, Jennifer S. H., and Elizabeth Vibert. *Reading beyond Words: Contexts for Native History*. Peterborough, Ont.: Broadview, 1996.

Cañizares-Esguerra, Jorge. *How to Write the History of the New World: Histories, Epis-*

temologies, and Identities in the Eighteenth-Century Atlantic World. Stanford: Stanford University Press, 2001.

Cantù, Francesca, ed. Guaman Poma y Blas Valera: Tradición andina e historia colonial. Actas del Coloquio Internacional, Instituto Italo-Latinoamericano, Rome, September 29–30. Rome: Antonio Pellicani, 2001.

Carruthers, M. J. The Book of Memory: A Study of Memory in Medieval Culture. Cambridge: Cambridge University Press, 1990.

Ceci, Lynn. "The First Fiscal Crisis in New York." The Second Coastal Archeology Reader: 1900 to Present, ed. James E. Truex, 97–106. Lexington, Mass.: Ginn, 1982.

——. "The Value of Wampum among the New York Iroquois: A Case Study in Artifact Analysis." Journal of Anthropological Research 38, no. 1 (1982), 97–107.

Clanchy, M. T. From Memory to Written Record: England 1066–1307, 2d ed. Oxford: Blackwell, 1993.

Clements, William M. Native American Verbal Art: Texts and Contexts. Tucson: University of Arizona Press, 1996.

Clendinnen, Inga. " 'Fierce and Unnatural Cruelty': Cortés and the Conquest of Mexico." New World Encounters, ed. Stephen Greenblatt, 12–47. Berkeley: University of California Press, 1993.

Cline, Sarah L. "Native Peoples of Colonial Central Mexico." The Cambridge History of the Native Peoples of the Americas, Vol. 2: Mesoamerica, Part 2, ed. Richard E. W. Adams and Murdo J. Macleod, 187–222. New York: Cambridge University Press, 2000.

Coe, Michael D. Breaking the Maya Code. New York: Thames and Hudson, 1999.

Coffler, Gail H. Melville's Classical Allusions: A Comprehensive Index and Glossary. Westport, Conn.: Greenwood, 1985.

Cohen, Marcel. La grande invention de l'ecriture et son evolution. Paris: Imprimerie Nationale, 1958.

Cohen, Matthew, and Jeffrey Glover, eds. Early American Mediascapes. Lincoln: Nebraska: University Press, forthcoming.

Colden, Cadwallader. The History of the Five Indian Nations of Canada, which Are Dependent on the Province of New York, and Are a Barrier between the English and the French in That Part of the World (1727–47), 2 vols., repr. ed. New York: A.S. Barnes, 1904.

Coles, Robert R. "Wampum Was More than Money." The Second Coastal Archeology Reader: 1900 to Present, ed. James E. Truex, 290–92. Lexington, Mass: Ginn, 1982.

Copway, George (Kah-Ge-Ga-Gah-Bowh). The Traditional History and Characteristic Sketches of the Ojibway Nation. London: Charles Gilpin, 1850.

Cover, Robert. "Nomos and Narrative." Harvard Law Review 97, no. 4 (1983), 4–68.

Cowan, William. "Objibwe Vocabulary in Longfellow's Hiawatha." Papers of the Eighteenth Century Algonquian Conference, ed. William Cowan, 59–66. Ottawa: Carleton University Press, 1987.

Daniels, Peter T., and William Bright, eds. The World's Writing Systems. New York: Oxford University Press, 1996.

Davis, Merrell R., and William H. Gilman, eds. The Letters of Herman Melville. New Haven: Yale University Press, 1960.

de Acosta, José. Historia natural y moral de las Indias, en que se tratan las cosas notables del cielo, y elementos, metales, plantas, y animals dellas: Y los ritos, y ceremonias, leyes, y *gouierno, y guerras de los Indios.* Seville: Impresso en Seuilla en casa de Iuan de Leon, 1590.

——. *Natural and Moral History of the Indies,* ed. Jane E. Mangan. Durham: Duke University Press, 2002.

de Alva Ixtlilxóchitl, Fernando. *Historia de la nación Chichimeca.* Madrid: Historia 16, 1985.

de Gamboa, Pedro Sarmiento. *History of the Incas,* ed. and trans. Brian S. Bauer and Vania Smith. Austin: University of Texas Press, 2007.

de Landa, Diego. *Yucatan before and after the Conquest,* trans. William Gates. New York: Dover, 1978.

de Las Casas, Bartolomé. *In Defense of the Indians: The Defense of the Most Reverend Lord, Don Fray Bartolomé de Las Casas, of the Order of Preachers, Late Bishop of Chiapa, against the Persecutors and Slanderers of the Peoples of the New World Discovered across the Seas,* ed. and trans. Stafford Poole. DeKalb: Northern Illinois University Press, 1992.

de Lom d'Acre, Louis-Armand. *New Voyages to North-America,* 2 vols., ed. Reuben Gold Thwaites. Chicago: A. C. McClurg, 1905.

De Matienzo, Juan. *Gobierno del Perú (1567).* Lima: Institut Français d'Études Andines, 1967.

de Montesinos, Fernando. *Memorias antiguas historiales y políticas del Perú,* ed. Jiménez de la Espada. Madrid: Miguel Ginesta, 1882.

de Murúa, Martín. *Historia general del Perú.* Madrid: Historia 16, 1987.

de Ondegardo, Juan Polo. *Notables daños de no guarder a los indios sus fueros (El mundo de los incas) (1571),* ed. Laura González and Alicia Alonso. Madrid: Historia 16, 1990.

de Porres, Diego. "Instrucciones que escribió el P. Fr. Diego de Porres para los sacerdotes que se ocuparan en la doctrina y conversion de los Indios" (1585). *Los Mercedarios en el Perú en el siglo XVI,* 4 vols., ed. Victor M. Barriga. Arequipa: Editorial La Colmena, 1953.

de Sahagún, Bernardino. *Historia general de las cosas de Nueva España: Fray Bernardino de Sahagún y los informantes aztecas.* Barcelona: Círculo de Lectores, 1985.

de Zárate, Augustín. *Historia del descubrimiento y conquista de la provincial del Perú (1555),* ed. A. González Barcia. Madrid: Zúñiga, 1749.

DeFrancis, John. *Visible Speech: The Diverse Oneness of Writing Systems.* Honolulu: University of Hawaii Press, 1989.

Deloria, Phil. *Playing Indian.* New Haven: Yale University Press, 1999.

Dening, Greg. *Islands and Beaches: Discourse on a Silent Land, Marquesas, 1774–1880.* Honolulu: University of Hawaii Press, 1980.

Dennis, Mathew. *Cultivating a Landscape of Peace: Iroquois-European Encounters in Seventeenth-Century America.* Ithaca: Cornell University Press, 1993.

Dilke, Christopher. *Letter to a King: A Peruvian Chief's Account of Life under the Incas and under Spanish Rule.* New York: E. P. Dutton, 1978.

Dimock, Wai-chee. *Empire for Liberty: Melville and the Poetics of Individualism.* Princeton: Princeton University Press, 1989.

Diringer, David. *The Alphabet: A Key to the History of Mankind.* New York: Hutchinson's Scientific and Technical Publications, 1948.

——. *Writing.* London: Thames and Hudson, 1962.

Dordillon, René Ildefonse. *Grammaire et dicionnaire de la langue des Iles Marquises: Marquisien-Français.* Paris: Institut d'Ethnologie, 1931.

Dorsey, Peter. "Going to School with Savages: Authorship and Authority among the Jesuits of New France." *William and Mary Quarterly* 55, no. 3 (July 1998), 399–420.

Druke, Mary. "Iroquois Treaties: Common Forms, Varying Interpretations." *The History and Culture of Iroquois Diplomacy: An Interdisciplinary Guide to the Treaties of the Six Nations and Their League,* ed. Francis Jennings, William N. Fenton, Mary A. Druke, and David R. Miller, 85–98. Syracuse: Syracuse University Press, 1985.

Drummond, A. M., and Richard Moody. "Indian Treaties: The First American Dramas." *Quarterly Journal of Speech* 39 (1953), 15–24.

Dunn, Dorothy, ed. *1877: Plains Indian Sketch Books of Zo-Tom and Howling Wolf.* Flagstaff: Northland, 1969.

Earenfight, Phillip J., ed. *A Kiowa's Odyssey: A Sketchbook from Fort Marion.* Seattle: University of Washington Press, 2007.

Edmonson, Munro S., trans. *The Ancient Future of the Itza: The Book of Chilam Balam of Tizimin.* Austin: University of Texas Press, 1982.

Erdrich, Louise. *Books and Islands in Ojibwe Country.* Washington, D.C.: National Geographic, 2003.

Evelev, John. " 'Made in the Marquesas': Typee, Tattooing, and Melville's Critique of the Literary Marketplace." *Arizona Quarterly* 48 (1992), 29–45.

Ewers, John C. "Introduction." *Howling Wolf: A Cheyenne Warrior's Graphic Interpretation of His People,* by Karen Daniels Petersen, 5–33. Palo Alto: America West, 1968.

——. *Murals in the Round: Tipis of the Kiowa and Kiowa-Apache Indians.* Washington, D.C.: Smithsonian Institution Press, 1978.

Fabian, Johannes. *Time and the Other: How Anthropology Makes Its Object.* New York: Columbia University Press, 1983.

Fadden, Stephen. "Beaded History: The Hiawatha Belt Is the Founding Document and Symbolizes the 'Constitution' of the Iroquois Confederacy." *Northeast Indian Quarterly* 4, no. 3 (1987), 17–20.

Fenton, William N. *The Great Law and the Longhouse: A Political History of the Iroquois Confederacy.* Norman: University of Oklahoma Press, 1998.

Février, James. *Histoire de l'écriture.* Paris: Payot, 1948.

Fiedler, Leslie. *Love and Death in the American Novel.* Normal, Ill.: Dalkey Archive Press, 1997.

Fischer, Steven Roger. *Rongorongo: The Easter Island Script: History, Traditions, Texts.* Oxford: Clarendon, 1997.

Fletcher, Richard M. "Melville's Use of Marquesan." *American Speech* 39 (May 1964), 135–38.

Fossa, Lydia. "Two Khipu, One Narrative: Answering Urton's Questions." *Ethnohistory* 47, no. 2 (2000), 453–68.

Foster, Michael K. "Another Look at the Function of Wampum in Iroquois-White

Councils." *The History and Culture of Iroquois Diplomacy: An Interdisciplinary Guide to the Treaties of the Six Nations and Their League*, ed. Francis Jennings, William N. Fenton, Mary A. Druke, and David R. Miller, 99–114. Syracuse: Syracuse University Press, 1985.

Foucault, Michel. *The Archeology of Knowledge: The Discourse on Language*. New York: Barnes & Noble, 1969.

Franklin, H. Bruce. *The Wake of the Gods: Melville's Mythology*. Stanford: Stanford University Press, 1963.

Frye, David, ed. and trans. *Felipe Guaman Poma de Ayala: The First New Chronicle and Good Government*. Indianapolis: Hackett, 2006.

Gates, William, trans. "Introduction." *Yucatan before and after the Conquest*, by Diego de Landa. New York: Dover, 1978.

Gelb, Ignace J. *A Study of Writing*. Chicago: University of Chicago Press, 1963.

Gell, Alfred. *Wrapping in Images: Tattooing in Polynesia*. Oxford: Clarendon, 1993.

George-Kanentiio, Doug. "Iroquois at the U.N." *Akwesasne Notes New Series* 1, nos. 3–4 (1995), 71.

Gilmore, Michael T. *Surface and Depth: The Quest for Legibility in American Culture*. Oxford: Oxford University Press, 2003.

Goodell, William. *The American Slave Code in Theory and Practice: Its Distinctive Features Shown by Its Statutes, Judicial Decisions, and Illustrative Facts*. New York: American and Foreign Anti-Slavery Society, 1853.

Goody, Jack. *The Domestication of the Savage Mind*. New York: Cambridge University Press, 1977.

——. *The Interface between the Written and the Oral*. Cambridge: Cambridge University Press, 1987.

Goody, Jack, and Ian Watt. "The Consequences of Literacy." *Comparative Studies in Society and History* 5 (1963), 304–45.

Goux, Jean-Joseph. *Symbolic Economies: After Marx and Freud*, trans. Jennifer Curtiss Gage. Ithaca: Cornell University Press, 1990.

Gray, Edward G., and Norman Fiering, eds. *The Language Encounter in the Americas, 1492–1800*. New York: Berghahn, 2000.

Greenblatt, Stephen. *Marvelous Possessions: The Wonder of the New World*. Chicago: University of Chicago Press, 1991.

Greenfield, Bruce. "The Mi'kmaq Hieroglyphic Prayer Book: Writing and Christianity in Maritime Canada, 1675–1921." *The Language Encounter in the Americas, 1492–1800*, ed. Edward G. Gray and Norman Fiering, 189–214. New York: Berghahn, 2000.

Grejda, Edward S. *The Common Continent of Men: Racial Equality in the Writings of Herman Melville*. Port Washington, N.Y.: Kennikat Press, 1974.

Guaman Poma de Ayala, Felipe. *El primer nueva corónica y buen gobierno (1615/1616)*. GKS 2232, 4. Royal Library of Denmark, Copenhagen. Available online at http://www.kb.dk/elib/mss/poma.

Gustafson, Sandra M. *Eloquence Is Power: Oratory and Performance in Early America*. Chapel Hill: University of North Carolina Press, 2000.

Hale, Horatio, ed. *The Iroquois Book of Rites* (1883). New York: AMS Press, 1969.

Hall, David D. *Cultures of Print: Essays in the History of the Book.* Amherst: University of Massachusetts Press, 1996.

Handy, Willowdean Chatterson. *Tattooing in the Marquesas.* Honolulu: Bernice P. Bishop Museum, 1922.

Heflin, Wilson. *Herman Melville's Whaling Years.* Nashville: Vanderbilt University Press, 2004.

Hemming, John. *The Conquest of the Incas.* New York: Penguin, 1970.

Herbert, T. Walter. *Marquesan Encounters: Melville and the Meaning of Civilization.* Cambridge: Harvard University Press, 1980.

Hewitt, J. N. B. "The Requickening Address of the Iroquois Condolence Council," ed. William N. Fenton. *Journal of the Washington Academy of Sciences* 34, no. 3 (1944), 65–85.

Hill Boone, Elizabeth. "Introduction." *Writing without Words: Alternative Literacies in Mesoamerica and the Andes,* ed. Elizabeth Hill Boone and Walter D. Mignolo, 3–26. Durham: Duke University Press, 1994.

——. *Stories in Red and Black: Pictorial Histories of the Aztecs and Mixtecs.* Austin: University of Texas Press, 2000.

Hill Boone, Elizabeth, and Walter D. Mignolo, eds. *Writing without Words: Alternative Literacies in Mesoamerica and the Andes.* Durham: Duke University Press, 1994.

Houston, Stephen. "Literacy among the Pre-Columbian Maya: A Comparative Perspective." *Writing without Words: Alternative Literacies in Mesoamerica and the Andes,* ed. Elizabeth Hill Boone and Walter D. Mignolo, 27–49. Durham: Duke University Press, 1994.

Howard, James H. ed. *Lakota Warrior: A Personal Narrative.* Lincoln: University of Nebraska Press, 1998.

Hyland, Sabine. *The Jesuit and the Incas: The Extraordinary Life of Padre Blas Valera, S.J.* Ann Arbor: University of Michigan Press, 2003.

Irwin, John T. *American Hieroglyphics: The Symbol of the Egyptian Hieroglyphics in the American Renaissance.* New Haven: Yale University Press, 1980.

Jackson, Virginia. "Longfellow's Tradition; or Picture-Writing a Nation." *Modern Language Quarterly* 59, no. 4 (December 1998), 471–97.

Jehlen, Myra. "The Literature of Colonization." *The Cambridge History of American Literature,* Volume I: 1590–1820, ed. Sacvan Bercovitch, 13–168. Cambridge: Cambridge University Press, 1994.

Jennings, Francis, William N. Fenton, Mary A. Druke, and David R. Miller, eds. "Glossary of Figures of Speech in Iroquois Political Rhetoric." *The History and Culture of Iroquois Diplomacy: An Interdisciplinary Guide to the Treaties of the Six Nations and Their League,* ed. Francis Jennings, William N. Fenton, Mary A. Druke, and David R. Miller. Syracuse: Syracuse University Press, 1985.

——. *The History and Culture of Iroquois Diplomacy: An Interdisciplinary Guide to the Treaties of the Six Nations and Their League.* Syracuse: Syracuse University Press, 1985.

Jensen, Hans. *Sign, Symbol, and Script: An Account of Man's Efforts to Write.* New York: G. P. Putnam's Sons, 1969.

Jogues, Isaac. *Novum Belgium* in *American Captivity Narratives*, ed. Gordon Sayre. Boston: Houghton Mifflin, 2000.

Julien, Catherine. "How Inca Decimal Administration Worked." *Ethnohistory* 35, no. 3 (1988), 357–79.

Kalter, Susan. "A Student of Savage Thought: The Ecological Ethic in *Moby-Dick* and Its Grounding in Native American Ideologies." *ESQ* 48 (2002), 1–40.

Klor de Alva, Jorge, trans. "The Aztec-Spanish Dialogues of 1524," trans. Miguel León-Portillo. *Alcheringa/Ethnopoetics* 4, no. 2 (1980), 52–193.

Kolodny, Annette. *In Search of First Contact: The Peoples of the Dawnland, the Vikings of Vineland, and American Popular Culture.* Durham: Duke University Press, forthcoming 2012.

Konkle, Maureen. *Writing Indian Nations: Native Intellectuals and the Politics of Historiography, 1827–1863.* Chapel Hill: University of North Carolina Press, 2004.

Lafitau, Joseph-François. *Customs of the American Indians Compared with the Customs of Primitive Times,* 2 vols., ed. and trans. William N. Fenton and Elizabeth L. Moore. Toronto: Champlain Society, 1977.

——. *Moeurs des sauvages amériquains, comparées aux moeurs des premiers temps.* Paris: Jesuit Society, 1724.

Lepore, Jill. *A Is for American: Letters and Other Characters in the Newly United States.* New York: Alfred A. Knopf, 2002.

Lienhard, Martín. *La voz y su huella: Escritura y conflicto étnico-social en América Latina 1992–1988.* Hanover, N.H.: Ediciones del Norte, 1991.

Lipsitz, George. *The Possessive Investment in Whiteness: How White People Profit from Identity Politics.* Philadelphia: Temple University Press, 1998.

Lisi, Francesco Leonardo. *El Tercer Concilio Limense y la aculturacion de los indígenas sudamericanos: Estudio crítico con edición, traducción y comentario de las actas del concilio provincial celebrado en Lima entre 1582 y 1583.* Salamanca: Ediciones Universidad de Salamanca, 1990.

Lockard, Joe. "The Universal Hiawatha." *American Indian Quarterly* 24, no. 1 (Winter 2000), 110–25.

Locke, L. Leland. *The Ancient Quipu or Peruvian Knot Record.* New York: American Museum of Natural History, 1923.

Lockhart, James. *The Nahuas after the Conquest: A Social and Cultural History of the Indians of Central Mexico, Sixteenth through Eighteenth Centuries.* Stanford: Stanford University Press, 1992.

Long, Richard C. E. "Maya and Mexican Writing." *Maya Research* 2 (1935).

Longfellow, Henry Wadsworth. *The Song of Hiawatha* (1855). Boston: Ticknor and Fields, 1860.

López-Baralt, Mercedes. "La persistencia de las estructuras simbólicas andinas en los dibujos de Guamán Poma de Ayala." *Journal of Latin American Lore* 5, no. 1 (1979), 83–116.

Luxton, Richard. "The Inca Quipus and Guaman Poma." *Colloquium Verlag Berlin,* 1979. Ibero-Amerikanisches Archiv N.F. Jg 5 H. 4.

Mackey, Carol, Hugo Pereyra, Carlos Radicati, Humberto Rodriquez, and Oscar

Valverde, eds. *Quipu y yupana: Colección de escritos*. Lima: Consejo Nacional de Ciencia y Tecnología, 1990.

Maeno, Shigeru. *The Sources of Melville's Quotations*. Tokyo: Kaibunsha, 1981.

Mallery, Garrick. *Introduction to the Study of Sign Language among the North American Indians as Illustrating the Gesture Speech of Mankind*. Washington, D.C.: Smithsonian Institution Bureau of Ethnology, 1880.

——. *Picture-Writing of the American Indians*, 2 vols. New York: Dover, 1972.

Mann, Barbara A. "The Fire at Onondaga: Wampum as Proto-writing." *Akwesasne Notes* 1, no. 1 (1995), 40–48.

Maranda, Pierre. "Marquesan Social Structure: An Ethnohistorical Contribution." *Ethnohistory* 11 (1964), 301–79.

Marchand, Etienne. *Journal de bord d'Etienne Marchand: Le voyage du solide autour du monde: 1790–1792*. Paris: Comité des travaux historiques y scientifiques (CTHS), 2005.

Marcus, Joyce. *Mesoamerican Writing Systems: Propaganda, Myth, and History in Four Ancient Civilizations*. Princeton: Princeton University Press, 1992.

Mariani, Giorgio. "Chiefly Known by His Rod: The Book of Jonah, Mapple's Sermon, and Scapegoating." *"Ungraspable Phantom": Essays on Moby-Dick*, ed. John Bryant, Mary K. Bercaw Edwards, Timothy Marr, and the Melville Society, 37–57. Kent, Ohio: Kent State University Press, 2006.

Marsh, Charles R. "Recent Studies on Guaman Poma de Ayala." *Latin American Indian Literatures* 6, no. 1 (Spring 1982), 27–32.

Marshall, Joyce, trans. and ed. *Word from New France: The Selected Letters of Marie de l'Incarnation*. Toronto: Oxford University Press, 1967.

Martien, Jerry. *Shell Game: A True Account of Beads and Money in North America*. San Francisco: Mercury House, 1995.

Marx, Karl. "Capital, Volume 1." *The Marx-Engels Reader*, ed. Robert C. Tucker, 312–22. New York: W. W. Norton, 1972.

Mauss, Marcel. *The Gift: The Form and Reason for Exchange in Archaic Societies*, trans. W. D. Halls. New York: W. W. Norton, 1990.

McLellan, Howard. "Indian Magna Carta Writ in Wampum Belts." *Akwesasne Notes New Series* 1, nos. 3–4 (1995), 64–65.

McNally, Michael D. "The Indian Passion Play: Contesting the Real Indian in Song of Hiawatha Pageants, 1901–1965." *American Quarterly* 58, no. 1 (March 2006), 105–38.

Melville, Herman. *Moby-Dick; or, The Whale*. Evanston, Ill.: Northwestern University Press, 2001.

——. *Omoo: A Narrative of Adventures in the South Seas*. Evanston, Ill.: Northwestern University Press, 1968.

——. *Typee: A Peep at Polynesian Life*. Evanston, Ill.: Northwestern University Press, 1995.

Memmi, Albert. *The Colonizer and the Colonized*. Boston: Beacon, 1965.

Merrell, James H. *Into the American Woods: Negotiators on the Pennsylvania Frontier*. New York: W. W. Norton, 1999.

Mignolo, Walter. *The Darker Side of the Renaissance: Literacy, Territoriality, and Coloniza-tion*. Durham: Duke University Press, 1995.

Miller, Huron, trans. *Turtle: Native American Center for the Living Arts Quarterly Edition Newspaper*. Winter 1980.

Moore, James T. *Indian and Jesuit: A Seventeenth-Century Encounter*. Chicago: Loyola University Press, 1982.

Moorhouse, Alfred Charles. *The Triumph of the Alphabet: A History of Writing*. New York: H. Schuman, 1953.

Mulford, Carla, Angela Vietto, and Amy E. Winans, eds. *Early American Writings*. New York: Oxford University Press, 2002.

Murra, John V., and Rolena Adorno, eds. *El primer nueva corónica y buen gobierno por Felipe Guaman Poma de Ayala (Waman Puma)*. Mexico City: Siglo Veintiuno, 2006.

Murray, David. *Forked Tongues: Speech, Writing, and Representation in North American In-dian Texts*. Bloomington: Indiana University Press, 1991.

Newman, Andrew. "Captive on the Literacy Frontier: Mary Rowlandson, James Smith, and Charles Johnston." *Early American Literature* 38, no. 1 (2003), 31–65.

Nicholson, H. B. "Phoneticism in the Late Pre-Hispanic Central Mexican Writing System." *Mesoamerican Writing Systems: A Conference at Dumbarton Oaks, October 30th and 31st, 1971*, Elizabeth P. Benson, ed., 1–46. Washington, D.C.: Dumbarton Oaks Research Library and Collections, 1973.

Nicolar, Joseph. *The Life and Traditions of the Red Man*, ed. Annette Kolodny. Durham: Duke University Press, 2007.

Nyland, Waino. "Kalevala as a Reputed Source of Longfellow's *Song of Hiawatha*." *American Literature* 22, no. 1 (March 1950), 1–20.

O'Brien, Lynne Woods. *Plains Indian Autobiographies*. Caldwell, Idaho: Caxton Printers, 1973.

Olaniayan, Tejumola. *Scars of Conquest/Masks of Resistance: The Invention of Cultural Iden-tities in African, African-American and Caribbean Drama*. Oxford: Oxford University Press, 1995.

Olson, David R. *The World on Paper: The Conceptual and Cognitive Implications of Writing and Reading*. Cambridge: Cambridge University Press, 1994.

Ortega, Julio. "Transatlantic Translations." *PMLA* 118, no. 1 (2003), 25–40.

Ossio, Juan M. "The Idea of History in Felipe Guaman Poma de Ayala." B. Litt. thesis, Oxford University, 1970.

Otter, Samuel. *Melville's Anatomies*. Berkeley: University of California Press, 1999.

Parker, Arthur C. *Parker on the Iroquois*, ed. William N. Fenton. Syracuse: Syracuse University Press, 1968.

Parker, Herschel. *Herman Melville: A Biography*, 2 vols. Baltimore: Johns Hopkins University Press, 1996–2002.

Parkinson, Richard B. *Cracking Codes: The Rosetta Stone and Decipherment*. Berkeley: University of California Press, 1999.

Pearson, Jonathan, trans. and ed. *Early Record of the City and County of Albany and Ren-sealaerswyck*, 4 vols., rev. ed. by A. J. F. Van Laer. Albany: Munsell, 1869–1919.

Peterson, Karen Daniels, ed. *A Cheyenne Warrior's Graphic Interpretation of His People*. Palo Alto: American West, 1968.

——. *Plains Indian Art from Fort Marion*. Norman: University of Oklahoma Press, 1971.

Porter, David. *Journal of a Cruise Made to the Pacific Ocean, by Captain David Porter, in the United States Frigate Essex, in the Years 1812, 1813, and 1814*, 2 vols. Philadelphia: Bradford and Inskeep, 1815.

Potter, Tiffany. "Writing Indigenous Femininity: Mary Rowlandson's Narrative of Captivity." *Eighteenth-Century Studies* 36, no. 2 (2003), 153–67.

Pound, Ezra. "Hugh Selwyn Mauberley." *Personae: The Shorter Poems of Ezra Pound*, ed. Lea Baechler and A. Walton Litz, 188. New York: New Directions, 1990.

Pozdniakov, Konstantin. "Les bases du déchiffrement de l'écriture de l'île de Pâques." *Journal de la Société des Océanistes* 103 (1996), 289–303.

Pratt, Mary Louise. *Imperial Eyes: Travel Writing and Transculturation*. New York: Routledge, 1992.

——. "Transculturation and Autoethnography: Peru, 1615/1980." *Colonial Discourse, Postcolonial Theory*, ed. Francis Barker, Peter Hulme, and Margaret Iversen Manchester, 24–46. England: Manchester University Press, 1994.

Quilter, Jeffrey, and Gary Urton, eds. *Narrative Threads: Accounting and Recounting in Andean Khipu*. Austin: University of Texas Press, 2002.

Rappaport, Joanne. "Object and Alphabet: Andean Indians and Documents in the Colonial Period." *Writing without Words: Alternative Literacies in Mesoamerica and the Andes*, ed. Elizabeth Hill Boone and Walter D. Mignolo, 271–91. Durham: Duke University Press, 1994.

Renker, Elizabeth. *Strike through the Mask: Herman Melville and the Scene of Writing*. Baltimore: Johns Hopkins University Press, 1996.

Revard, Carter. "Beads, Wampum, Money, Words, and Old English Riddles." *American Indian Culture and Research Journal* 23, no. 1 (Winter 1999), 177.

Richter, Daniel K. *Facing East from Indian Country: A Native History of Early America*. Cambridge: Harvard University Press, 2001.

——. *The Ordeal of the Longhouse: The Peoples of the Iroquois League in the Era of European Colonization*. Chapel Hill: University of North Carolina Press, 1992.

——. "Ordeals of the Longhouse: The Five Nations in Early American History." *Beyond the Covenant Chain: The Iroquois and Their Neighbors in Indian North America, 1600 to 1800*, ed. Daniel K. Richter and James H. Merrell, 11–28. Syracuse: Syracuse University Press, 1987.

Robinson, Andrew. *Lost Languages: The Enigma of the World's Undeciphered Scripts*. New York: McGraw-Hill, 2002.

Romero, Lora. "Vanishing Americans: Gender, Empire, and New Historicism." *The Culture of Sentiment: Race, Gender, and Sentimentality in Nineteenth-Century America*, ed. Shirley Samuels, 115–309. New York: Oxford University Press, 1992.

Rosaldo, Renato. *Culture and Truth: The Remaking of Social Analysis*. Boston: Beacon, 1993.

Rousseau, Jean-Jacques. "Essay on the Origin of Languages." *On the Origin of Language: Two Essays by Jean-Jacques Rousseau and Johann Gottfried Herder (1754–91)*, ed. J. H. Moran and A. Goode, 17. New York: Frederick Unger, 1966.

——. *Essay sur l'origine des langues*, ed. Charles Porset. Bordeaux: Ducros, 1969.

Rowe, John Howland. "Inca Culture at the Time of the Spanish Conquest." *Handbook of South American Indians*, 7 vols., ed. Julian H. Stewart, 2:183–330. New York: Cooper Square, 1963.

Roys, Ralph L., trans. *The Book of Chilam Balam of Chumayel*. Norman: University of Oklahoma Press, 1967.

Salisbury, Neal, ed. *The Sovereignty and Goodness of God, Together with the Faithfulness of His Promises Displayed; Being a Narrative of the Captivity and Restoration of Mrs. Mary Rowlandson and Related Documents*, ed. Neal Salisbury, 1–60. Boston: Bedford, 1997.

Salomon, Frank. *The Cord Keepers: Khipus and Cultural Life in a Peruvian Village*. Durham: Duke University Press, 2004.

——. "How an Andean 'Writing without Words' Works." *Current Anthropology* 42, no. 1 (February 2001), 1–27.

——. *Native Lords of Quito in the Age of the Incas: The Political Economy of North Andean Chiefdoms*. Cambridge: Cambridge University Press, 1986.

Sampson, Geoffrey. *Writing Systems: A Linguistic Introduction*. Stanford: Stanford University Press, 1985.

Sanborn, Geoffrey. *The Sign of the Cannibal: Melville and the Making of a Postcolonial Reader*. Durham: Duke University Press, 1998.

Sanders, Thomas E., and Walter W. Peek, eds. *Literature of the American Indian*. Beverly Hills: Glencoe, 1976.

Sandoz, Mari. "Introduction." *A Pictographic History of the Oglala Sioux* by Amos Bad Heart Bull, ed. Helen H. Blish, xix–xxii. Lincoln: University of Nebraska Press, 1967.

Sayre, Gordon. *Les Sauvages Américains: Representations of Native Americans in French and English Colonial Literature*. Chapel Hill: University of North Carolina Press, 1997.

Schele, Linda. *Maya Glyphs: The Verbs*. Austin: University of Texas Press, 1982.

——. *The Proceedings of the Maya Hieroglyphic Weekend*, 3 vols. United States: Phil Wanyerka, 1987–94.

Schellhas, Paul. "Fifty Years of Maya Research." *Maya Research* 3 (1936), 138.

Schoolcraft, Henry R. *The American Indians: Their History, Condition and Prospects, from Original Notes and Manuscripts*. Rochester, N.Y.: Wanzer, Foot, 1851.

Schousboe, Karen, and Mogens Trolle Larsen, eds. *Literacy and Society*. Copenhagen: Akademisk Forlag, 1989.

Scozzari, Lois. "The Significance of Wampum to Seventeenth Century Indians in New England." *Connecticut Review* 17, no. 1 (1995), 59–69.

Sealts Jr., Merton M. *Melville's Reading: A Check-List of Books Owned and Borrowed*. Madison: University of Wisconsin Press, 1966.

Shueller, Malini Johar. "Colonialism and Melville's South Seas Journeys." *American Fiction* 22 (1994), 3–15.

Silko, Leslie Marmon. *Yellow Woman and the Beauty of Spirit: Essays on Native American Life Today*. New York: Simon and Schuster, 1996.

Slotkin, J. S., and Karl Schmitt. "Studies in Wampum." *American Anthropologist*, new series 51, no. 2 (1949), 223–36.

Smith, Linda Tuhiwai. *Decolonizing Methodologies: Research and Indigenous Peoples*. Dunedin: University of Otago Press, 1999.

Smith, Mary Elizabeth. "The Relationship between Mixtec Manuscript Painting and the Mixtec Language: A Study of Some Personal Names in Codices Muro and Sánchez Solís." *Mesoamerican Writing Systems: A Conference at Dumbarton Oaks, October 30th and 31st, 1971, 47–98*. Washington, D.C.: Dumbarton Oaks Research Library and Collections, 1973.

Smith, William. *An Historical Account of the Expedition against the Ohio Indians, in the year 1764*. Philadelphia: W. Bradford, 1765.

Sollors, Werner, and Marc Shell, eds. *The Multi-Lingual Anthology of American Literature: A Reader of Original Texts with English Translations*. New York: New York University Press, 2000.

Speck, Frank G. "Functions of Wampum among the Eastern Algonkian." *Memoirs of the American Anthropological Association* 6 (1919).

Spivak, Gayatri. "Subaltern Studies: Deconstructing Historiography." *Other Worlds: Essays in Cultural Politics*, 197–221. New York: Routledge, 1988.

Stearns, R. E. C. "Ethno-conchology: A Study of Primitive Money." *Annual Report for 1887*. Washington, D.C.: Smithsonian Institution.

Stern, Steve J. *Peru's Indian Peoples and the Challenge of Spanish Conquest: Huamanga to 1640*. Madison: University of Wisconsin Press, 1993.

Stewart, Charles S. *A Visit to the South Seas, in the U.S. Ship Vincennes, during the Years 1829 and 1830; with Scenes in Brazil, Peru, Manilla, the Cape of Good Hope, and St. Helena*, 2 vols. New York: John P. Haven, 1831.

Street, Brian. "What's 'New' in New Literacy Studies? Critical Approaches to Literacy in Theory and Practice." *Current Issues in Comparative Education* 5, no. 2 (2003), 4.

Sturtevant, William C., general ed. *Handbook of North American Indians*, 20 vols. Washington, D.C.: Smithsonian Institution Press, 1978.

Sullivan, James, and Alexander C. Flick, eds. *The Papers of Sir William Johnson*, 14 vols. Albany: State University of New York Press, 1921–65.

Supno Collapiña y otros quipucamayos, Relación de la descendencia, gobierno y conquista de los Incas (1542). Lima: Biblioteca Universitaria, 1974.

Taylor, Isaac. *The History of the Alphabet*, 2 vols. New York: Scribner's, 1899.

Tedlock, Dennis, trans. *The Popol Vuh*. New York: Simon & Schuster, 1985.

Tercer Concilio Limense, 1582–1583: Version Castellana original de los decretos con el sumario del Segundo Concilio Limense. Lima: Facultad Pontificia y Civil de Teologia de Lima, 1982.

Thomas, Alan G. *Great Books and Book Collectors*. New York: Excalibur, 1975.

Thomson, Robert. *The Marquesas Islands: Their Description and Early History*, 2d ed., ed. Robert D. Craig. Laie, Hawaii: Institute for Polynesian Studies, 1980.

Thwaites, Reuben Gold, ed. *The Jesuit Relations and Allied Documents: Travels and Explorations of the Jesuit Missionaries in New France, 1610–1791*, 73 vols. Cleveland: Buroughs Brothers, 1896–1901.

Todorov, Tzvetan. *The Conquest of America: The Question of the Other*, trans. Richard Howard. New York: Harper and Row, 1984.

Trachtenburg, Alan. "Singing Hiawatha: Longfellow's Hybrid Myth of America." *Yale Review* 90, no. 1 (January 2002), 1–19.

Trigger, Bruce, ed. *Handbook of North American Indians, Volume 15: Northeast.* Washington, D.C.: Smithsonian Institution Press, 1978.

Ugarte, Rubén Vargas. *Historia de la iglesia en el Perú, Volume 2: 1570–1640.* Burgos, Spain: Aldecoa, 1959.

Unger, J. Marshall, and John DeFrancis. "Logographic and Semasiographic Writing Systems: A Critique of Sampson's Classification." *Scripts and Literacy: Reading and Learning to Read Alphabets, Syllabaries, and Characters,* ed. Insup Taylor and David R. Olson, 45–58. Dordrecht: Kluwer, 1995.

Urioste, George L. "The Spanish and Quechua Voices of Waman Puma." *Latin American Literature and Arts Review* 28 (January–April 1981), 16–19.

Urteaga, Horacio, ed. *Discurso sobre la descendencia y gobierno de los Incas, by Collapiña and Supno and other Khipukamayuqs.* Lima: San Martí y Cía, 1921.

Urton, Gary. "From Knots to Narratives: Reconstructing the Art of Historical Record Keeping in the Andes from Spanish Transcriptions of Inca Khipus," *Ethnohistory* 45, no. 3 (Summer 1998), 409–38.

——. *Signs of the Inca Khipu: Binary Coding in the Andean Knotted-String Records.* Austin: University of Texas Press, 2003.

——. *The Social Life of Numbers: A Quechua Ontology of Numbers and Philosophy of Arithmetic.* Austin: University of Texas Press, 1997.

Van Doren, Carl. "Introduction." *Indian Treaties Printed by Benjamin Franklin 1736–1762,* vii–xviii. Philadelphia: Historical Society of Pennsylvania, 1938.

Van Doren, Carl, and Julian P. Boyd. *Indian Treaties Printed by Benjamin Franklin 1736–1762.* Philadelphia: Historical Society of Pennsylvania, 1938.

von den Steinen, Karl. *Die Marquesaner und ihre Kunst: Studien über die Entwicklung primitiver Südseeornamentik nach eigenen Reiseergebnissen und dem Material der Museen (1925–28),* 3 vols. New York: Hacker Art Books, 1969.

von Krusenstern, A. J. *Voyage round the World, in the Years 1803, 1804, 1805, and 1806,* 2 vols. London: C. Roworth for John Murray, 1813.

von Langsdorff, Georg H. *Voyages and Travels in Various Parts of the World, during the Years 1803, 1804, 1805, 1806, and 1807,* 2 vols. London: Henry Colburn, 1813–14.

Walker, Cheryl. *Indian Nation: Native American Literature and Nineteenth-Century Nationalisms.* Durham: Duke University Press, 1997.

Wallace, Paul A. W. *White Roots of Peace.* Saranac Lake, N.Y.: Chauncy, 1986.

Wardrop, Daneen. "The Signifier and the Tattoo: Inscribing the Uninscribed and the Forces of Colonization in Melville's *Typee.*" *ESP* 47 (2001), 135–61.

Warkentin, Germaine. "In Search of 'The Word of the Other': Aboriginal Sign Systems and the History of the Book in Canada." *Book History* 2, no. 1 (1999), 1–27.

White, Richard. *The Middle Ground: Indians, Empires and Republics in the Great Lakes Region, 1650–1815.* New York: Cambridge University Press, 1991.

Whitman, Walt. "The Spanish Element in Our Nationality." *Complete Poetry and Collected Prose,* 1146–48. New York: Library of America, 1982.

Wilcox, U. Vincent. "The Manufacture and Use of Wampum in the Northeast." *The*

Second Coastal Archeology Reader: 1900 to Present, ed. James E. Truex, 295–305. Lexington, Mass: Ginn, 1982.

Wildschut, William. "A Crow Pictographic Robe." *Indian Notes* 3, no. 1 (1926), 28–32.

Williams, Mentor L., ed. *Schoolcraft's Indian Legends from Algic Researches, the Myth of Hiawatha, Oneónta, the Red Race in America, and Historical and Statistical Information Respecting . . . the Indian Tribes of the United States.* East Lansing: Michigan State University Press, 1956.

Williams, Robert A., Jr. *Linking Arms Together: American Indian Treaty Visions of Law and Peace, 1600–1800.* New York: Routledge, 1999.

Wogan, Peter. "Perceptions of European Literacy in Early Contact Situations." *Ethnohistory* 41, no. 3 (Summer 1994), 407–29.

Wolf, Eric. *Europe and the People without History.* Berkeley: University of California Press, 1983.

Womack, Craig. *Red on Red: Native American Literary Separatism.* Minneapolis: University of Minnesota Press, 1999.

Wong, Hertha. *Sending My Heart Back across the Years: Tradition and Innovation in Native American Autobiography.* New York: Oxford University Press, 1992.

Wright, Nathalia. *Melville's Use of the Bible.* Durham: Duke University Press, 1949.

Wroth, Lawrence C. "The Indian Treaty as Literature." *Yale Review* 17, no. 4 (1928), 749–66.

Wyss, Hilary E. *Writing Indians: Literacy, Christianity, and Native Community in Early America.* Boston: University of Massachusetts Press, 2000.

Yupanqui, Titu Cusi. *An Inca Account of the Conquest of Peru*, ed. Ralph Bauer. Boulder: University Press of Colorado, 2005.

Zuidema, R. Tom. "Guaman Poma between the Arts of Europe and the Andes." *Colonial Latin American Review* 3, nos. 1–2 (1994), 37–86.

BIRGIT BRANDER RASMUSSEN is an assistant professor of American Studies and Ethnicity, Race, and Migration at Yale University. She is the co-editor of *The Making and Unmaking of Whiteness* (Duke, 2001).

Library of Congress Cataloging-in-Publication Data
Brander Rasmussen, Birgit, 1968–
Queequeg's coffin : indigenous literacies and early American literature /
Birgit Brander Rasmussen.
p. cm.
Includes bibliographical references and index.
ISBN 978-0-8223-4935-8 (cloth : alk. paper)
ISBN 978-0-8223-4954-9 (pbk. : alk. paper)
1. Indian literature—History and criticism. 2. Indians—Languages—Writing.
3. America—Literatures—History and criticism. I. Title.
PM155.B73 2012   897—dc23   2011030871